The Consumption of Mass

A selection of previous *Sociological Review* Monographs

Life and Work History Anaylses[†]
ed. Shirley Dex

The Sociology of Monsters[†]
ed. John Law

Sport, Leisure and Social Relations[†]
eds John Horne, David Jary and Alan Tomlinson

Gender and Bureaucracy[*]
eds Mike Savage and Anne Witz

The Sociology of Death: theory, culture, practice[*]
ed. David Clark

The Cultures of Computing[*]
ed. Susan Leigh Star

Theorizing Museums[*]
ed. Sharon Macdonald and Gordon Fyfe

Consumption Matters[*]
eds Stephen Edgell, Kevin Hetherington and Alan Warde

Ideas of Difference[*]
eds Kevin Hetherington and Rolland Munro

The Laws of the Markets[*]
ed. Michael Callon

Actor Network Theory and After[*]
eds John Law and John Hassard

Whose Europe? The Turn Towards Democracy[*]
eds Dennis Smith and Sue Wright

Renewing Class Analysis[*]
eds Rosemary Crompton, Fiona Devine, Mike Savage and John Scott

Reading Bourdieu on Society and Culture[*]
ed. Bridget Fowler

[†] Available from The Sociological Review Office, Keele University, Keele, Staffs ST5 5BG.
[*] Available from Blackwell Publishers Journals, PO Box 805, 108 Cowley Road, Oxford OX4 1FH.

The Sociological Review Monographs

Since 1958 *The Sociological Review* has established a tradition of publishing Monographs on issues of general sociological interest. The Monograph is an edited book length collection of research papers which is published and distributed in association with Blackwell Publishers. We are keen to receive innovative collections of work in sociology and related disciplines with a particular emphasis on exploring empirical materials and theoretical frameworks which are currently under-developed. If you wish to discuss ideas for a Monograph then please contact the Monographs Editor, Martin Parker, at *The Sociological Review*, Keele University, Newcastle-under-Lyme, North Staffordshire, ST5 5BG. Email m.parker@mngt.keele.ac.uk

The Consumption of Mass

Edited by Nick Lee and Rolland Munro

Blackwell Publishers/The Sociological Review

First published in 2001

Blackwell Publishers
108 Cowley Road, Oxford OX4 1JF, UK

and
350 Main Street
Malden, MA 02148, USA

British Library Cataloguing in Publication Data

A CIP catalogue record for this book is available from the British Library

Library of Congress Cataloging-in-Publication Data applied for

ISBN 0 631 22819 5

Printed and bound by Page Brothers, Norwich

This book is printed on acid-free paper.

The Sociological Review are grateful to Patricia Wirz for granting permission to use the painting 'Fundamental' by her late husband J.P. Wirz.

Contents

Introduction

Rolland Munro

Keep you doped on religion, sex and TV
And you think you're so clever, classless and free
But you're still fucking peasants, as far as I can see
John Lennon, *Working Class Hero*

Mass is the heart of darkness. Mass is that which evades identity; substance that takes meaning – principally non-meaning – from its *lack* of representation. Akin to primeval slime, mass suggests extension without shape, viscosity without direction and density without definition. Inchoate, formless, undifferentiated, mass seems the very Other of understanding.

So what is mass? The idea seems all too vague. How can something which so lacks identity be brought to analysis? In the putative reality of a world composed of 'things', mass can have no presence: the term registers more an *absence* of representation. Within formal theory, for example, anything that cannot be represented slips to the edges of research. Mass becomes the 'residual', what cannot be accounted for. It is the unknown, or error term, the absence lurking in the background – always threatening explanation, but never entering it.

Sociologically, the concept of mass seems also overworked. In one line of thinking, mass invited analysis to go beyond the near and familiar; and think about the *whole*. As such, conceptions of mass lie behind many key terms, such as population, society, solidarity, structure and social movement. It would be a mistake, however, to think of these matters as identical with mass. As Marx (1972/1939: 100) noted about 'population', far from helping us begin with 'the real and the concrete', such terms are often mere abstractions. If mass invites, it also eludes.

In another line, several important concepts – especially mass production and mass consumption – have gestured less to the mysteries of substance and aspire, instead, to grasping a scale invoked by unimaginable numbers. Far from approaching the sublime, however, tropes like that of 'mass communications' and 'mass murder' usually imply a lowest common denominator, the crudity of the only too familiar. Other terms, such as norm, deviation, consensus and average not only depend on numerical conceptions of mass but also point to traditional assumptions about the importance of measuring mass.

Perhaps for these reasons, vagueness, overuse and ambiguity, mass has become a somewhat discredited term. Yet, more recently, mass has become a pressing issue in sociological research. For over two decades, analysis has focused on such related concepts as the body, embodiment and materiality. It is as if dissatisfaction with abstraction has returned analysis to the real and the concrete; a kind of return to basics. In addition, topics such as governmentality explore the effects that disseminate from the use of statistical techniques, or a reliance on questionnaires and other forms of 'mass survey'. Here it seems to go without saying that the invention of mass is a critical prior to later talk about individuation and the 'making up' of persons.

Given the so-called 'crisis of representation', this renewed attention to mass today might be less than surprising. When something escapes representation, it can also become of consumate interest. And it is surely this very absence of identity that presents a challenge for contemporary social theory. How to *account* for mass? How does mass work? What does mass affect? When do these effects appear?

The massifying of subjects

'Mass' once occupied a key place within social theory. Here the term refers to the concept of *undifferentiated wholes*. Analytically, these are units of analysis for which no further discrimination or division into parts is either thought necessary – as in the case of a society envisaged as an economy – or possible – in the case of a society whose very scale makes the polis inoperable as a community (cf Nancy, 1991). Thus, even at the cost of a conflation between 'the all' and 'the same', references abound to crowds as 'the mass', or to the bulk of society as 'the masses'.

Much of the systematic nature of the early writers is due to this tendency to address social phenomena in aggregate terms and conceptualize society in terms of its being a whole. As social philosophers, Weber and Durkheim were critically concerned with the creation and reproduction of a social mass, the web that *binds*. So Weber could theorize the rise of bureaucracy and speculate about disenchantment and the creation of the iron cage. Durkheim could go beyond the vagaries of individual suicides and posit the homogenous tendencies of society as an organic entity. Unlike Marx's proletariat which took its identity from being both the means of production and the means of revolution – one bound and we are free – they portray an unthinking solidarity. Unthinking in as much as each envisaged it as becoming a *mass culture*, one in which the mode of consumption is dictated for Weber by rationalism and, if notoriously for Durkheim, wherein the social actor becomes figured as a cultural dope.

In an early paper on mass culture, Zygmunt Bauman discusses what is usually (if problematically) meant when the term mass is applied to a culture.

Where culture, he claims, would normally *differentiate* into subcultures, he sees the reverse happening to present day society:

> Its acquisition of a 'mass' character in fact amounted to a disappearance of these subcultures and their replacement by a universal culture, common to all the members of a society. (Bauman, 1972/1966: 62)

Bauman, typically, is pointing to conditions which facilitate the *production* of mass culture. For a culture to acquire their 'mass' character, he suggests the social situations of the members of the society must become standardized.

The appearance of mass culture, in Bauman's analysis, is thus a reversal of the more 'natural' process of differentiation. This reversal involves a rendezvous with three specific conditions, namely the market, organization and technology:

> Man becomes dependent upon the market, on organization and on technology because he cannot by-pass them on the road from the expenditure of his creative energy to the acquisition of the good indispensible for its regeneration. (71)

With much of the economic framing seemingly turned over to systems of mass production, mass distribution, mass communication and mass transportation, it must have seemed inevitable that society would gravitate to an ever-increasing homogeneity.

With the aid of more contemporary ideas of culture, much of this diagnosis and concern about mass culture seems misguided, limiting itself to one particular mode of consumption – mass consumption – and to one particular mode of production – mass production. Here Bauman's own analysis was more prescient. In a reflective moment, Bauman questions the notion of need and notes that, while 'deficiency needs' disappear when they are satisfied, what Maslow calls 'Being needs' are further *stimulated* by their satisfaction.

This is where the story of mass takes an unexpected twist. It is not these Being needs of the individuated subject that begin to dominate. In a world of choice, what might be better called 'identity needs' become endlessly demanding. Instead of self-actualization slowly becoming 'psychological universals' leading to the 'birth and triumph of mass culture' (73), as Bauman in this early piece suggests, consumption shifts into a mode of identity.

The effect is to create a paradox of consumption in which display through consumption is governed neither by the culture of community, nor by individual subjectivities, but by the chimera of choice. But before discussing the conceptual interconnections between choice and identity, and their potential break from the mode of production, something more needs to be said about the nature of mass.

The turn of choice

A return to mass, a preference for the embodied and the material over the conceptual and the abstract, comes late in the history of sociology. It comes at a time of supreme distrust over categories and other modes of inquiry which, from Aristotle on, have been largely concerned to *amass* facts.

The project of representation has been to build up knowledge from secure foundations – the categorical, the indubitable. But how can this mass of knowledge re-enter the world? The traditional point of entry is through reason; but an unintended consequence of reason, explicit in Weber's analysis (Walker, 1992: Hennis, 1988), is the loss of the very individuality that the Enlightenment also prized. A difficulty that the pragmatists also notice: 'The method must be such that the ultimate conclusion of *every man shall be the same*' (Peirce, quoted by Rose: 164, emphasis added). The humanist symbols of Enlightenment reason and progress stand awkwardly therefore against the motif of mass culture. For the mass is precisely the huddle into which reason, the light of knowledge and rationality, cannot penetrate. Mass lacks identity, aims and definition.

Even anti-humanists rail against mass culture, the averageness of *Dasein* and this 'leveling down' of all possibilities of being:

> The They prescribes what can and may be ventured, it keeps watch over everything exceptional. Every kind of supremacy gets silently suppressed. Overnight, everything that is original gets glossed over as something long well-known. Everything gained by a struggle becomes just something to be manipulated. Every mystery loses its force. (Heidegger, quoted by Collins and Selina, 1999: 69)

Collins and Selina are mistaken to presume that Heidegger valorizes bourgeois culture and is particularly opposed to popular culture. The enemy of thinking for Heidegger is rather the insistence on 'correctness', which he sees as usually confused with truth.

Both views, the humanist and the anti-humanist, greatly underestimate the effects of the later stages of mass production. During periods where many of the goods of mass production, including education, remain relatively scarce, an appearance of mass consumption may be generated: any colour of automobile as long as it's black; any theory as long as it is within the canon. Increasingly, however, choice is accommodated by the manufacture of a range of models, even within each marque; or by the range of specialist options within each discipline.

Far from being erased, choice becomes the *point* of consumption. Unceasing production, as Dan Rose's chapter further explores, puts into circulation a mass of goods. But this mass becomes so rich, as to surpass all previous visions of mass culture. Thus, rather than bring about a mass culture in terms of a levelling – where all aspire to eat, drink and speak the same – the effect is to intensify the importance of choice. (And with this, consumption.) Where once people might have died for their beliefs, or their country, now they can display their brand of choice in what they read, wear or eat.

Yet we should not jump to thinking that people simply become captive to brands. As Douglas and Isherwood (1980) insist, any purchase of goods is a display of culture. So the display is not so much one of a preference for any brand *per se* – although this kind of fetishism inevitably happens. Or even for what the purchase of a brand ostensibly tells us about the person. Goods, like any other artefact, are *expressive*. And what they express is culture (and identity).

Identity and choice

The question, however, is what sort of culture? This is where the insight of Douglas and Isherwood's analysis may be more limited than previously noticed. For a contemporary display of goods no longer implies the kind of belonging to a community that they imagined.

In our view, display, increasingly, comes to display choice itself. Choice becomes the ultimate, inescapable fate: who are you if you can't choose? Brands can be said to have appeal because what they signal is the *exercise* of choice. The power to choose. And the more a brand symbolises a power to choose, the greater its premium for identity work.

Identity work is governed by a display of this power to choose. This is what much purchase today symbolises: a culture in which choice is the mode of domination, legitimation and signification. Thus, the ability of goods to stand for choice, rather than for themselves, explains perhaps why fashion labels are so sought after (Friedman, 1990) and why MacDonald's take-aways in the US appeal so strongly to the immigrant poor. But purchase is not the only alternative.

Identity can also be marked as much by a *refusal* to purchase certain key goods, such as televisions and mobile phones, or even drugs and designer clothes. Identity can focus instead on 'investment' goods, such as private education; or on making 'collections' of any production of goods that has been limited, such as first editions, or 'Beanie Babies'.

Possibly this is why distinction – class, gender or ethnic distinction – tends to take place in different *arenas* of choice. Just as the eighteenth century upper class turned thin when upwardly mobile tradespeople grew prosperous and fat, so those who already have the security of certain forms of identity can withhold from certain forms of consumption. So, too, can they turn to other forms of expenditure in which to discriminate themselves from each other.

The motility of mass

With the individual secure in an empire of choice, a return to the discredited notion of mass might seem odd. But our question is not about mass consumption, or its variants. It is about a *consumption* of mass. Understood in traditional terms, this idea constitutes something a scandal. If consumption is about goods, and mass is what has not yet become goods, there seems a contradiction in terms. How could mass be consumed?

In Heidegger's view we wake up to thinking. The things of the world are *already* in use – he would say *zuhanden* (ready-to-hand) before they are *vorhanden* (present-to-hand). So that we have learnt to use technology – and 'master' it – before we question technology (Heidegger, 1977). In this sense, Heidegger gives the consumption of things – including the 'things' of knowledge – its priority. A priority, that is, over their production. Thrown from birth into an on-going production of social realities, we consume well before we choose what to produce.

But this priority that Heidegger gives to the ready-to-hand is far from self-evident. In many cases, its opposite seems to be the case. Tautologically, it is the *present-to-hand* that commands our attention. In representing things, we engage categories. And the effect is to centre consciousness in ways that bring the world, as it seems, to us. What matters here is that representation not only effects a *disposal* of mass, a would-be correspondence of signifiers and signifieds in which mass dissipates and words lie like a veil over things. It is more that representation appears to leave mass *at* our disposal. A matter of mood, or attitude. One moment, the world is heavy on our soul; the next, we ride it lightly. One moment, there is someone pressing at our elbow; the next moment, we see it is only a beggar. We bring the things of the world near, or make them far. By changing categories we can make the things of the world appear and dissappear.

The sovereign effects of our gaze, and its susceptibility to discourse, have been well discussed and need not delay us here. What matters is that the mass of the ready-to-hand does not so easily slip about. Or, rather, it can slip its categories. Here Heidegger contrasts the hammer which slips in the hand. One moment the tool swinging in our hand is all arm, invisible in our attention on the nail; the next moment, we are staring at a heavy lump of metal hanging loosely over a rising bruise on the thumb.

Mass might be absent from representation, but it cannot be voided entirely. Just as there is a passage between the *zuhanden* (ready-to-hand) and the *vorhanden* (present-to-hand) – in which objects of the earth are turned into objects of contemplation – so, there is a re-seepage. A re-disposal. Whatever it seems, mass is not entirely at the disposal of language: by the laws of motion, only mass can move other mass.

Extension

Let's take things more slowly. First we should clarify what we mean by consumption. As already indicated, consumption is about the iterative processes by which persons make up the world. It is through their engagement with goods, artefacts and symbols, that people create social realities and display their identity or express their sense of belonging. We refer to this process as *extension* (cf Strathern, 1991; Munro, 1996).

Conventionally, it is through their attachment to materials that persons add on parts, such using a wooden leg, or swinging a hammer, or listening through a stethoscope. Strathern, however, makes a turn towards the notion of *performance* by stressing the idea that 'parts' are also dramatic: Long John Silver, the DIY Dad, the nurse playing doctor. The adding-on of parts (material objects) also extends the range of parts (performances as subjects) (Munro, 1996: 260). Object and subject, as effects, move hand in hand.

Strathern explicates this doubling of 'parts' in respect of the dances Wantoat people put on at the time of the festivals:

> Performers literally magnify themselves. They wear barkcloth and bamboo extensions ... carried by being tied on to the body of the dancer .... In some cases, such figures triple the dancer's height .... The whole edifice gives the appearance of a tree with a man at its base. (Strathern, 1991: 63).

Importantly, Strathern also notes how the parts making up a performance are never forgotten entirely as materials. Those watching at the festival move *between* two figures: between a focus that on the one hand keeps body and bamboo apart and a focus on the other hand that sees the trees. At one moment there is a recognition of a mechanical attachment and, in the next, a seeing of 'towering trees'.

Strathern here is giving full play to the term *attachment*, first as attach-ment, movement to and from something, and second as attachment, feelings of belonging to something:

> By keeping both meanings of attachment alongside each other, Strathern prevents the latter experience being made disjunct as (merely) subjective, or rejected as an e-motion. Her image of attach-ment *as* detach-ment, and vice versa, tells us what is important about the relations between self and identity. Extension is always a 'doubling' of parts; a prosthesis of attachment/detachment that adds motility to performance. (Munro, 1996: 262).

As audience, we are also in extension: we move *from* figure *to* figure. Back and forth, in watching, we shift between the extension as a figure of dancer plus bamboo and a catching of the image of 'towering' trees.

The motility of mass is critical. Crucially, as in a gestalt switch, the seeing of the second figure, the mass of 'towering trees' involves a 'forgetting' of the parts of the first figure, the barkcloth and bamboo. For cultural performances to take place, there needs to be not only a social memory, capable of understanding what is being materialized. In order to appear and dissappear, the material parts themselves have to be disposable; attachable or detachable, as if by choice. Yes, people magnify themselves through goods – to be visible they need to be seen as attached to these. But they also wish to be admired *apart* from their goods, as if they could be 'valued' for themselves.

The circulation of mass

One challenge, we think, is to try to incorporate mass in terms of *embodied relations*. To see mass no longer as an additional variable, but as emblematic of a more general movement of contemporary theory away from the 'thing' view of the world. Yet in seeking to 'body forth' (see Latimer, this volume) ourselves *as* individuals, would any material do? We think not. Lyotard's point about mass production is that it consumes us, just as much as we consume mass products.

Even in the thrall of choice, the consumption of mass has a dark side which should not be forgotten. As Cooper (this volume) suggests, the nature of mass production in the modern techno-sciences has to be understood not just as objects, but as an endless dispersion of events in movement. In this powerful sense, the consumption and production of mass turns out to be about the 'drama of individuation, the tracing and erasing of those boundaries without which there would be no phenomenal world, no individual life' (Bersani and Dutoit, 1993: 144)

In all this endless 'making up' of Euro-American selves *as* individuals, Bauman's three specific conditions, the market, organization and technology, appear to be coming together in an unexpected way. Over matters of choice, reason and custom are giving way to the market. Only the goods of the market – it seems – can display choice. By contrast, reason – either in the form of organization or as technology – suggests incarceration, a compulsory mode of being.

In respect of choice, then, the unceasing production of goods is driven into a new frenzy of circulation. For it is a condition of choice that we should no longer need to wait. The consequence is to create a new kind of mass. Not the mass of the earth, of primeval substance, but a mass of fabricated materials – a world of goods – that is kept in unceasing motion.

Technology, as Heidegger (1977) predicted, is busy creating the world as a 'standing stock'. For example, rivers no longer run their course, but are damned up, or diverted, in order that their power may be drawn from them on demand. So, too, the materials of the earth are turned into goods that are 'standing in advance'. It is not that consumption runs ahead of production. More that, in a world of choice, production must *anticipate* consumption as well as respond to it.

This is the mass of a world that is waiting *in advance* of choice. Insofar as goods are 'standing in advance' and are not produced for anyone in particular, they return to being a kind of mass. The peculiarity of this mass, however, is that it is kept in *circulation*, in advance of consumption. Without this circulation, the goods would become unavailable for immediate purchase and so choice would be restricted. If we want something, we invariably want it *now*!

The difficulty is to know what this mass is for, apart from satisfying dogmas of choice. As an elicitation of culture, perhaps the best that can be hoped for is a kind of pastiche: a virtual memory of the famous, of those 'who have gone before' – down the catwalk, or starred in a television soap. Madonna as Marilyn Monroe, or *Pulp Fiction* as a string of 'references' to early B movies. So it is not yet all choice: as with the brand, getting the reference in popular culture is still the deadly serious business of getting the joke.

About this volume

For the moment, mass remains one of the least theorized concepts in social theory. Excepting insights in the work of Walter Benjamin, few theorists have carefully examined the notion. For Benjamin, as Cooper remarks (Chapter 1 of this volume), mass is movement – displacement, dissolution, dispersal and self-multiplication. Yet this emphasis on movement has failed to delegitimize the more static conceptions of mass. Most work to date is in line with assumptions of inertness and meaninglessness that lie behind early conceptions of mass production and mass consumption.

In attending to the consumption of mass, the aim of this book is to move contemporary debate away from its dependence on these more static assumptions about mass as substance. Certainly mass is that which evades analysis. But this is hardly the end of the matter. For mass has its active effects – and its desires – to which the chorale, communion and other forms of mass bear witness (Hopfl, Chapter 3; Munro, Chapter 6). Mass is *involving* – it is not to be dismissed as some primeval slime from which we have devolved.

Even so, to talk about a consumption of mass is still to engage in mundane sociological research. As chapters in this collection illustrate, 'consumption' is a useful and productive way of probing perennial topics like art, fashion, luck, war, nationhood, music and passion. Of course, this is not to make the mistake of treating these kind of topics as things in themselves – matters simply to be surveyed passively over time. Sociologists increasingly ask about the relations which are at stake. So we want to know about the *demands* of glamour (Lee, Chapter 10), or our *engagement* with art (Cooper, Chapter 1) and the *call* of war (Munro, Chapter 6). And ask questions about the social framing of luck (Parish, Chapter 7), the poetry in passion (Latimer, Chapter 9), the contusion of bass (Beeston, Chapter 4), or the 'spin' on nationhood (Stuart, Chapter 8). In basic questions about who gets consumed (Pallí Monguilod, Chapter, 11), or how materials like salt get related to talk (Rose, Chapter 2) and in new concepts like that of 'peg communities' (Bauman, Chapter 5), or in giving space for auto-critique (Grafton Small, Chapter 12), we sharpen our understanding about occasions in which relations are embodied as well as mobilized.

Added to this, we want to know more about the *un*consumable. What elides analysis? What activities or people become excluded from what passes as social life? At stake are not only standard questions of class, race, age or gender; or even the critical importance of asking: who benefits? If conduct increasingly turns towards the 'shopping experience', what then becomes marginalized or missed out? Here there are also key anthropological concerns. Once custom and reason are abandoned for the market, do 'persons' disappear? Can social memory become fragmented and frail? Are ways of knowing sacrificed, or extended, by a current trend to 'pick and mix'? And, within either tradition, there are vital questions to ask about what exactly *is* being consumed: class or fashion, ethnicity or racism, gender or destiny, knowledge or ideology, individuality or discourse? Or even, as suggested in this introduction, choice itself?

To think about consumption, then, is also to inquire in a way that asks some of the newer questions that burden recent social theory – questions of political and practical philosophy that have been emerging over the closing century of the second millenium. Here questions arise about the nature of culture, the ethics of language, the sociality of self, or the dictat of choice. These are questions that not only confront paradox by bringing together terms previously held apart: the very question of mass seems predicated on a multiplicity and precariousness of our ideas of culture and sociality.

References

Bauman, Z., (1972), A Note on Mass Culture: on infrastructure, 1966, reprinted in D. McQuail (ed.) *Sociology of Mass Communications*, Harmondsworth: Penguin.

Bersani, L. and Dutoit, U., (1993), *Arts of Impoverishment: Beckett, Rothko, Resnais*, Cambridge, Mass.: Harvard University Press.

Collins, J. and Selina, H., (1999), *Introducing Heidegger*. Cambridge: Icon Books.

Douglas, M. and Isherwood, B., (1980), *The World of Goods: towards an anthropology of consumption*, Harmondsworth: Penguin.

Friedman, J., (1990), Being in the World: globalization and localization, *Theory, Culture & Society* 8, (4): 311–328.

Hennis, W., (1988), *Max Weber: essays in reconstruction*, trans. K. Tribe. London: Allen & Unwin.

Marx, K., (1973/1939), *Grundrisse: Foundations of the Critique of Political Economy (Rough Draft)*, trans. M. Nicolaus. Harmondsworth: Penguin.

Munro, R., (1996), A Consumption View of Self: extension, exchange and identity. In S. Edgell, K. Hetherington and A. Warde (eds) *Consumption Matters: the production and experience of consumption.*, pp. 248–273. Sociological Review Monograph, Blackwell.

Nancy, J.-L., (1991), *The Inoperable Community*, trans. P. Cooper *et al.*, Minneapolis: University of Minnesota Press.

Rose, D., (1990), Quixote's Library and Pragmatic Discourse: toward understanding the culture of capitalism. *Anthopology Quarterly*, 63, (4): 155–168.

Strathern, M., (1991), *Partial Connections*. Maryland: Rowman & Little.

Walker, R., (1992), Violence, Modernity, Silence: from Max Weber to international relations. In D. Campbell and M. Dillon, *The Political Subject of Violence*. Manchester: University of Manchester.

Part 1: Imagining Mass

Introduction to Part 1

'Grant first of all that humans are composed entirely from the materiality of the world'.

Dan Rose's request, in Chapter 2 of this volume, is hardly unusual. His request is made, after all, within a culture that is aware of the materialist outlook that forms the backdrop of scientific research practice.

Even within such a culture, however, such a bald request will not go unchallenged. Many of the concepts used to distinguish human life (and mark it out for special consideration) are, in Western cosmologies, thought through the ethereal and insubstantial and in opposition to mass and matter. A mundane dualism between mass and human essence – each setting the other apart – has long informed our freedoms of speech, thought and imagination.

Lying beyond mass, the imagination is understood to leap and spark about. Its weightless speed makes it precious to those who desire worldly change. Our human values, our human spirit, traditionally weigh nothing. They are beyond mass. Weightless, they can be used to call any balancing acts of cost and benefit, any ethical materialism, into question.

So the spirit, the imagination, the human freedom to envisage alternatives – all these elements that might challenge a close articulation of scientific and ethical materialisms – find their safety instead in an unworldliness, an immateriality and a transcendence. Held aloft, they preserve their purity and gain strength from a strict seclusion, leaving the hermitage only rarely like a starved ascetic with blazing eyes.

But what if this relationship between mass and humanness could be re-imagined? What if 'human becomings' could be understood as a set of results from the busy, ongoing commerce and conversation of mass? Could we then seek out what we value in human life by acknowledging our involvements and dependencies, rather than by bidding for escape velocity? As with several of the later essays in the book, the following four essays in this section make a contribution to re-imagining this *mutuality* of mass and humanness.

In his wide-ranging essay, **Robert Cooper** begins by converting a traditional epistemological separation of unformed and formed matter (a distinction between disorganized mass and organized structure) into an ontological *tension*. For Cooper, mass names *transitions* between moments of dispersal on the one hand and moments of collection on the other. So, too, the populace is made up of countless *material* dependencies, involvements and associations. Thus, sociability means that, at any time, relatively dispersed patterns of association may cohere and collect, while other (useful) stabilities of coherence disperse. Yet in order to grasp the essence of mass, his concern is less with oscillation – as it appears to us – and more with *mutability*. Here the freedom and openness of Simmel's play-form of association seems suggestive. Plastic, as seen by Barthes, is paradigmatic, able to be converted into so many different shapes, forms or parts. And DeLillo's 'white noise', the movement of mass in the form of electrical energy that courses through all aspects of living.

In his chapter, **Dan Rose** asks about relations between humans and mass by interrogating language *and* matter. Together. There is a need, he suggests, to theorise 'matter and humans within a single intellectual framework'. In the face of rich Euro-American and Japanese societies being overwhelmed with so many objects and commodities for sale – a mass requiring so much *movement*? – he begins by raising a simple question about the correlation of movements of table salt with certain human utterances. How can speech move salt? How can language associate with (and affect) matter? As Rose observes, much 20th century linguistic theory has language move matter by *first* moving mind. Language and matter are permitted to associate only through the privilege of a third party – human mind. This makes for a situation in which correlations between material movement and utterance are either explained by a simple schema of securely coordinated intentions and comprehensions (in which minds are granted the independence of overseers), or they becomes themselves a mystery. Rose teases us into considering a rather different answer, one that fully acknowledges the place salt has in making mind possible.

Heather Hopfl, in Chapter 3, considers two parallel meanings of mass; mass as body, particularly the female body, and Mass as a religious practice of ordering. On her account, Christ's need to be born of a woman has long posed a tricky problem for the patriarchal orthodoxies of Christianity, a problem at once theological and practical. Embodiment, experience and motherhood have all been figured as 'necessary evils', posing problems wherever faith is turned into a way of life. So how are these necessary evils to be brought under control? Embodiment becomes 'temptation', and is to be answered by abstinence. Experience borders on 'heresy', and is overcome by orthodox teaching. And (the embodied experience of) motherhood, the ultimate in 'impurity', is banished by the Blessed Virgin Mary, an ethereally compliant body. In each case, the faithful are called to turn away from the associability and mutability of their own mass, numbing truth by endless recitation.

Rob Beeston's piece emerges from an unusual set of questions about sound, experience and creativity. Sound is perhaps the least 'massy' of the sensible registers. How does it take on bulk in the ear, move the body and so transport us? Against 'spirit' and 'transcendence', one might read music for its immanence, becoming materialist about its conditions of production and reception. To do this, however, would risk ignoring music's specificities and power to transport.

Beeston's materialism is rather different. Taking the consumption of bass in contemporary electronic music to be one of the definitive mediums of mass, he considers the rewriting of a production code. In particular, drawing on the work of Plastikman, he details the process of 'falling out' of production – moments of knob twiddling and mouse-clicking in which the sound waves of the synthesiser are allowed to speak, to reveal their mass free from the translation of uptake and remake. Beeston suggests these are moments of high consumption in which machines, people and sounds remake each other.

Interpreting mass: collection/dispersion

Robert Cooper

Mass is a term that resists easy interpretation. It has a variable history, with different meanings for different people at different periods. Its early, religious interpretation saw it as prodigious, life-giving matter that could be shaped into the multifarious creative expressions of human culture. Later, in classical science, it was physical substance that could be handled, weighed and measured. Later still, through the relentless interrogations of modern science, mass seemed to evade precise characterisation; its mutable nature exposed it to infinite interpretation; it could only be expressed as a specific product of a specific experimental set-up. Its popular meaning associates it with quantity and bigness of scale, which we see in such common expressions as *mass consumption, mass production, mass media* and *mass culture*. These expressions of social and economic mass not only indicate large numbers and quantities but also, as the dictionary suggests, 'bewildering abundance'. Mass seems profligate, difficult to tame.

This chapter explores these features of mass as the ceaseless movement of collection and dispersion, production and consumption, that specially characterizes mass society as it becomes more globalized. Mass is viewed not in the traditional sense of physical substance and volume but as a mutable and inexhaustible source from which worlds are continually being made through the repeated double movement of collection and dispersion. The incessant transmission of mass through collection-dispersion is elaborated through the analyses of mass phenomena by, among others, Georg Simmel and Walter Benjamin, and illustrated in the practical settings of newspapers, film, the supermarket, the city, computerized electronic space-time, as well as in the enhanced role of the mass media in producing an ever more mobile reality through 'electronic mass'. Beneath the agitated mettle of the modern world, mass appears as a relentless and prodigious power that resists the very forces that give it social and cultural form.

The prodigality of mass is stressed in Raymond Williams's (1983) cultural and social history of the term. Despite the variety of modern interpretations of mass, they all seem to reflect two basic earlier meanings: 'something amorphous and indistinguishable' and 'a dense aggregate' (Williams, 1983: 194). Mass is so dense that it is without distinguishable form. Put another way, mass is boundless, unfinished, infinite in the most basic sense of defying comprehension and resisting interpretation. Some sense of this boundlessness can be seen in the general use of words in language. No word exists in itself but is dialectically constituted by its difference from its wider linguistic context, how it differs from other terms. Just as mass itself seems to escape positive definition, so words gain their meanings from a curious process of deferral and continuous motion in a mutable space that resists precise location (Saussure, 1966). This is the way that Georg Simmel (1971) sees the energy of social life in what he calls the 'pure essence of association' (128): individuals exist but only as part of the flux and flow of abstract relationship that Simmel calls *sociability*. Sociability as pure association is the social energy or drive that circulates autonomously throughout the social body and is thus independent of individuals' intentions and meanings. Conversation, for Simmel, exemplifies sociability in one of its purest forms. Conversation is simply the play of words in the endless circulation of pure relationship, 'a social space in which signs circulate endlessly as weightless fragments of repartee, stripped of practical content – that of information, argument, business ...' (Krauss, 1998: 63). In conversation, words never arrive at a destination but are carried indefinitely in a continuous motion of deferral and postponement. In the same way, sociability as the endless circulation of pure relationship treats social agents and social objects as continuously deferred and postponed moments and events. Like words, agents and objects come and go, appear and disappear, change meaning and form, always against a background that seems massive, beyond human grasp, and even 'too much'. Mass appears as the endless circulation of energy in the social body in which individuals – whether words, objects or human agents – are carried along.

Simmel extends this image of the social body as the boundless circulation of energy to the urban mass. In contrast to the 'more smoothly flowing rhythm ... of small town and rural existence', urban life is energized by rapid and sudden changes of tempo and sensory stimuli, the 'telescoping of changing images, pronounced differences within what is grasped at a single glance, and the unexpectedness of violent stimuli', all of which intensify emotional life through 'the swift and continuous shift of external and internal stimuli' (Simmel, 1971: 325). From crossing the street and driving in traffic to the agitated 'tempo and multiplicity of economic, occupational and social life' (325), the energy of the urban mass presents itself as a hyperactive challenge to the meaning and stability of individual existences. Simmel's interpretation of the urban mass underlines mass as the energy of dense, continuous movement and mutability that underlies the conventional understanding of social mass as a collection of passive individuals such as we see in the concepts of the crowd or the public. What we normally think is individual and self-contained is really a transient arresting or slowing down of mass's endless motion. It is a way of binding the boundless or what Simmel, in the context of the hyperactive urban mass, calls 'a protective organ ... against the profound disruption with which the fluctuations and discontinuities of the external milieu threaten' the urban individual (Simmel, 1971: 326). Mass products – whether human agents or cultural objects – are by definition transient. They are transient in the multiple sense of being evanescent, incomplete and moving on. They are forms that are provisionally captured out of the radical impermanence of mass's dynamic energy.

When Walter Benjamin (1970) analysed the social and cultural character of the urban mass, he too stressed its resistance to clear and stable forms. The urban crowd is a flow of amorphous energy in which individual forms alternately appear and disappear. Benjamin illustrates the dialectical nature of the appearance-disappearance of mass forms in the example of the passerby who emerges out of the crowd as a momentary form only to be just as quickly reabsorbed into its inchoate mass. The ephemeral appearance of the passerby as an individual depends upon the mass in a double sense: the perceptual recession of the crowd gives form to the passerby while the passerby's disappearance lends a shadowy presence to the crowd. Passerby and crowd are thus expressions of each other's shared mutability. Benjamin presents mass as *movement* that exceeds all attempts to pin it down. Perception is at best a tentative arresting of mass's continuous movement in order to produce a visual object. There is no permanent subject that sees a substantive object. Both subject and object are themselves products of a strategy of framing which creates a provisional perspective with the viewing subject at one end and the seen object at the other. Outside this perspective, the subject and the object are actively suspended in a dynamic field of mutability and impermanence symbolised, for Benjamin, by the passing urban crowd. Benjamin thus offers us an alternative way of thinking mass: instead of clear, stable objects in static frames which persuade us to see *the* crowd, *the* public, *the* mass media, we are asked to see mass as a dynamic, mutable ground from which we extract the myriad changing forms that lend a degree of *apparent* stability to our world. Benjamin's passerby becomes a symbol of modern mass society in which the visual object emerges out of raw, inchoate mass and returns to it in a continuous process of appearance and disappearance, loss and retrieval. Passing away and constant change mark the movement of mass in all its mutable forms.

In Benjamin's interpretation of mass products, subjects and objects are more like moving and ambiguous *profiles* rather than fixed and bounded structures. They are like the words of language that get their significance from the peripheral contexts of which they are simply material transformations. Mass products, according to Benjamin, are the results of a continuous and complex practice of collection and dispersion. They thus reflect the basic logic of language and communication which collects letters into words, words into ideas and ideas into variable human worlds, and then disperses them in the double sense of distributing them as messages to a wider community *and* releasing them to return to their alphabetic and verbal sources where they lie waiting for the call of another collection. The communication of social and cultural forms rests on the continuous collection of letters and words which, like the urban mass, constitute an ever present background source of new and possible forms. Collection (from the Latin *colere*, to till, cultivate, and *legere*, to pick, choose) is the cultivation and selection of material elements from primal mass in order to construct visible and thinkable worlds. Collection in this sense is like identifying a figure from an imperceptible background on which the figure necessarily rests and to which it is constantly liable to return, just as Benjamin's figure of the passerby disappeared into the urban crowd. The act of collection is thus always shadowed by an act of dispersion. It is this double act of collection-dispersion that specially characterizes the movement and mutability of mass. The products of the social and cultural worlds oscillate around and between the double axis of collection-dispersion to create not simply an experience of constant change but, more radically, a disquieting sense of a power that not only exceeds human understanding but shatters and scatters – that is, disperses – every attempt to re-collect it. Mass is thus massive, 'too much'.

In his analysis of modern mass society as the *society of generalized communication*, Gianni Vattimo (1992) draws out the essence of social and cultural mass as constant, unremitting movement which denies any attempt to give it stability and permanence. The mass media, for example, engage in 'superficial games' that transmit 'novelties ... like those of fashion' and which generate overall 'a strange air of fragility and superficiality' (Vattimo, 1992: 57) in a way that reminds us of Simmel's (1971) analysis of conversation as an example of sociability or the endless circulation of pure relationship devoid of all practical content. Instead of stability and permanence, mass society produces a heightened degree of continuous change that is experienced by its members as 'an ongoing disorientation' (Vattimo, 1992: 53) which is yet another way of describing the multifarious mutability of mass. In other words, mass repeatedly disperses all acts of collection, which are then compelled to repeat themselves in acts of re-collection that never arrive at final states of stability or security. Vattimo pursues the theme of disorienting change through the philosopher Martin Heidegger's images of Earth and World. Earth is like mass in that it serves as the raw matter for the production of social and cultural worlds. Earth is also like mass in that it can never be located, never be pinned down, but is forever mutable. World is our collective human attempts to locate Earth, to give it human shape and significance, to found and form ourselves in matter that resists foundation and firm form. What we normally understand as mass society which creates itself through the mass production of consumer goods and media information is merely one way of expressing World. Modern mass society is the hyperactive translation of Earth's invisible mass into the visible and thinkable – and thus not merely consumable – forms and objects that we call the modernized world.

World founds itself as a 'system of significations' which it imposes on Earth as a system of interpretations and meanings to be transmitted in the endless circulation of energy that underlies the 'ongoing disorientation' of the social body (Vattimo, 1992: 53). Earth is 'the obscure and thematically inexhaustible depths in which the world of the work is rooted' but because Earth is 'not a system of signifying connections', because it is totally 'other, the nothing, general gratuitousness and insignificance', it can never serve as a stable foundation for the significations and meanings of World (Vattimo, 1992: 53). Earth is 'like a sort of nucleus that is never used up by interpretations and never exhausted by meanings' (Vattimo, 1988, 71); like the massiveness of mass, Earth is 'too much', it exceeds, shatters and scatters all attempts to fix it in a framework of human meanings. Earth and World are thus bound together in an energetic conflict in which the forms of World depend for their fleeting existences on the active and continuous withdrawal of Earth. World produces Earth only to lose it, like Benjamin's passerby who momentarily emerges out of the urban crowd to be just as quickly reabsorbed by it. World generates forms: Earth degenerates them. For this reason, we should not talk of objects or things with fixed and bounded structures that give a sense of solidity and permanence to the world and against which the degeneration of forms is seen as marginal. Instead, the degeneration of Earth should be seen – precisely because of its strategy of debasement and decay – as that hidden power which forces the work of World ceaselessly to redeem itself through the repetition of reproduction. World redeems itself from Earth as the reproduction of *events* rather than solid, self-enclosed objects and things. Events are happenings or occurrences that come and go, appear and disappear; they are more like moving and ambiguous profiles rather than fixed and bounded structures. Events are products of collection-dispersion by which World brings together disparate elements and parts into signifying patterns and which Earth simultaneously works to undermine and scatter. Earth thus appears as an expression of Williams's (1983) characterization of mass as that which is amorphous, indistinguishable and dense. World is that which translates and transforms Earth's mass into transient collections and recollections of meaningful and thus 'readable' forms and signs. What we understand as *mass society* is exactly this perpetual transaction of collection-dispersion between World and Earth but on a hypertrophic and hyperactive scale. In this interpretation of mass society, it is the sense of mass as recession and decline that prevails. Instead of mass society as a system of massive, dependable structures that serve as background support for the advancement of civilized life and culture, we are left with an image of the feverish movement of events and outline forms whose continuous dispersion and disappearance provides the implausible basis of what we still call *advanced* industrial society.

The production of mass

When Benjamin (1970) began to study modern society as a society of mass he chose to emphasize its dynamic mobility. Mass society was a matrix of moving and changing forms. Benjamin did not see mass as a vast collection of objects and things that could be clearly distinguished and thus clearly seen; he did not see mass society as the proliferation of individuals aggregated for the exchange of goods or information in a reticulation of production and consumption.

20

Modern society was to be more radically understood as a mass of events and moving outlines rather than the creation of large-scale structures of popular needs and wants and their satiation. Modern technologies revealed the world as an infinite source of ever-changing possibilities; they unveiled mass as a boundless origin of social and cultural forms. Film was one such technology. Film opened the eyes of the social mass to the hidden possibilities of a world it had previously considered obdurate. The camera expands space with the close-up; movement is extended in time with slow motion. The routinely familiar act of walking is transmuted into a strangely supernatural event. The habitual act of reaching for a lighter or a spoon is dramatized as the creative movement of the hand in its dealings with the world. Film reveals the mass of the world as an 'unconscious optics' in which the camera with 'its lowerings and liftings, its interruptions and isolations, its extensions and accelerations, its enlargements and reductions' (Benjamin, 1970: 239) foregrounds the experience of event and outline instead of the conventionally conscious perception of solid things. Film production is itself based on the production of transient events and outlines in that it takes 'shots' of its subject matter, 'cuts' and edits them in order to make them 'readable' for a mass audience. Production in this sense is a result of a mutual yet contestatory action between collection and dispersion. Film does not merely represent an already-existing world; it actively participates in the production of that world. It circulates images of the world as material fragments of contrasting degrees of physical light on moving frames of film. The material fragments of film begin to look like Saussure's (1966) words that simply circulate as pure deferral, without necessarily referring to objects or things in the solid world.

Film as a complex act of collection-dispersion is like all forms of the mass media in that it captures momentary events in transient outlines which it then places in the communication flows of mass society. Newspapers work in the same way. At one level, they report news of events that happen in the real world. At the level of pure circulation – Simmel's (1971) sociability – the material signs of words and pictures carried by the newspaper serve only as a vehicle for the transmission of the energy that animates social mass. In itself, the material sign – like the letters of the alphabet or the isolated word – is an indeterminate fragment; it begins to take on meaning when it is placed in the context of other material signs such as a sentence or a news report. The distinctive feature of modern mass society is its continuous and repeated acts of work on such indeterminate fragments in order to give them some sense of order and meaning, however temporary and ephemeral. This is the work of collection that makes the material mass of the world 'readable'. The material sign as indeterminate fragment is the dispersion of collection and therefore of meaning. Circulation as dispersion and indeterminacy represents mass as pure movement and mutability. Without collection and the constraint that goes with it, there is 'no real message, only an interminable, indeterminate, unbounded verbal flow that carries no messages prior to the transmitting stations that constitute them' (Bersani and Dutoit, 1993: 61).

Mass production and consumption are defined by the ceaseless and correlative movements of collection and dispersion which give modern mass society its peculiar ethos of ephemerality. Products are made *not to last* and give the impression that they simply serve as vehicles for activity and movement. They compel the human mind to move with them. The technologies of mass consumption display their multifarious products in a perceptual space of systematic distraction. The superstore concentrates a massive range of merchandise in a circumscribed space so that the consumer's attention is dispersed rather than focused. The newspaper commodifies news in the same way, presenting a kaleidoscope of international and home news, politics, comment, sport, fashion and advertising that systematizes distraction and thus reduces the singular significance of the story reported. This is what Benjamin (1970) intended with his idea of *distracted perception* as a defining feature of mass society. The social mass of mass society sees the world not in a focused or concentrated way but as a movement of ambiguous and passing forms; it consumes by absorbing everything around it as if in a reverie. Benjamin contrasts the distracted mass with the concentration the serious spectator of art brings to the work of art. The art lover is absorbed by the art work, by its transcendental significance, its technical bravura. By definition, the social mass sees things collectively and in the half-light of a continuously moving and ambivalent background of counteracting events. For the social mass, art is experienced marginally, not as a uniquely auratic event but is absorbed into the general ingestion of mass living. Architecture is Benjamin's example of an art that is distractedly perceived by the social mass. Architecture is always significantly present but rarely noticed as a taken-for-granted background of daily life in much the same way that the urban crowd moves as an imperceptible mass in and through all the activities of an individual's lifeworld. When Benjamin discusses the correlative nature of collection and dispersion, he makes the point that collected forms are always also informed or inhabited by a bias to disperse or scatter. Distraction is a form of dispersion and we see it demonstrated in the very structure of the word itself, for *distraction* is also *destruction* and *de-striction*.

As destruction, distraction is a destructuring or loss of collected structure; as de-striction, it is the removal of strictures or commands to act or 'read' a situation in a specific order and form. In interpreting *distraction* in this way, Benjamin reminds us of Williams's (1983) emphasis on mass as profligate matter that is difficult to tame and that language itself is simply another expression of mass that is subject to the twistings and turnings of dispersion and mutability. To talk of the *production of mass* is to recognize the work of dispersion and distraction in the very act of collection. For *production* as both word and act is a collection of dispersed, disparate meanings. Conventionally, it refers to the making of a product often with consumption or use in view. But it has a latent and generally unrecognized meaning: *prediction*. Production produces products which structure the future and the way we as producers and consumers think about tomorrow. The 'shelf life' of the thousands of products in a food supermarket is not just an indicator of a product's freshness and edibility; it is a major vector that directs the whole production-consumption system of the mass food industry. A product in this sense helps realize a mass of individual lifeworlds; it becomes less a consumable item and more an object through which to think. In the all-embracing mass production-consumption system of the modern world, we too have our 'shelf lives' which the system, in order to maintain its productive vigour, has to continually monitor through a strategy of 'seeing off that which has served its time, which has passed in accordance with its term, which has been accomplished' (Vattimo, 1993: 122). The special character of mass production-consumption as continuous *reproduction* underlines the interpretation of production as the continuous *remaking* of a world that is continuously menaced by the dispersed and disparate pressures intrinsic to the mass that production works on. Production in this basic and general sense is prediction as the control of the bias of mass to dispersion, scattering and decline.

The society of mass production is essentially to do with the *production of mass* in the special sense of producing and reproducing the mutability and 'bewildering abundance' intrinsic to mass. The products of mass production take their places in a society distinguished by incessant transmission and an inexorable movement of decline. They are dedicated to ephemerality and are born to die. The cultivation of mass as mutability and prodigality produces a sense of the world's impermanence, its intrinsic lack of founding principles, and even a hint of arbitrariness. The timeless values of transcendental truth and harmony associated with traditional culture are themselves subject to dispersion and decline in modern mass society. Traditional culture privileged permanence over change, stability over instability. Its products were realized out of materials such as gold, silver and marble which symbolized durability and the perpetual. In contrast, the products of mass culture are made from evanescent materials such as paper and plastic, and seem designed specifically for decline. Modern art has addressed itself as a form of social commentary to the fading away of traditional culture through the strategic volatility of mass society. Modern artists such as Picasso and Braque developed the technique of *collage* – a version of collection – in order to highlight the creative possibilities and general cultural significance of the new mass methods of production that began to burgeon at the beginning of the twentieth century. Collage is a form of art that brings together on a picture surface disparate ready-made objects such as newspaper cuttings, bottle labels, cigarette packets, wallpaper and from these creates a complex composition which not only questions the role of traditional, representational art as the conveyor of universal and superior human truths but which also underlines art as the creation of transitory events and outline forms. In Picasso's collages, the creative possibilities provided by the new mass-production system are celebrated by showing how its various products can be brought into *play* and thus express some of the more latent and less apparent capacities offered by the mutability and prodigality of mass. Picasso's collages thus essentially express the *play-form of association* that

Simmel (1971) sees as the essence of sociability. Picasso wants us to see the dynamics of mass society as a play-form of sociability in which bits and pieces of information and objects simply circulate as vehicles of communication that are wholly distinct from the practical and functional purposes and meanings we normally ascribe to the activities of daily life. Collage reveals the underlying nature of mass society to be the production of mass: the endless collection and dispersion of things, their continuous combination and permutation, in the play of mutability that is the special feature of mass.

Not self-contained, substantive things but *relations*. This is what Picasso's collages try to make us see. Not products as conveniences of life but products as the movement of complex and variable relations. Collage undermines the conventional perception of the human world as a collection of naturally stable and reliable things which are either already there or can be adapted for the use and ease of living. Collage tells us that things come together and then fall apart, that relations are ephemeral, even ghost-like, events we cannot physically see or touch, that possibilities rather than actualities constitute the fabric of our world. All this Picasso senses in the comings and goings of the society of mass and which he celebrates in collage as the simultaneous collection and dispersion of fragments and parts of the industrial and commercial world. Collage is itself the exaggerated performance of the production of mass: a newspaper cutting of small advertisements is 'scissored into the shape of a seltzer bottle, its lines of type upended' so that the small type of the advertisements gives the impression of rising bubbles (Krauss, 1998: 49); the title of a newspaper, *Le Journal*, is cut in half and the *Le Jou* bit is collaged with other products such as wallpaper and sheet-music to suggest – despite the gravity of the news reports of battles and financial collapses – the infinite and unstoppable *play* that underlines and motivates the work of mass production and consumption, of which the newspaper is merely one expression; posters of well known industrial products are collaged with factory outlines to suggest a dynamic figure-ground interaction between mass products and their industrial sources. Picasso is always careful to depict the mass product as a fragment or part that occurs as a transitory relation with other fragments and parts and not as a self-sufficient whole. The mass product is a collection that is already a dispersion. The vision of the mass product given in Picasso's collages is based on suggestion, impression, hint rather than the conventional perception of an object as self-evidently clear in shape and purpose. In the collage of the seltzer bottle, the small type of the upended newspaper cutting *suggests* rising bubbles and is not intended to represent them directly. Picasso offers a way of seeing and thinking mass society as transient event and outline that reminds us of Benjamin's vision of social mass as mass *movement* and the passerby who comes and goes with the urban crowd. Mass production becomes the production of mass or the creation of fragments and parts that can be combined and recombined in an infinite, flowing pool of relations in which – and this is what Picasso stresses – fragments and parts implicate and define each other as *con-verses* of interchangeable relations. Picasso's collage technique thus provides additional insight into Simmel's sociability as *conversation* in which words and ideas change places and dislocate each other in endless, non-functional exchange. For this reason, collage as the collection-dispersion of fragments and parts in playful exchange might be called the *convertibility* of mass since it especially calls attention to the mutually *convertible* and interchangeable nature of mass's intrinsic mutability as expressed in the generalized dynamic dispersion and distraction that characterizes modern mass culture where, for example, it becomes difficult to distinguish high art from the artful and insidious artifices of the modern mass-production system, as Picasso set out to demonstrate.

The history of mass production shadows the loss of objecthood and the emergence of a culture that recreates itself more and more out of dense and amorphous aggregates (Williams, 1983). Objects become secondary products in a system geared increasingly to the production of mutability and hence the creation and circulation of evanescent signs and images, fleeting events and forms. Traditional craft production revolved around the identifiable terms of the unique maker, the made object such as a table or a vase, and the client for whom the object was specially made. The made object was fashioned directly from raw material. All this changed with mass production. Instead of the unique client, mass products follow no one in particular but anyone and everyone. Instead of the unique maker, the act of making is distributed – we might also say dispersed – among an anonymous many. Mass production 'substitutes collective presence for individual presence' and in doing so foregrounds *relations among parts* of the general collective rather than the individual identities of the collective's constituent members and products (Fisher, 1991: 243). The collective presence of the mass production-consumption system includes the human body and especially its parts as raw material for social and cultural reproducibility. Collective presence is the continuous collection and recollection of parts and fragments of bodies and objects which, like the pieces of a jigsaw, can be assembled, disassembled and re-assembled. It is in this sense that we can understand the human body and its parts as *con-verses* of the objects that relate it to the world, for 'the edges of the body have never been absolute' (Fisher, 1991: 244) and require their *con-verses* in the external world in order to work, produce and reproduce: the arms and legs of a chair *con-verse* with the arms and legs of its human occupant, the lip of a cup *con-verses* with the human lips that drink from it, a spoon *con-verses* through its handle with the hand that holds it and through its bowl with the mouth it fits into. Chair and limbs, cups and lips, spoon, hand and mouth are thus *convertible* into each other. Each object – chair, cup, spoon – can never be separate and self-contained; by definition, it is always partial, a *con-verse* in a dynamic network of *convertibilities*. The body, too, is necessarily partial, momentarily defining itself through assemblage with another partial object. The understanding and definition of the human agent as essentially purposeful and self-directive now takes second place to agency as the general collection and dispersion of parts and fragments which co-define each other in a mutable and transient assemblage of possibilities and relations.

Instead of voluntary human agency expressing its conscious desires, we see human action as the interactions between body parts and external objects in what Philip Fisher has called the *materialization of acts* in which, for example, the spoon as object materializes the act of eating or a bridge over a river materializes on a bigger scale the smaller bodily act of leaping across a stream (Fisher, 1991: 245). Body parts and objects *con-verse* with each other in a form of material sociability (Simmel, 1971). Materialized acts represent mass as the endless circulation of energy in the social body in which objects and human agents are carried along. Mass production-consumption as the production and consumption of mass is itself essentially a system for the materialization of acts *through the production of parts*. The modern industrial system has concentrated on the production of part-based products rather than whole objects. The modern factory focuses on parts and their assembly. The finished product – the motor vehicle, the television set – is a secondary feature of the part-assembly activity and of the mass production system more generally. In a wider sense, the finished product is still unfinished: the motor vehicle and the television set are incomplete or partial objects which seek further connections with their human users. Again, we see the work of the partial object which seeks to complete itself – at least momentarily – as materialized act. The *part* (from the Latin *partire, portare,* to bear, carry, share, distribute) expresses transience, movement and dispersion rather than stable objecthood. In mass production, the 'central set of parts is like the letters of the alphabet, open to assembly into infinite combinations – words' (Fisher, 1992: 247). The industrial part capitalizes on its degrees of freedom to be assembled and reassembled and this weakens the sense of the object as a self-sufficient whole. This is exactly what Picasso's collages exaggerate and dramatize in their speculations on the radical implications of mass production-consumption systems for the way we act, think and see in mass society. The withdrawal of the object into a background role transfers 'reality to the system as a whole and to the play of transformations and possibilities that it invites' (Fisher, 1991: 249). Collection-dispersion as the continuous combination and permutation of parts makes social and cultural reality into a system of infinite *convertibility* in which the incompleteness of things is emphasized at the expense of their wholeness.

Desire

The human agent as producer and consumer is necessarily included as an assemblage of incomplete parts that can be continuously combined and permutated in a system of infinite *convertibility*. The human agent is forever redefined in a collage of *con-verses* and ephemeral relations which resist wholeness and objecthood. Agency in this context is the continuous collection and recollection – the recovery, if you like – of the individual human image from the flux and flow of dispersion and the sense of looseness and loss it implies. The persistence of the individual's self-image depends on its recovery or the making and remaking of itself from the human body and its parts that serve, in association with non-human part-objects, as raw material for social and cultural reproducibility. This urge to recover and remake the human image, whether individual or collective, lies at the heart of *desire* as a basic and essential force that keeps the social body moving. Desire is a force or energy that depends directly on dispersion and loss for its regeneration; it actively seeks dispersion and can be said to be itself an expression of dispersion (as we see in the Latin term for desire, *desiderium*, a longing for that which is lost, and the French *déchirer*, to tear apart or disperse). Identities have no natural location; they are constituted by repetition out of the flux and flow of the 'placeless relational mobility' of dispersion (Bersani and Dutoit, 1993: 76). The act of social collection that locates an individual *I* or *you* helps us 'to locate where we stop and others begin, but at the same time the beginnings of others are inseparable from the consciousness of self ... . There is no moment of self-identification that is not also a self-multiplication or dispersal' (Bersani and Dutoit, 1993: 75). Desire in this sense is the *energy* of collection-dispersion as well as Simmel's (1971) drive of sociability that circulates autonomously throughout the social body. Here it is important to distinguish the common-sense understanding of desire as the wish for specific objects and the pursuit of specific goals from desire as the pure energy or play of the *convertibility* that moves collection-dispersion. Common-sense desire already knows what it wants and its knowledge is therefore always conscious of some identifiable object that it lacks; it seeks to satisfy a known lack or need in order to make itself whole again. Common-sense desire is thus the desire of a self-contained, self-directing human agent that seeks always to augment its sense of individual self. Desire in its wider sense is the desire for the freedom and openness of Simmel's (1971) *play-form of association* that goes beyond the specific and local; it desires dispersion, looseness, even loss. Collection is that act which responds to the desire for the specific and locatable, for meaning and significance; dispersion, to the desire for the general and the transcendent, for what exceeds the limited meanings of the local and specific. In identifying these two spaces of desire, we should also acknowledge that they too are subject to the interplay that marks the mutuality of collection-dispersion: the local and specific is a product of the more general, diffuse space of dispersion, while the general and transcendent is that indeterminate space that gets its calling power from the limits that define the local and specific.

Walter Benjamin's (1970) analysis of the urban mass and its movements reflects this distinction between the two spaces of desire: his passerby who momentarily emerges out of the crowd only to be just as quickly returned to it is a motif that Benjamin employs in various forms to catch the idea of the continuous oscillation between specific, identifiable spaces and a more general, indeterminate space that specially characterizes the movement of mass in urban societies. Benjamin's motif of social mass as oscillation and mutability is taken up by Philip Fisher (1985) in his analysis of the development of urban life in

America at the end of the nineteenth century. Fisher explores the changing nature of individuality and social relations in the Chicago of the 1890s through the novels of Theodore Dreiser; he shows how Dreiser's novels work as social analysis by introducing a set of ideas that complement and extend Benjamin's (1970: 157–202) commentary on Paris at roughly the same period: transient worlds, dynamic movement, the incomplete self, decline and renewal, all discussed within the wider context of desire as collection-dispersion.

The city – Chicago, Paris, London – represents the dense, unremitting movement of social mass. Beneath a veneer of active purposefulness, the city is a collection of worlds – commercial, manufacturing, political, family, leisure – that together produce an overall effect of hyperaction and agitation. The many worlds of the city seem to be going somewhere, seem to be reaching out for specific goals while at the same time suggesting that their activities are driven by a relentless and instinctive force which their conscious purposes simply gloss over. For Fisher (1985), this force is desire as collection-dispersion. The city represents the 'translation of desires' or the transformation and translation of mass as raw, placeless matter into structured vehicles that will carry our thoughts and feelings: buildings are never just the raw materials of brick, concrete or glass out of which they are made 'but restaurants, churches, brothels, shoe stores, apartments, offices, and factories' that 'translate into places the desires for food or God, sex or various coverings, shelter or work' (Fisher, 1985: 131–2). Desire in this sense is a *covering* and a *re-covering*, however temporary, of the human world from the non-human world of mass. Desire's repetitive acts of *re-covery* translate the city-world of physical substance and solid objects into vehicles of *convertible* forms, moving profiles rather than fixed and bounded structures: 'Things within the city have lost substance, what 'they' may be is a kind of film over what we can see as our own want' (Fisher, 1985: 132). The motions *between* objects express the 'energy of desire' rather than the objects themselves. Desire is the acting *out* of the self through the fabric of the cityscape which surrounds 'the body like a second, more spacious suit of clothing' (Fisher, 1985: 131). The display of goods in a department store is part of the *con-versation* of desire, it 'defines the process of yearning, choosing and imagining the transformations of the self by things, by others, and by places that the city proposes' (Fisher, 1985: 133). The goods and commodities of the city are not desired as property or as simple utilities: 'With property a person absorbs a thing into his life' whereas desire as *con-versation* seeks 'to be absorbed temporarily into the magical life of the things' that make up the city as 'a market for the rental of aura' (Fisher, 1985: 134). Aura is auratic, even erotic, desire to lose oneself in the dynamic otherness of the cityscape: 'For a man inside the city his self is not inside his body but around him, outside the body (Fisher, 1985: 134).

The transient energy of desire, its resistance to identity, to being located in places and objects, its dispersive turbulence, all find their optimal genesis in the mutable, temporary worlds of the city. As a collection of temporary worlds, the city is a 'fragile, ad-hoc world' (Fisher, 1985: 139) that continually transforms itself in much the same way as Vattimo's society of generalized communication with its 'strange air of fragility and superficiality' (Vattimo, 1992: 57). Fisher's city of temporary worlds reconnects us with Vattimo's discussion of Heidegger's images of World and Earth where World is the human attempt to give expression and significance to the massive mutability and excessiveness of Earth. World and Earth are locked together in a mutually generating conflict in which the continuous withdrawal of Earth knee-jerks World into those transient reconstructions of significations and meanings that Fisher calls temporary worlds. Picasso's collages also exemplify the dynamic *convertibility* of the city's mutable and temporary worlds; the collage's fragments and parts combine and recombine as *con-verses* of interchangeable relations. In Fisher's examples, the city becomes a gigantic ever-moving collage: a portion of pavement becomes an overnight bed for a homeless person, a newspaper is turned into an ad-hoc umbrella at a sudden outbreak of rain. In the constantly moving collage of the city, people are not self-sufficiently themselves, never persons in possession of themselves, but always reflections of others from whom they 'borrow their being' and from whom they get their 'selves' 'moment by moment as a gift from the outside' (Fisher, 1985: 140–1). The hotel is a world from which its guests and employees 'borrow their being'. As a world, the 'hotel has more being, more reality than anyone within it. To each it rents out a part of its self ...'. (Fisher, 1985: 147). The factory and the department store are also worlds that rent out the aura of desire: the clothes they make and sell are vehicles by which the person is able to express multiple selves and enhance their capacity for social movement in the various worlds of the city that beckon them.

The self in the city is always a 'self in anticipation' (Fisher, 1985: 157). Ever incomplete, always desiring, the urban self is never fully present to itself; it does not occupy present time but always either the future or the past. The 'anticipated self' is moved by prospective desire, by auratic hope. But just as there is prospective desire of hoped-for and hopeful future worlds, so there is the desire of 'retrospective being' (Fisher, 1985: 160), of worlds the self has either lost or known only in dreams. Always driven by anticipation, desire's future is implicitly already a past. Desire in the city is a mixture of the 'might-be', the 'has-been' and the 'might-have-been'. These are desire's ways of saying collection and dispersion and the continuous movement in space *and* time they provoke. The newspaper is an urban product driven by desire's tension between past and future; the present does not concern it; it prints what has already happened and is already geared up to report the future as the past. The self that reads the newspaper is itself defined by the temporary worlds the newspaper both represents and records. Like the temporary worlds it inhabits, the anticipated self is a version of *production* as *prediction*. The newspaper joins with the thousands of products on the shelves of the food supermarket; both newspaper and food product have their limited 'shelf lives' which the production system *as a vehicle of anticipative desire* has to monitor continually in order to see off 'that which has served its time, which has passed in accordance with its term, which has been accomplished' (Vattimo, 1993: 122). Production in this sense is also prediction or the anticipation of worlds that are yet to come but which are already destined to be past. Desire as production-prediction, as collection-dispersion, embraces both generation and decline in its unrelenting quest for expression. Fisher illustrates the continuous and co-defining work of generation *and* decline in the city through Darwin's theory of evolution which emphasizes the collectivity rather than the individual in the survival – or what we might call the production-prediction – of an organic world. As well as reminding us of the incompleteness of the individual and its dependence on the collective, evolution stresses the *energy* of generation in much the same way as mass appears as the endless circulation of energy by which individuals – words, objects, human agents – are carried along in the social body. In the extreme, this energy disperses all collection, shatters all sensible and meaningful collocations of the human mind, all reasoning power, and momentarily reduces the knowable world to a 'tangled mass' of dense, amorphous passion (Fisher, 1985: 172). The climax of desire is the point where individuality and selfhood lose themselves in the experience of pure mass in a magnification of the more domesticated desire that moves the city dweller 'to be absorbed temporarily into the magical life of the things' that make up the city (Fisher, 1985: 134). All expressions of desire in the city follow a pattern of generation, decline and regeneration. The energy of desire shadows the life history of the city and the partial selves who live through it: 'This life history is that of products and objects which are best when new or fresh and then become worn out and discarded. The life history of a shirt is one of continual decline. All goods are used up and replaced' (Fisher, 1985: 175). The city is a collection of worlds in which generation and decline are hyperbolized as definitive features of human life. As products decline, so do human lives and their worlds shrink with loss of energy, eyesight and mental faculties until they become finally extinct. The city thus becomes a vast production site which produces not individual products for individual consumers but multiple worlds of energetic desire which rise and fall as the repetition of collection and dispersion. The city emerges as an evolutionary machine that is hyperactively preoccupied with the recovery of human worlds from the non-human world of dense, amorphous, boundless mass.

In his semiological commentaries on modern mass culture, Roland Barthes (1972) has thematized the role of mass as raw matter in the modern production-consumption system. Matter, for Barthes, 'is much more magical than life' (Barthes, 1972: 88), for it provides human life with infinite possibilities; its excessive prodigality, its exuberant mobility, constantly presses us to rework it as the source for our own recovery. In a short essay on the nature of plastic as a symbol of matter's producible power, Barthes (1972: 97–9) reminds us of the significance of raw matter in general for the production of human worlds – a significance submerged by our familiarity with products as taken-for-granted supports of daily living. Like all matter, plastic is much more than mere substance: 'plastic is the very idea of its infinite transformation; as its

© The Editorial Board of The Sociological Review 2001

everyday name indicates, it is ubiquity made visible' (Barthes, 1972: 97). Plastic's infinite transformability or *convertibility* 'into a multitude of more and more startling objects' of everyday use – Barthes' thoughts were the result of seeing an industrial exhibition of plastic's production potential held in Paris in the 1950s and which included practical demonstrations of the transformation of 'heaps of greenish crystals' into finished products such as suitcases, brushes, car-bodies, toys, buckets, jewellery – prompts 'a perpetual amazement, the reverie of man at the sight of the proliferating forms of matter, and the connections he detects between the singular of the origin and the plural of the effects' (Barthes, 1972: 97). Barthes is less concerned with the finished products and their use values than with recognizing plastic as a mutable and mobile source of commercial and social energy. While plastic clearly has 'utilitarian advantages' and prosaic uses, its latent character lies beyond the functions the everyday world imposes on it (Barthes, 1972: 98). Like mass in general, it is densely amorphous and so resists all attempts to understand it in worldly terms. Its implicit character is beyond our grasp, for we can only really place it and know it in its specific contexts of production and consumption. In this respect, the latency of plastic is an example of Earth's invisible mass which can never be located since it is intrinsically mutable and without firm foundation; like Earth, plastic withdraws at every attempt by World to pin it down, to give it human shape and meaning (Vattimo, 1992). Plastic simply uses the names of the world to signal its negative presence. It is, for Barthes, a new 'poetic substance' revealed by the alchemy of modern techno-science, and thus a harbinger of a new universe of *convertibility* where 'the whole world *can* be plasticized, and even life itself since, we are told, they are beginning to make plastic aortas' (Barthes, 1972: 99). Not so much a substance but an 'infinite transformation', plastic is 'ubiquity made visible'; 'it is less a thing than the trace of a movement' (Barthes, 1972: 97). Plastic underlines desire as mobility, not possession; it reveals production as the movement of complex and variable relations rather than products as the conveniences of life. Plastic is like collage in the fundamental sense of disclosing mass as the movement of *convertibility* which continually undermines the idea of a world of fixed locations and stable identities. Plastic is the expression of desire as search and seeking for its own sake; and which, by definition, has no specific goal, no object, no place, no end. Desire *is* plastic – plastic energy: infinite, boundless, unlocatable mobility.

Both Barthes and Fisher see raw matter as movement, energy, vitality. Their urban products are vehicles for the activity and movement of generation and decline, collection and dispersion. And we cannot see the movement of matter. Plastic matter, Barthes tells us, 'is less a thing than the trace of a movement' (Barthes, 1972: 97). This reminds us that mass production is less to do with the production of objects and more to do with the production of mass as the creation and circulation of evanescent signs and images, fleeting events and forms. In his fictive essay on modern America as an advanced production-consumption system, Don DeLillo (1985) traces the movement of mass as electrical energy or 'white noise' that courses through all aspects of living:

television, radio, the supermarket, techno-science, the computer, the newspaper. Behind what we once knew as a world of meaningful, stable objects, there now emerges a sense of phantasmatic mutability where formerly identifiable things recede into the indistinguishable, amorphous mass of 'white noise' just like Benjamin's passerby who recedes into the urban crowd. Even the self is no longer sure it thinks its own thoughts since these are now 'a question of brain chemistry, signals going back and forth, electrical energy in the cortex' (DeLillo, 1985: 45). A nerve impulse is activated and 'suddenly I want to go to Montana or I don't want to go to Montana. How do I know I really want to go and it isn't just some neurons firing or something?' (DeLillo, 1985: 45). The person that used to be recedes into the cortical mass of invisible neuronal movement. We are suspended as *traces* between the solid objects of the world and the indistinguishable raw matter from which these objects are made. Even the familiar names of the production-consumption system seem to reflect a world of energetic phantoms: Kleenex Softique, Dacron, Orlon, Lycra Spandex, Tegrin, Denorex, Selsun Blue call to us from the supermarket shelves and the television commercials. The product names are made electronically *convertible* through consumer codes provided by the generic magic of MasterCard, Visa, American Express. The proliferation of product images, brand names and electronic passwords in due course creates an experience of distracted perception or 'brain fade' in which 'people's eyes, ears, brains and nervous systems have grown weary' so that they lose the ability to look and listen attentively (DeLillo, 1985: 67). Like Benjamin's passerby absorbed by the crowd, the consumer is absorbed by the 'white noise' of the electronically simulated and ambiently insinuative messages of the production-consumption world. Desire becomes automatic, mechanical, until it is wrenched out of its sleep-walk by an event that recovers for us the extraordinary powers behind the everyday routine of mass products when they are revealed to us as the production of mass. The narrator of DeLillo's novel hears his daughter repeat a product name in her sleep: *Toyota Celica*. At first he does not realize it is the brand name of a car; out of context, it sounds 'beautiful and mysterious, gold-shot with looming wonder ... like the name of an ancient power in the sky'. And yet it was only a 'simple brand name, an ordinary car ... near-nonsense words, murmured in a child's restless sleep ... She was only repeating some TV voice. Toyota Corolla, Toyota Celica, Toyota Cressida. Supranational names, computer-generated ... Part of every child's brain noise, the substatic regions too deep to probe' (DeLillo, 1985: 155). Yet he is awe-struck by the utterance, as if he were in the presence of something 'much more magical than life' (Barthes, 1972: 88). Whatever it is, it seems too massive, too prodigal, to be comprehended. It reappears in the supermarket in the electronic language of the terminals with their holographic scanners which 'decode the binary secret of every item' (DeLillo, 1985: 326). Beneath the display of its edible and usable images, the supermarket speaks an other-worldly, transcendental language, 'the language of waves and radiation, or how the dead speak to the living' (DeLillo, 1985: 326). Like plastic, the supermarket 's wares mediate between recognizable, worldly things and the electronic 'traces of movement' that resist meaning and location (Barthes, 1972: 97). The only strategy left to us in the face of this remote, mutable and mute energy is *creative pretence*. Creative pretence is production-prediction as *making it up* as we go along. The more that techno-science reveals the world as raw matter which, like Earth, 'is other, the nothing, general gratuitousness and insignificance' (Vattimo, 1992: 53), the more we as desiring agents have to *make believe* a world of human possibilities by *making over* the unhuman possibilities of Earth. Creative 'pretence is a dedication' to recover and remake the human image from the mute and mutable energy of mass (DeLillo, 1985: 319).

Electronic mass

DeLillo's America is a cybernetic system of electronic communication where people and things take second place to their movement as incomplete parts. Like Fisher's depiction of modern industrial production as a system of combinable and permutable parts, computer-based cybernetics creates a *convertible* reality of evanescent signs and fleeting images. Collection and dispersion as combination and permutation require the translation of raw, mutable mass into discrete parts as a first step. In conventional languages, this initiating step is the setting up of an alphabet of separate letters which then provide enormous freedom for combination and permutation. In the computer, the binary digit is the basic device that translates electronic energy into vast mind-like cybernetic systems of information forever on the move. Electronic brains, argues Italo Calvino (1987), model human brains and living systems more generally as incomplete parts that play with each other through combination and permutation. Through the computer, we now see even the writing of literature as 'purely and simply a process of combination among given elements' (Calvino, 1987: 17). Literature becomes a 'machine' and we can no longer talk of an individual writer's 'genius' or 'talent', of poetry as 'a matter of inspiration descending from I know not what lofty place, or welling up from I know not what great depths', of creative spirit or intuition (Calvino, 1987: 14). How can we detect and describe the route by which these phantom concepts are 'transformed into a series of black lines on a white page' (Calvino, 1987: 14)? The black lines on the white page 'write' the writer just as the writer writes them. Writer and lines are thus *con-verses* of each other in a *materialized act* (Fisher, 1991: 245). The writer as author disperses into a haze-like world of relations where former things are now converted into mutable profiles. For Calvino, literature is an electronic brain which creates new worlds by endlessly combining and recombining the material marks of letters and words. Literature takes on that sense of permanent incompleteness that Saussure (1966) saw as a chief feature of words which get their meanings from being continuously deferred in a mutable space that resists precise location. At this elemental point, the marks of writing begin to suggest the amorphous mutability of mass:

cybernetics and literature begin to look indistinguishable; they call to each other from within their own disciplinary boundaries as if to say they are materially more than they seem. Both are 'combinatorial games' that play on the mutable possibilities of mass and that release into consciousness, often unexpectedly and by chance, the surprise or even shock intimations of 'hidden ghosts' that lie within the material folds of the rational glosses we place on consciously managed *systems* of communication (Calvino, 1987: 22).

By definition, electronic mass undifferentiates and dedifferentiates the bounded structures of the conventional world. The bounded self is dispersed in networks of *con-verses* and *convertibilities*, mind becomes a play of pulses and signals in electronic space and time, the nervous system moves out of the living body to become a computerized collective organism, the languages of the world merge together in the universal linguistic community of the binary digit. Electronic mass means the dissolution of the conventional distinction between living organisms and machines. Darwin's theory of evolution maintained that only living organisms could self-evolve and that machines, being inorganic, were merely part of the world of dead matter. Electronic mass implies a symbiosis of neural communication between human organism and electronic machine: 'Everything that human beings are doing to make it easier to operate computer networks is at the same time, but for different reasons, making it easier for computer networks to operate human beings' (Dyson, 1998: 10). This is the mutable and ambivalent movement of mass where conventional distinctions begin to falter and where perception becomes distracted and subject to the dynamic oscillation of collaged *convertibilities*. Pulses and fibres constitute electronic mass and they move collectively, not individually; their final expression as information is a statistical product of their complex interactions, a coalition of digital relations that momentarily come together and make a temporary sense rather than a discrete message: 'A successful, if fleeting coalition, in our mental universe, may surface to be perceived – and perhaps communicated, via recourse to whatever symbolic channels are open at the time – as an idea' (Dyson, 1998: 158). This is Don DeLillo's America where products are consumed as neural images transmitted by 'the language of waves and radiation' (DeLillo, 1985: 326) and where production is less to do with the provision of usable commodities and much more to do with the statistical *prediction* of mass in the form of mutable and mobile electronic worlds. Production as prediction is always about *probabilities*, about the likely behaviour of collectives rather than the more unpredictable behaviour of individuals. The supermarket, through its vast range of mass products, is more a means of ensuring the collective future than a satisfier of individual wants and tastes. Electronic mass speaks collectively through the statistical language of the nervous system in which things are *probable* rather than *certain*. Probability requires the unknown or the 'too much' of mass in order to do its work. Cybernetic information is that which we did not know before; it is 'news' in the radical sense of being 'new'; it depends on the unknown and is in this radical sense a form of desire which seeks to regenerate or re-'new' itself through dispersion and loss. Information in the cybernetic context is thus another way of talking about the production of mass with its cycles of production and consumption, generation and decline, collection and dispersion, all of which echo in their different ways the making and loss of form that cybernetic information implies. Electronic mass dramatically emphasizes the dynamic mutability between the formless and the formed. The growth of modern cybernetic systems in which electronics and biology merge to create giant, world-wide mental webs through the computer-telecommunications link are themselves products of this universal desire for the unknown, the formless, for mass that 'bewilders'. In the cybernetic age, the production of mass reappears as a 'digital wilderness' (Dyson, 1998: 228).

The electronic world of the computer and its associated technologies brings us all significantly nearer to Benjamin's (1970) world of mass movement in which the urban mass and its mass products move within a dynamic background of ephemeral, fleeting impressions. The mass world created by electronic machines is also Vattimo's (1992) society of generalized communication in which the electronic-based media hyperactively circulate signs and images to create an overwhelming sense of rapid movement as 'ongoing disorientation' (Vattimo, 1992: 53). The computer is a machine that seems almost destined to bring human beings nearer to their origins in dense, amorphous mass: the electronic pulse as binary movement is the computer's way of expressing raw, placeless matter. As a vehicle of electronic mass, the computer in its developing symbiosis with both ourselves and other machines is a production system increasingly geared to the creation and circulation of fleeting signs and images and ephemeral worlds. But, and perhaps more significantly, it has the capacity to reveal new worlds through its more direct communication with the possibilities intrinsic to mass as mutable matter. In other words, electronic mass is a potential *hyperworld* of hypermedia and hyperspace. The hyperworld is a formless space that invites, even challenges, us to give it shape and meaning, however temporary; like mass and Earth, it is *hyper*, too massive and 'too much', it exceeds all attempts to fix it in a framework of human meanings; and yet it is that primal source from which cybernetic information gets its originating urge to make form out of the formless. In contemporary computer language, we call this translation of the hyperworld, *hypertext*.

Hypertext is a form of collection and dispersion that reveals information as a complex, moving process rather than a simple, fixed commodity. Conventional text is what represents for us a world 'out there' that is (somehow) already ordered for us as a linear, sequential, fixed and unitary set of objects; it makes the world and its information readily 'readable' for us. In contrast, hypertext is like Picasso's strategy of collage: it reveals and displays information as the play of form's plastic potential, its possibilities for combination and permutation, its 'readability' is not already there for us but has to be created. Hypertext is a form of 'nonsequential writing' which collates text, sound, images, diagrams and maps and allows them to be variously combined on a computer screen (Landow, 1992: 4). It has the power to make available the vast resources of libraries, museums, art galleries, and other information resources to a single computer user. As an advanced form of electronic collection-dispersion, hypertext is a means of revealing form and information as the *convertibility* of parts and fragments in an endless process of *con-versational* assemblage and re-assemblage or play-form of association that Simmel (1971) sees as the primitive basis of sociability. Significantly, this aspect of hypertext returns us to the culture of 'preliterate man' who thought nonsequentially, mutably and fragmentally (Landow, 1992: 62). If hypertext is 'preliterate', it is because it returns us to a stage of human experience that more closely expresses the dense, amorphous and profligate nature of mass.

Electronic mass is that energetic, mutable and mobile field that computerized cybernetics discloses to us. As an expression of electronic mass, hypertext hints at 'something' we can never directly grasp and which we can only approach laterally; it indicates the *virtual* as opposed to the full presence of its subject matter, a tentative outline that seems to mediate between ungraspable, mutable mass and a world of fixed and solid things. Hypertext redefines information as an endless dialogue between form and unform: 'There is no Final Word. There can be no final version, no last thought. There is always a new view, a new idea, a reinterpretation' (Theodor Nelson, an originator of hypertext, quoted by Landow, 1992: 58). It is this newness of the infinite, the forever unfinished and inexhaustible, that hypertextual information foregrounds as a temptation for desire. In the practical technology and vocabulary of hypertext, the tension of virtual form is expressed as *intertextuality, multivocality*, and *de-centering* (Landow, 1992: 8–13). Intertextuality is a complex, plastic process of combining and permutating the parts and fragments that constitute the resource lexicon of hypertext; it retraces that basic logic of the collection and dispersion of letters and words that language uses to make and communicate its variable human worlds. Intertextuality stresses the potential of parts over wholes; like the modern system of industrial production, it expresses the work of parts and their constant re-assemblage as temporary connections rather than fixed and stable structures. The multivocality of hypertext tells us that there is no one authoritative voice in the hypertextual lexicon but a communal yet variable voice made up from the anonymous raw material of its parts and fragments. Just as a letter of the alphabet or a word has no identifiable, originating author, so the varied elements of hypertext are open to variable use and interpretation. Multivocality is hypertext's way of saying profligate mass. De-centering means that there is no privileged focus or perspective for interpreting hypertext, only 'an infinitely re-centerable system whose provisional point of focus depends upon the reader' (Landow, 1992: 11). Eminently plastic, hypertext provides only transient centres of understanding which, by the indefiniteness of their definition, can be at best only temporary resting places for the mind. Intertextuality, multivocality and de-centering are hypertext's strategies for engaging with the prodigality of mass; they defer to mass's intrinsic resistance to fixed locations and ultimate meanings; they are traces of mass's dense mutability and might almost be said to be its messengers. As a final gesture of electronic mass's resistance to objectification, hypertext signals the 'erosion of the self' (Landow, 1992: 71–77). The self we used to know, that thought for itself, that made its own decisions, that authored its own messages, is absorbed into the mobile interweavings of neural information that courses through the generalized nervous system that underlies the surface interpretations of hypertext. In the equivocal world of hypertext, the thinker is thought, the reader is read, the writer is written, and the author is authored. The self is freed from itself to become a freely moving point through which information passes and is reconvened, at least momentarily.

The computer as generalized electronic mind blurs the conventional distinction between self and other; self is now transformed into 'a transindividual system of signs' that 'no longer belong to anyone in particular, but are the medium of collective or "polylogical" thought' (Miller, 1992: 37). Mind is no longer in us; we are in mind. Computerized mind is a mediatized mind where the medium 'has its material base ... in the invisible arrangement of electrons on the disc where it is stored' (Miller, 1992: 36). Electronic mass in this particular quasi-form has yet to be made 'readable'; it is still amorphous. The 'readability' of electronic mass begins with the translation of electronic pulses into binary digits and with binary digits into systems of structured signs. This is the beginning of the electronic production-prediction of mass in which electronic mind has to be repeatedly made or re-covered (in the sense of covered over or hidden from view) out of 'something' that is strangely 'unreadable'. This repeated operation has been aptly called 'a perpetually iterated anamorphosis of the real' (Miller, 1992: 58), for what underlies 'reality' as that which is 'realized' is the translation of amorphous or formless raw matter into anamorphous and hence 'readable' structures. This 'perpetually iterated anamorphosis of the real' characterizes the essential nature of hypertext in its continuously creative attempts to figure out a world that resists meaningful capture. The mutable mass that lies behind the world is always 'there' to remind us that we depend upon its intrinsic recalcitrance as a necessary and originating force in the repeated acts of constituting our own worlds. As an example of this perpetual work of self-constitution, the computerized world of multi-media production well illustrates the exigent dependence of mass culture on the cultivation of mass as 'something' essentially amorphous: in the 'realm of multi-media reproduction ... pictures, music and words are all treated the same way by the computer' where they become digitised electronic marks where pictures, music and words 'coincide before their separation into the different sign functions of picturing and writing' (Miller, 1992: 36, 74). The electronic mark is where the different computer graphics – word, image, sound – converge in the raw matter that presages the emergence of identifiable signs. Mass culture in whatever form can be seen as the repetitive translation of the amorphous into the anamorphous yet still mutable events and outlines through which we tentatively 'read' the autonomously self-constituting mind we call our world.

Mediations of mass

Technology in general shows the social and cultural world to be a source of plastic possibilities. For this reason, Benjamin (1970) chose film to express the plastic mutability of raw mass, whether natural or human, that modern technologies were beginning to reveal. With its 'shots' of the world and its edited 'cuts', film displayed its products as versions of mass *convertibility* in which mass audiences *took part*. Film actively contributed to the production of the new mass world and that included the production of the mass audience. Film can be seen as a forerunner of hypertext in the specific sense that it broke with the traditional assumption that our perceptions and thoughts simply mirrored a world of already-existing stable forms by showing them – perceptions, thoughts and forms – to be productively pliable and massively *convertible*. Hypertext dramatically expands this perceptual and mental agility as well as calling on its users to collaborate more actively in the vision it offers. At the same time, both film and hypertext forcefully exemplify a newly emerging insight into the latent character of the technologically challenged modern world – its 'ongoing disorientation' or 'unfounding' of previously looked-for and taken-for-granted stabilities (Vattimo, 1992: 53). Instead of firm foundations, the techno-scientific production systems of the modern world create a constant and universal sense of dispersion and dissolution. The production of mass is the generation of mutable and ephemeral forms; less directly concerned with the manufacture of usable objects, techno-scientific production concentrates on creating pools of material elements that can then be assembled and re-assembled in a manifold of protean forms and images. Collection-dispersion becomes the prime mover of modern production-consumption; movement itself, its main reason for being. What we call the mass media are the major cultural means by which collection-dispersion moves itself. The media are literally devices for *mediating* or *moving between* positions and locations; the positions and locations they present and represent are secondary to the movement of collection-dispersion they were set up to promote. Film, radio, television, video, telephones, faxes, computers – all are nodal points in the transmission and translation of raw, amorphous mass into 'readable' signs and messages. They themselves are prime examples of this translation process. The computer translates digitized, electronic marks and sounds into pictures, words and music. But it is their intermixing to make a hyperworld and hyperspace of *hypermedia* that multiplies their capacity to *plasticize* the world, to make it infinitely mobile and transformable (Barthes, 1972: 99). It is this capacity of the electronic media and (what he calls) compu-telecommunications technology that Mark Taylor (1995) indicates in his concept of the *mediatrix*. 'New spaces and new times are opening in our midst. Spaces and times that no longer conform to the spacings and timings of the past or present. Openings that open a midst that is not precisely "our" midst' (Taylor, 1995: 24). The new mediatrix redefines the sense of *midst* or *being amidst* by refining the notion of *media* as that ambient reality which we are always *amid*. Our reality is structured by the media that supposedly represent it to us: 'The structure of the real is indistinguishable from the structure of the medium. In more familiar terms, the medium is not only the message but is nothing less than reality itself' (Taylor, 1995: 26–7). The mediatrix is thus much more than an advanced electronic mind; it is the very fabric that *mediates* our world and from which we can never distinguish ourselves. We are the mediatrix just as much as the mediatrix is us, and it is in this novel sense that Taylor uses the term *midst* to signify a condition that is suspended hyperactively as a 'between' in which 'things neither come together nor fall apart' and which is 'not closed but open, constantly changing, and repeatedly shifting' (Taylor, 1995: 34).

The significance of the mediatrix is its expression as electronic mass and its more general reflection of modern techno-science's drive to reveal the basis of the humanly constructed world in 'ongoing disorientation' and 'unfounding' (Vattimo, 1992: 53). Techno-scientific production systems such as the electronic media or biotechnology are less concerned with the production of specific products to satisfy specific needs than with the production-prediction of futures that by definition must be currently improbable and even unknown. At this level, we participate as ordinary consumers in the consumption of products as information and images that have their sources at the frontiers of techno-scientific exploration where dense, amorphous mass is constantly being challenged to submit itself to the anamorphic strategies of modern production methods. But the increasing dependence of mass production-consumption on techno-scientific exploration means that the production of the anamorphic must always be secondary to the production-prediction of that which is intrinsically obscure and uncertain. In other words, techno-science seems more like an expression of the desire for freedom and dispersion rather than a quest for solutions to problems. This is perhaps saying no more than Taylor (1995) says about the electronic mediatrix where the media technologies of comput-telecommunications networks actually constitute the reality they also represent and where mediation as *being amidst* summarizes the strange quandary of collection-dispersion as that suspended condition in which 'things neither come together nor fall apart' (Taylor, 1995: 34). This, of course, was Benjamin's (1970) point in stressing the correlative nature of collection and dispersion in which collected forms are also always informed or inhabited by a bias to disperse. The production and movement of mass had a natural tendency to disperse or scatter the perception of stable forms in what Benjamin called *distracted perception* and which he saw as a special feature of mass society. The distracted mass seemed to see things of the world as though they were being absorbed into a background of oscillating impressions just like the passerby who was reclaimed by the urban crowd or the mesmerizing distraction of 'white noise' and 'brain fade' that DeLillo (1985) noted as major features of the electronic mass that characterizes modern America. Benjamin contrasted distracted perception with the more collocated and collected attention that the art lover brings to the singularity of the work of art. The art lover is thoroughly absorbed by the human and cultural significance of the painting, its historical and transcendental meaning. In contrast, distracted perception sees only mutable, flickering outlines in which forms seem to 'neither come together nor fall apart' (Taylor, 1995: 34). Distracted perception brings us closer to the experience of mediation as mediatrix, as *being amidst* that mediated reality which we can never distinguish and from which we can never distinguish ourselves. When *distraction* moves towards *destruction* and *de-striction* it demonstrates its own instinctive susceptibility to dispersion.

The singular art work when viewed perhaps in the quiet of the museum and thus distinguished from the distractive mass activity of the outside urban world was Benjamin's chosen example of pure, unmediated collected perception. Architecture, in contrast, was his example of an art form that was seen only obtusely, as background to the mixed activities of daily life in the city. Architecture might be art but, since it also partly constitutes the common medium of everyday living, we do not normally see it as art or something that deserves our concentrated, focused attention. The art of architecture gets lost in the 'white noise' and 'brain fade' of hyperactive urban life. Architecture becomes merely yet another 'product' in the vast crowd of moving signs and images that populate the modern urban scene. It was precisely this theme that the artist Andy Warhol addressed in recognizing that the reality of modern American life was indistinguishable from its mediatized culture of production and consumption. Warhol also saw himself and his work as being indistinguishable from the production technologies and products that his works commented on. He set up his own business, Andy Warhol Enterprises, together with an industrial workshop he called the Factory which produced pictures of industrial products such as Campbell's soup cans and boxes of Brillo pads – all attempts to obliterate the traditional distinctions between art and life, between high culture and common products. American life in the 1950s and 1960s was beginning to assume that culture of *creative pretence* noted by DeLillo (1985) in which the products that supported daily existence became aestheticized objects of desire. The shopping mall looked more like a museum in displaying itself as a collection of designs and images borrowed from Ancient Greece or Renaissance Italy. In this criss-cross culture, art and industrial production began to create a new, dispersed space in which they became each other and where their traditional identities were hyperactively suspended in a 'between' in which they neither came together nor fell apart (Taylor, 1995: 34). Where the shopping mall borrowed its images from ancient civilisations, Warhol borrowed his from newspapers, advertisements, magazines, film and television, and, like these mass-production media, his art works were produced as numerous copies; the singularity of the conventional art work was deliberately dispersed and a form of distracted perception took its place. As well as the distraction of the art work, Warhol's identity became 'distracted'; the figure of the originating, inspired artist disappeared in the 'double copying' that the products of Warhol's Factory re-presented – the copying of the images of industrial products *and* the further copying of these copies on Warhol's assembly line: 'Instead of a lonely genius, the artist in the Factory was more like a supervisor who oversees workers on the assembly line, or a film editor who repackages footage shot by others' (Taylor, 1992: 180). In this shadowland of lost identities and placeless forms, we are reminded yet again of Fisher's (1991) analysis of the logic of the modern industrial system with its production of parts rather than whole objects and where the withdrawal of the whole object into a secondary role transfers 'reality to the system as a whole and to the play of transformations and possibilities that it invites' (Fisher, 1991: 249). Warhol was obsessed with the images of famous film and television celebrities whom he further reproduced in his assembly-line pictures: Elizabeth Taylor, Marlon Brando, Joan Crawford and (perhaps the best known of his reproductions) Marilyn Monroe. Since these stars were known less as real people and more as disseminated cinematic images, it seemed more appropriate to Warhol to view them as filmic transmissions which the mass cinema and television audiences considered more real than the psycho-physical selves behind the projected images. For this reason, he understood his work not as art nor as the representation of a reality 'out there' but as the manufacture of reality itself in much the same way that film created an *apparently* real world or a world of real *appearances*. It is in precisely this sense that we are asked to understand Warhol's work as the practical expression of the argument that reality and medium are the same: 'The structure of the real is indistinguishable from the structure of the medium. In more familiar terms, the medium is not only the message but is nothing less than reality itself' (Taylor, 1995: 26–7). Once the medium disappears, so does the reality. Signs and images are as ephemeral as the media that create them. Preoccupied as he was with reproducing famous images created by the media, Warhol was equally intent on revealing the intrinsic transience of media images: the death and decline of reality – through hospital scenes, funerals, skulls, car crashes, suicides – were reproduced as the other side of the media creation of images. Following a period of reproductive fascination with the assassination of President John F. Kennedy, Warhol himself was gravely wounded in an assassination attempt by an actress and, as if to validate his fundamental belief that we are all potentially raw matter for the creation of images, the *New York Times* featured the pictured story on its front page. Like the dense amorphousness of mass, a medium for Warhol was essentially invisible and therefore void; it had to be shaped and formed in word and image in order to become 'real'. This was the interpretation of raw mass that he applied to all kinds of products, whether industrial, cinematic or political. He imagined the supermarket as a vast, empty space with its shelves waiting to be filled with the edible and usable images of soup cans and scouring pads; he imagined the empty television screen demanding to be filled with desirable social and cultural images. Like the unseeable space of raw mass, the supermarket and the television cannot be seen until they are filled with the transient images that mediate our desires. Warhol realized his own amorphousness – he continually described himself as 'nothing', inexistent –

and used it as the basis for re-covering and reproducing himself as a series of mediatized images. In this very basic sense, he was no different from the mediatized reality created and transmitted by the supermarkets, the television and the cinema whose products he both re-collected and dispersed in his project to make art works into products and products into art works.

Warhol's life and work re-enact for us Benjamin's (1970) portrayal of modern mass society as a mass of dynamic movement which resists being disciplined into stable forms and permanent truths. Warhol himself can be compared to Benjamin's passerby who appears and disappears as a transient product of the forever flowing urban mass; like his image-products, he was a 'moving label' and a 'captive snapshot' momentarily and repeatedly collected and dispersed against the background of mass's bewildering prodigality (Foucault, 1977: 189); he sought to produce and reproduce himself out of the 'white noise' of America's electronic mediatrix, realizing at the same time that his so-called self was part of 'a transindividual system of signs' that belonged to no one in particular and was merely 'the medium of collective or "polylogical" thought' (Miller, 1992: 37). Warhol's medium – including the screen on which he 'painted' as well as the cinema and television screens – was a source of 'ongoing disorientation' and 'unfounding' for him because, like Heidegger's concept of Earth, it was totally 'other, the nothing, general gratuitousness and insignificance' (Vattimo, 1992: 53) which stared him in the face – he would sometimes say he would look into the mirror and expect to see nothing there – like a threatening void. But it was precisely this void, this sense of gazing into the formless and inchoate, that stimulated Warhol's fundamental insight into the nature of human production systems in general and that provoked him to work always 'between' art and industry – namely, that all production is the never-ending pre-diction or formation of collective signs and images out of mute and mutable mass.

References

Barthes, R., (1972), *Mythologies*, London: Jonathan Cape.
Benjamin, W., (1970), *Illuminations*, London: Jonathan Cape.
Bersani, L. and Dutoit, U., (1993), *Arts of Impoverishment: Beckett, Rothko, Resnais*, Cambridge, Mass.: Harvard University Press.
Calvino, I., (1987), *The Literature Machine*, London: Secker and Warburg.
DeLillo, D., (1985), *White Noise*, London: Picador.
Fisher, P., (1985), *Hard Facts: Setting and Form in the American Novel*, New York: Oxford University Press.
Fisher, P., (1991), *Making and Effacing Art: Modern American Art in a Culture of Museums*, New York: Oxford University Press.
Foucault, M., (1977), *Language, Counter-Memory, Practice*, Ithaca, N.Y.: Cornell University Press.
Krauss, R.E., (1998), *The Picasso Papers*, London: Thames and Hudson.
Landow, G.P., (1992), *Hypertext: the Convergence of Contemporary Critical Theory and Technology*, Baltimore, MD.: The Johns Hopkins University Press.
Miller, J. Hillis, (1992), *Illustration*, London: Reaktion Books.

Saussure, F. de, (1966), *Course in General Linguistics*, New York: McGraw-Hill.

Simmel, G., (1971), *On Individuality and Social Forms*, Chicago: The University of Chicago Press.

Taylor, M.C., (1992), *Disfiguring: Art, Architecture, Religion*, Chicago: The University of Chicago Press.

Taylor, M.C., (1995), 'Rhizomic fields of interstanding', *Tekhnema*, 2, 24–36.

Vattimo, G., (1988), *The End of Modernity: Nihilism and Hermeneutics in Post-modern Culture*, Cambridge: Polity Press.

Vattimo, G., (1992), *The Transparent Society*, Cambridge: Polity Press.

Vattimo, G., (1993), *The Adventure of Difference: Philosophy after Nietzsche and Heidegger*, Cambridge: Polity Press.

Williams, R., (1993), *Keywords: a Vocabulary of Culture and Society*, London: Fontana.

Pass the salt: how language moves matter

Dan Rose

Introduction

'*cum grano salis*'

The question I want to ask is: How do human beings use language with one another and in so doing bring new materials fabricated as products into the realm of the contemporary world? The rich Euro-American and Japanese societies very nearly drown in stuff – in the mass of things, objects, and commodities for sale.[1] My point here is to theorize about how human society produces mass for its consumption.

There are two egregious absences in twentieth cultural theory into which I wish to pitch this text; these omissions occur in theories of language and society. The idea is not to refute those theories and then attempt to correct them for what they fail to do, but to point toward a different direction for inquiry. I will briefly mention their inexplicable neglect, and then work toward stimulating thinking about the object-world that requires our serious attention.

Omissions 1 and 2

1st Omission. In the decades after Durkheim's establishment of sociology and the perpetuation of the idea that society must be understood in its own terms, through Weber and Parsons almost to the end of the twentieth century, there was very nearly no theory of, and, therefore, no way to address the material world in the human sciences. Nor can one yet find quite an adequate theorization of autos, pleasure boats, nylon jogging suits, tract houses, or culinary dishes (whether Szechuan or Northern Italian) that are at one and the same time nature and culture.

One might construct an infinite list of bangles and baubles that cannot be satisfactorily explained because there is no theoretical approach to the materials from which they are fashioned. Merely to call commodities *fetishes* proved a self-limiting tactic.[2] Materialist anthropology, despite its aggressive title, fared only slightly better. With one or two notable exceptions (Latour, 1993), the sociology of science has had little to say about physical stuff, often eliding iron and steel or elementary particles by restricting itself to the discussion of texts or social practices.[3] Feminist theory, by revising our most fundamental notions of the female body and planetary raw materials, offered precious hints but does not constitute itself as a theory of the physical world. Donna Haraway considers that material elements are like the native American trickster, Coyote, which never does exactly as one would wish (1991). Elaine Scarry, following Marx, considers human technology to be extensions of bodily functions and activities (1985). Although her claim appears on the surface of it, irrefutable, the problem I have with it is that it seems to answer questions rather than ask new ones.

2nd Omission. Twentieth century linguistics which does not account for materials might actually be rather too neatly summarized by Chomsky's famous formal, nonsense phrase: 'Colorless green ideas sleep furiously'. Although he illustrated in this sentence an impeccable grammatical order, we derive precariously little meaning, except perhaps to the language poets.[4] On the one hand meaning was problematic to the formalist and structuralist. On the other, structure was problematic to the student of contexted discourse – ethnomethodologist or sociolinguist. Yet physical materials of the planet and commodities were nearly wholly absent from both except as appearances in a grammatical order. Given the history of language theory there is no reason to expect that there would be formal or other accounts of objects appearing in a grammatical order.

The point I want to make here is that no major linguist taught us in a body of ideas interior to language usage how language might move or recombine matter, whether the masses were human, vegetable, or mineral. In addition to the notion of the arbitrariness of the sign or the phoneme, linguists have been overwhelmingly absorbed with order, and a formal one at that, an innate attribute, finally, of the way the mind was believed to work. So both in the body of twentieth century social thought and in linguistic work there is no theoretically adequate accounting for the stuff of which we and the world are made.

A turnaround appears on the horizon. With a growing number of largely descriptive and entertaining publications about such things as minor commodities to the historical importance of the screw (Rybczynski, 2000) written by journalists and scholars, there is attendant and growing interest in theorizing material life and culture from academics in various fields from archaeology (Schiffer, 1999) through cultural anthropology (Rose, 1995) and the sociology of science already mentioned, to literature (Brown, 1998).

Matter

I contend that each utterance makes a difference in the hearer, at once physical and cultural. There is no docility to language. Any difference is also a material one. On perceiving a sight or sound such as reading a sentence or hearing an exclamation, the hearer (or reader) has been altered, even if it were a few molecular changes in the brain, an assertion easily enough witnessed with current medical imaging technology. Obviously there are lesser and greater differences to be made as the brain registers inputs from the sensors throughout the body; as when the body dreams, or engages the world by eye and hand. Language moves matter, and if we would like, we could begin with the brain, and can trace the translation of instructions to the hand, the foot, and hence to the machine, and the machines that the machine controls. More anon.

In this case the proposed theory of matter is about agency, the ability of all things in the universe to act and more importantly to interact and to influence one another. From the complex interior of an atomic nuclei to all matter in this universe, things have energy – or power – and, perhaps, mass. What we need to theorize, and Durkheim, notably under the influence of Kant, could not, is matter and humans within a single intellectual framework. There is no need, as some sociobiologists still assert, to reduce behaviour and biology to physics. Nature and humans – who are also nature – are all active agents affecting and being affected.

To say this is to state an epistemology of engagement – where one energetic thing contacts and subsequently relates to and affects and is affected by some other energetic entity. Both the stuff of nature and humans, simply put, exhibit the same constitutive agencies.

On such a far-reaching note, consider that scientists who contend verbally with one another, daily simulating and moving around biological and chemical agents, thereby modify those materials in quite specific directions. Scientists pass on the newly formed agents as prototypes that they have developed, such as a vaccine, to engineers who fabricate from them life-prolonging objects that consumers might use. Engineers in turn pass on the formulas to manufacturers and marketers. Large batches are made up and salesmen call on doctors who will deploy the vaccines, now a complex of natural and manufactured agents to reduce infectious diseases. Patients through their health care providers will pay for access to the injections.

The retail marketplace, in this model of materials and talk, reaches backward financially from the money transactions with the patient through the health care system and doctor to the manufacturing, engineering, and research firms to animate the entire sophisticated and very complex linguistic processes of human-agents and natural-agents interactions. All of this is accomplished by complex speech genres that have been developed in order to move even the most microscopic and delicate objects around! Through language and its power to activate humans and their relationships with energetic materials, nature and culture are being bonded in new ways in the laboratory, the medicine cabinet, and our bodies.

Language can be used to affect profoundly, and irreversibly, the agency of nonhuman matter. That is, language is used to affect or amplify the ability of nonhuman materials to act concertedly in very particular, designed ways.

Through the medium of listening and acting, human speech can be used to move matter and to recombine numerous elements in ways not given in nature. Indirectly, human pragmatic utterances, the daily talk of physicians, sales people, assembly workers, engineers, and research scientists, are all priced on the world market. Words that affect things and the things themselves receive a range of monetary values. One wonders whether or not many salaries aren't a price given to utterances that have the power to stimulate the (re)animation of naturally occurring elements.

In what follows, I wish to emphasize that human language is a physical power evolved within the agency repertoire of humans. I am attempting to hold up a mirror to the site of commerce, as the central motif, as the animating, reality-producing locus of our time. Concealed within the marketplace is a dynamo which when understood reveals that the ingredients of the world are consumately lively and vivaciously interacting with one another.

Salt

'*Pass the salt*'.

This request or command to pass the salt from one end of the table to the other could serve to stand for the most ancient origin of a human language-that-moves-material (see Figure 1).

A

B

C

(S)

D

Figure 1

Persons A, B, C, and D are sitting, roughly, in a line. The sodium chloride (S) is closest to person D. On this occasion, with this arrangement among persons and a naturally occurring object of nature, a speech act can be fictitiously reconstructed. By hearing words, others can respond to what the first person said in any number of appropriate ways.

From today's great temporal distance we can weigh what sort of things a group of very early ancestors might be saying to one another. We can consider this moment or one something like it as a language game by which better to understand one aspect of language in our own time, in this case, how language – speech, writing, and small images including arrows and diagrams – serves to manipulate the material world.

The *utterance* of a human, heard by another human can be translated by that second person through hand and external prosthesis in order to move objects. Thus the speaker may be said to move things at a distance through the medium of others.

Humans have evolved over millions of years and in the process they were successful in a Darwinian sense. They adapted, they beat out competitors and outran predators; they flourished. When language emerged, perhaps sixty to a hundred thousand years ago, there is no evidence that linguistic ability was less adaptive for them than the other, less loquacious animals; if anything it was just the opposite. One can assume that the very earliest uses of language had something, if not everything, to do with human adaptive successes in physical ways.

We could imagine that this earliest language has in a fundamental sense never been superseded. We are at some substratum of everyday existence continuing to employ the language of material effects even in our most unconscious moments. For example, listen to a conversation near you in a public place. Nearly every sentence will include references to numerous material objects ranging from other humans through all the plethora of stuff people own and use in everyday life. Speech not only helps move physical things around, it surrounds objects with stories and accounts. The speaking genres that we use today concerning material things, I think, are deeply akin to those employed by our predecessors two thousand generations ago.

This buried stratum of the archaeology of human speech is important to think with, for we have needed to resurrect our consciousness of it after centuries of philosophical and scientific omission. The linguists, seduced by the script in the codex, have purveyed the implicit but confused notion that language was best understood through writing. With the interior fastening of spoken and written language onto the transactions of global markets, we can no longer ignore the ways in which our linguistic and material engage one another in an inner way.[5] The market demands our speech and prices it. Rhetorical tropes concerning objects such as beer or shampoo, government policy or information, and corporate strategy or press releases are highly rewarded; and evidence for this appears in the quantities of monies billed to clients for the words and images that are engineered for the world market by advertising agencies, corporate gurus, and spin doctors. This host of language affects how matter is commercially produced and consumed.

Person D hears A say, 'Pass the salt'. D picks up the salt, hands it to C who then hands it to B who in turn passes it to A. If we edit from the scene the speech and individuals then we witness salt being moved from one location to another. In a view with human presence edited out, salt moves jerkily through the air from position *d* to position *a* at the table. The materials of the world appear, remain stable, and are used again and again in this picture of how humans engage and circulate natural objects. In this language-with-matter game, we foreground the physical substances and background the human activities in order to return later to such uses of language as the lifting of salt and passing it to another grasping hand.

We could imagine a matter game more primitive than this. Person A gestures with hand signs that everyone understands (pass the salt): but D is not looking at her. Will C then place his hands in front of D and make the proper sign for A? Why should he, or what would compel him to do so?

If there were neither hand signs nor sounds from the mouth, how would A acquire the salt from three positions away? In other words, how would material move through the inter-human world? Would its passage not be remarkably slow and up to each person to acquire? Person A might walk in front of D and pick up the salt, its short journey to the first seat would then be in the hand of A.

Where might salt have come from in the first place? Who brought it from the mine to the table? Did D himself bring the salt?

There may be a more formidable question. Why was salt brought by humans from the ground into the human realm?

Was salt, perhaps (internal and external to the human body), making a demand on the body, on the body's culture to recognize it and move it from the mine to the table and from there into the body? Was salt insistent in its claims on the mind or on consciousness attendant to the uses of it by the body? The mind proves accompaniment to the body's engagement with the world. Nature, out of which humans are composed, clamours for human attention. Is there an epistemology of *clamour*? Does the engagement of one object by another arise out of clamour?

Person A says, 'Pass the salt', but we have been also asking: Is it that the salt exerts some effect on humans in order to get itself moved? We might ask here: How does nature which is greater than language and outside it, enter language? How do stars in the night sky, for example, get notated into a system of signs called constellations?

In *Tristes Tropiques* Levi-Strauss observed that the Nambikwara of Central Brazil, a little-contacted native group he visited in the late 1930s, used no salt or spices in their diet (1992: 350). But the human organism and that of all animals must have appropriate amounts of sodium chloride at the level of the cell in order to function properly. The Nambikwara were able to ingest enough salt through their consumption of plants, and especially other animals which included fish and rodents. Salt is crucial in animals for it enables the continuing actions of the nervous system. Without sodium chloride there would be no action potential in the cells of the nerves. As the nerve is stimulated, the movement of oppositely charged sodium and chloride ions flood across the plasma cell membrane which effects rapid neural transmission. Thus for the brain to think and the body to act requires a critical saline balance at the cellular level. To think and write about salt, to ask for it and to pass it up the table, all require that sodium channels in the nerve cell open and that the ratio of positive outside ions alters in relation to the negative inside ions, initiating very rapid movement along the length of the nerve. In a real sense the animal body clamours for salt and the effects it enables.

Salt is thought with what it can do and like all objects of the planet it is active at the molecular level and potentially available to be sensed at the level of human phenomenal awareness.

To think of salt or with salt is to construct a mental scenario of its activity. Very little with its essence, if there is one. Perhaps there are no essences, just complexes of active agencies all the way down. Consider a brief list of thoughts about agency:

All the physical objects of this, or any world, exhibit agency; they exhibit material effects on other materials.

Nature evolves its agencies into more complex entities. Agencies cluster with agencies. As a result the world may be thought of as complexes of active ingredients.

In this metaphysic, consider that the universe has evolved humans so that humans will in turn accelerate the pace of natural evolution. Intelligence is applied to matter through the language and physical manipulations of the sciences that are, in turn, motivated by the necessity to exchange one's intellectually energized products on the world market. Intellectually energized products we refer to as technology, and it is through technology that humans intervene in and accelerate natural processes.

The universe sends us to itself. We humans produce nature's culture. The human body is also culture's nature. The agency of nature acts upon itself through the vehicle of human agency.

Objects

And reflections on objects:

Objects are composed of other active, energetic objects.

Objects connect to other objects and both become modified.

Objects engage humans: Lightning demands a response. Flood demands a response. Fire demands a response. The response may be named a creature or figure or spirit by the humans.

Humans respond with words and rites and physical manipulation to the active objects of the planet.

Objects join society with a name given by humans: pear, livre, email, codfish, the list goes on.

Objects are brought into commercial society with legal status. They are owned:

© ©

® ®

Trademark^{TM}

Objects confront and colonize human consciousness through the medium of the human body. Because objects are not docile they can be consumed by one another, destroyed by one another, infected by one another, deployed by one another. Objects demand organization, some would say they self-organize. Actively, objects can construct predator-prey relations or cooperative relationships, can co-evolve with one another or extinguish one another.

Humans engage active ingredients

Making-and-talking, and using-and-talking are tightly bundled complexes of possibilities for manipulation and modification.

Humans manipulate with the hand, foot, eye, mouth, voice;

Humans as they work together alter things.

Humans divide their labour and their speech among themselves.

Humans think with objects and talk about them.

Humans can use speech to get others to engage objects.

Are there communal speech-object engagement plans?

How do humans collectively make an object? What are the Aristotelian speech figures regarding objects? What are the Bakhtinian speech genres regarding the objects-world?

To what extent do objects by themselves, in collections, or as complex assemblages condition or demand or suggest subsequent human action?

Future talk appears in plans, intentions, thoughts, suggestions, discussions, or ideas for the deployment of objects including the human organism in space and contact with others ...

Think of looking at objects, the language of manipulation, thought (thinking with an object's activities ...), and the physical moving of objects **as a single production**.

Objects connect to other objects and taken together form identities, families, networks, communities of things and people. These complexes as yet have no name which suggests the new frontier of such inquiry.

We need to comprehend the inter-active richness of the objects-world and the powers of humans who have all evolved from within it.

In what does this plethora lie? In the activities of the world and a realization of the energies all around us, within us, in the efficacy of things, and the power, the agency of objects. Atomic nuclei, molecules, photons, viruses, cells, creatures, plants, planets, weather systems, the entire universe is made up of agents acting upon agents, powerful forces engaging and shaping other ingredients and in turn being affected by them.

Humans engage the world as a primordial soup of possibilities. We imagine our future as we begin to understand the implications of changing everything around us and changing our selves, our machines, our bodies (through genomics), as well as the plant and non-human animal kingdoms.

There are as many agencies as there are objects. The full agency of objects is difficult to know. To observe influences, engagements, and effects of objects is a long, perhaps never ending process, though in a market economy, *why* questions give way to the less demanding *how* questions which are pragmatic rather than axiological.

Humans are increasingly engaging all that is. They engage one another with rhetoric when they wish to persuade others' hearts and minds. They engage one another with pragmatic discourses when they wish to plan, design, or make alterations in matter. They mix the two master tropes rhetoric and pragmatic when they persuade, as in televised commercials, to purchase one product over another. In the ads, the pragmatic often exhibits itself, particularly as a story of the use of the product. Directions (pragmatic) can be persuasive, for example, if I ask and you give directions to the city then it can be inferred that I know how to move my machinery and body in order to get there. Persuasion can offer directions.

Objects as active agents are coming under increasing judicial scrutiny and litigation often with such legal individuals as corporations as co-defendants: Prozac (a serotonin re-uptake inhibitor), silicon (breast implants), autos (that explode or burn on impact).

We offer one another through the marketplace possessions with which we feel comfortable. These possessions are often compadres or aides, machine cohorts or helpers. Think of our relationships with the miniature cyborgs, such as a toaster or water heater. They are largely silent or make humming or singing noises. Person A cannot call out to the salt, 'Travel up here next to me!' or 'Place yourself in my hand!' Although the salt has abilities, moving itself is not one of them. However, we must imbricate human compadres with one another in our material projects. That salt can neither hear nor move does not mean it is without power, for it can preserve fish or meat. The different powers of nature and of machines are highly distributed. Humans not only engage nature but remodel its various ambient integrities into highly energized machines that have abilities but act in ways as highly specialized as salt. Humans must engage one another with material-relevant speech in order to deploy the machines or natural objects.

Toiletries we tend to use mutely without the help of other persons. To engineer and manufacture them requires millions of hours of human speech-that-coordinates-human-activities-with-objects.

Huge invisible communities form with human-machine-natural objects. What should we name these concealed but pragmatic interrelationships between humans and the physical *welt* on which we are interactively reliant? Are these governments of disparate but operating materials over which humans at best partly preside? What would this government without parliament or adequate representation be called? Is it not largely corporate? The landscape, the elements of earth, all private property – *stuff* in a strange translation – becomes intellectual property and subsequently precisely priced. Laboratories are machine complexes that turn nature into intellectual property embedded in and surrounding machine sidekicks that are bought and sold on the world bourse.

As mentioned above, objects are themselves made up of other objects. The objects form communities, networks, associations, complexes, these vital relationships of subcomponent parts may be viral, parasitic, predator-prey, co-evolutionary, co-operative, agonistic, or whatever. Polyglot relating to one another with electrochemical languages in vast networks of influence and engagement, that object-community cuts across any and all relevant human communities, discourses, relationships, disciplines, ecumenae, and stitches a lesser or greater macro-community of natures-cultures. Such is the automobile, electricity, the internal combustion engine, oil, silicon chips, telecommunications.

The subjects which I am addressing are not encompassed by ontology, epistemology, or metaphysics. I cannot rely upon categories of distinction, grids of specification, or mechanics of proof but upon something like a world picture where all the ingredients are boiling – but, from the vantage point of the observer, in slow motion.

Design

Humans take a design or a plan for the making-manipulation of active objects and work together toward their construction.

If draftspeople work together on a design, is this site a pragmatic theatre of design performance with its own language of making, stage sets such as pens, trace, finished drawings, CAD stations, audiences (clients), and the rest?

And are not consumption sites, such as the kitchen, the bathroom, the office, also places of public or private consumption-theater-with-objects-of-use?

In the morning shower who are the actors? Your body, the soap, the shampoo, the conditioner, the powder, or the body lotions? Surely it is all of them but who is the star of the series?

Language

Our most fundamental idea of language should be situated not in the codex, but in the bourse. By doing so we may discover the oldest form of human discourse. Now the boisterous clamour of the global market has breathed new life into our most routine conversations.

Is language, then, made up of utterances that vitally contact, engage, and manipulate active agents? Everyday talking, especially in the economically developed countries, reveals the work-horse genres that humans use with one another to alter the materials, machines, and other humans in factories, fields, and offices. In the settings of labour we will find the formal or formalizable features of language, ancient as they are, that join humans and other objects in the two-way street of manipulation and being manipulated. Each of the following list of language items is a gloss of a conversation genre in which physical matter is routinely referenced with the potential for immediate effect.

1.0 Commands 'Pass the salt, now!'

1.1 Requests 'Please pass the salt'.

1.2 Suggestions 'It would be appreciated if someone passed the salt'.

1.3 Hints 'This steak is too bland'.

2.0 Instructions (Directions) 'D, if you pick up the salt and hand it to C, and, C, if you pick up the salt and hand it to B ...'.

2.1 Descriptions 'Salt can be grasped by the human hand. D actually did this ...'.

2.2 Recipes 'For salt to move from position d to position a at the table, seat four people in a row ...'.

3.0 Questions and Answers 'Did D pass the salt yesterday at lunch?' 'No, he did not'.

3.1 Promises 'I will always (never, sometimes) pass you the salt..'.

4.0 Assertions (Declarations) 'This handing of salt from one to the other is the act of moving a naturally occurring substance, salt ...'.

5.0 Accounts 'D passed the salt to C, who then passed it to B, who then handed it to A'.

5.1 Narratives (Stories) 'Once upon a time there were four people sitting at a table ...'.

These pragmatic speech genres are not logically exclusive of one another but overlap and often one can be transformed into another using much of the same stock of language. Several of them achieve similar effects. In the salt example, each type of utterance contains a speech plan that can animate an engagement plan – that is, the request to pass the salt indicates an immediate encounter with the stuff of nature. The commands through the accounts may all be caught up in and thus found in the narrative, for a story is a form that deploys and is dependent upon a number of other speech genres.

The interest here is not pointed toward the pragmatic genres, or the pragmatic potential of what we think of literary genres, and their endless re-deployment within the narrative, but the fact that much of language contains the ingredients of the physical world and uses these ingredients over and over and potentially manipulates them as the objects are passed from speech genre to speech genre. It is as if salt can exist within language use in innumerable contexts all of which give additional gravitas and cultural potential to the saline substance.

Utterances can engage the entire human body; an utterance activates (with an activity-speech plan) your being-there; the utterance is addressed to you, the speech of which contains all sorts of directives, possibilities, and codes for your subsequent activities, a next utterance, and what physical engagement are called for.

Speech genres include *engagement genres* and manipulation plans whether in everyday life or the scientists laboratory. The activeness of language spoken from one to another directly connects the active ingredients of the natural, human, and machine worlds. Some genres take the engagement of humans with physical elements into the Cartesian reductive separation of objects into components or the chemists' new molecular soups. A recipe is an engagement genre.

Just as there are spheres of human communication, there are spheres of human making-with-language and using-with-language, but these have not been mapped.

Such spheres include the vocally co-ordinated extraction labourers, work cleaning crews, committee meetings of production engineers and assembly line workers, and members of research departments, executive offices, and nurseries. In this way objects are transformed and work gets done.

If we do want to begin outside language with objects of the world, the whole world of humans in it, we can begin with salt. How did salt first come to the attention of humans such that salt appeared next to D at the end of the row and that A wanted it? Did salt *announce* itself?

Salt has no voice.

Was there some kind of nearly explicit hunger on the part of humans so that salt became an object of search by the humans? Is hunger a knowledge? Or is it the knowledge of things that can slake the hunger that are paramount such that hunger can be fed, a state of the body altered? What comes first, the feeding of hunger with its appropriate foods, properly prepared, or the hunger for something? Humans and their hunger and what satisfies it evolve together.

Language must have responded to a necessity to move physical objects in order to satisfy hunger, acquire food, comfort children, direct migration, kill animals, or construct ever more sophisticated machinery.

Was there a picture in the early humans' heads before the language arrived such that A could say to D, 'Pass the salt?' Was the picture (if it was a picture and not a feeling or thought) of salt put there by the absence of salt, not by another human being or language but by one part of the body communicating to another part of the body – the digestive system without adequate salt inquires of the brain, 'Can you help provide us with more sodium?'

If we were to add up all the ingredients of nature that acted upon the human body-mind, would there be, a) a catalogue of active substances and b) a notation of their insistence on the organism and c) how the organism translated the insistence of the active agents into thoughts, images, words, gestures, calculations, and engagements with or against the material features – the item from the catalogue of active substances, d) a set of tables that included the catalogue of active substances, how the substances exerted themselves directly on the human organism, and how the human body translated the effect of natural agents into the mind's ability to act or picture or, say, tell an anecdote about, or have the hand perform, dig, throw, build, or gesture as in a command or in despair?

What does *water up to the ankles* produce in the human organism? What if A, B, C, and D had to stand in water that deep day and night? What would they then say about it?

What does a pinch of salt on the tongue do to thought? How was it thought that the salt could be pinched and deposited there in the first place? Why would it be? Was it an experiment in culinary delight? How is the salt thought with? How does one think with *water up to the ankles*? Are not such acts of nature vivid in the human mind as a set of possibilities for thinking how one ought to act on the world and its substances, particularly in concert with others?

Things influence humans. Humans too are things. Humans talk endlessly to one another about how to influence other things.

Doesn't water up to the ankles lead one to think: I'm going to have to find someone who can get this out of here, perhaps make a pump? One can think water into and through a machine that will remove it. Thinking with materials and placing that thought into speech can influence several people to act in concert, one to make or find a hose, another a bellows, a third a valve, a fourth who can fit it all together and so on. And someone, perhaps A, the first person, to operate the pump. In concerted work many of the same forms of language are used, such as the request in 'Pass the salt', except that at the end of the string of utterances, we have assembled a pump, a contribution toward getting rid of unwanted, excess water and a contribution to knowledge as the know-how of invention.

We do not operate as active agents of nature – which we are – only through some passive registering of sense impressions, or making only descriptions, or sophisticated critiques, but through finding ourselves, as some subset of a collectivity of active objects in situations that require we engage and modify features of the local context. Language modifies; it arises in the moments required to alter the material world. Is it possible, for example, to think of an utterance that does not contain within itself the potential, if uttered in the relevant situation, to modify other materials or one another?

Natural events are translated by the body into speech that influences one's fellows to take an action (with tools, with one another) on the natural events in order to effect some modification.

One could reverse the above order and say that humans make endless demands on and modify the world, but to begin there takes something away from the world. Nothing of the world is passive, it is all active and can affect, at least potentially, humans in endless ways.

It would be a short step to say that rather than merely offering sense impressions, water acts through us, salt acts through us, coffee beans or soy beans act through us: Or we could more globally say the planet engages itself through us: Nature acts its way through us, or the universe acts through us/we who are ourselves, planet, nature, and universe in our locality.

If on other similar planets there are intelligent creatures something like ourselves who intervene in the nature that has evolved them, will we not all converge at some point and achieve some significant interventions in the unfolding of the universe that evolved us all?

A recipe may not be a formula – each made thing tastes slightly different than its predecessor. A recipe may be more like an heuristic for subsequent action or a reminder, or suggestions that provide the possibility for improvisation.

I think with the active ingredient salt. I think with its flavour, with where it is deposited, with ways to acquire it by hand, how to trade for it, etc. I think how I might classify salt with a set of other active ingredients. By itself there is no thinking, only thinking *with*. What are the possible sets of with? This question opens infinite material possibilities.

Objects resist. They cannot be talked into doing what they cannot do.

Things and events in the world enter language via descriptions, classifications, and naming. But things can also enter language or at least awareness indirectly through commands, 'Pass the salt', even when one has never heard the word salt before. If there is a strange substance in front of D and a strange sound (salt), through inference, D can figure that the new sound is a name for the new substance and the act of passing the object tests whether or not the word salt names the substance in front of him by the response A makes to his passing the white grains.

Probably everyone who touched the salt thought with it in some way.

Motors

Machines made up of natural elements are enhanced physical agents that in turn amplify the agency of other naturally occurring objects and of cultural processes. Objects of nature are engines, motors of X. Actors, active ingredients, motors. The salt motor. The photon engine. The DNA engine. Nano-engines. Primate engines.

After the end of humanity will there be something like the book of humans that tells a whole story of their rise and demise? But why bother to write it since there will be no one to read it? What will all the moral lessons have added up to?

We have some pretty good ideas of where we've come from but we are entranced by where we are going. I don't think it will be into the dead end of eternity. We will use the materials of nature to give birth to other stars, but can we once having done that climb aboard? How in the future will we code our beings in order to transport ourselves over interstellar distances? As photons? For now we have no clue and cannot have, due to the mass our bodies in this current form would amass traveling at light speed.

Grant first of all that humans are composed entirely from the materiality of the world. Imagine second that humans are embedded in the awesome materiality of the world: air, wind, sun, sand, road, trees, water, earth of all kinds, machines, tools, fabrications of all sorts, buildings, autos, kerbs, pavement, sidewalks, glass, aluminum, steel, cement ... this is where the human sciences must begin anew. Must start. The new beginning for the *sciences humaine*. We begin in the materiality of the market, the context of speech and materials made for it and changing hands there. We address how in our utterances with one another we assemble matter, use machines, move materials throughout the human realm, and act as consumers in mass society. A voice:

Pass the salt.

D reaches out and grasps the container. The human hands act as motors activated by another's voice, to move an energetic portion of the world toward other human beings thereby modifying them all – nature *and* culture – in an irreversible way. Then others may tell a story, write a novel, or a chapter in a book, attempting to capture in other tropes a scene where salt moves through the human sphere, from nature – the salt mine, to culture – onto the table, into language, and back again to nature – digested within the body.

Notes

1. This chapter follows and seeks to extend some of the ideas in 'Active Ingredients' (Rose, 1995) and is indebted most to Aristotle's *Rhetoric* and to Bacon (1989), Bakhtin (1986), and Wittgenstein (1953).
2. Members of the Frankfurt School did not advance Marxist materialism any further than did Marx for whom it was not so much material, anyway; it was labour (see Brown, 1998: 952–956).
3. Evidence for this assertion are found in Bijker and Law (1992, see Latour's article therein). Latour's work (1993) does suggest a new and post-Marxist materialism.
4. Chomsky first used his well-known example in 1957 (15), but thirty years later commented that 'a small industry has been spawned by one linguistic example ... which has been the source of poems and arguments and music and so on' (1988: 28–29). The language poets who were influenced by linguistic theories, such as Chomsky's, are best known for drawing words and notions from formal linguistics into their poems: Language about language about language. This move allows them to appropriate words and phrases from scholarly sources and transpose them into a poetic trope thereby reversing the analytical uses of poetry by linguists. The best-known language poet is Charles Bernstein (Andrews and Bernstein, 1984) and a critical review of the movement is found in Perloff (1999). For the cognoscenti, the unpublished and archived *oeuvre* of James Oppen at the University of California at San Diego remains the most exciting unexplored body of work. A newer journal, *The Germ: A Journal of Poetic Research*, publishes the work of a younger generation and recoups some of the unpublished pieces from the past. The most avid followers might claim that the language poets have snatched the English language lyric poem from the graveyard of obsolete genres, of which the most famous decedent is the epic.
5. The poet Ezra Pound in his 1930 essay, 'How to Write', makes provocative points about language. Ardizzone in an introduction to some of his writings from that period comments: 'If 'logopoiea' is to 'charge language with meaning', then language will be saturated with nature (as we know it through scientific knowledge); it will be carried back to that unity of word and thing which, according to Pound, Aristotelian metaphysics obstructs'. (1996: 24) My complaint is that the saturation is working but our theoretical understanding of the associated phenomena is not.

References

Andrews, B. and Bernstein, C. (eds), (1984), *The L-A-N-G-U-A-G-E Book*. Carbondale, IL: Southern Illinois University Press.

Bacon, F., (1989), *New Atlantis and the Great Instauration*. Arlington Heights, IL: Harlan Davidson. (Original work published in 1627).

Bakhtin, M., (1986), *Speech genres and Other Late Essays*, trans. V. McGee. Austin: University of Texas Press.

Bijker, W. and Law, J. (eds), (1992), *Shaping Technology/Building Society*. Cambridge: Cambridge University Press.

Brown, B., (1998), *How to Do Things with Things (a toy story)*, Critical Inquiry, Vol.24, Summer, 935–964.

Chomsky, N., (1957), *Syntactic Structures*. The Hague: Mouton.

Chomsky, N., (1988), *Manufacturing Consent: the political economy of the mass media*. New York: Pantheon.

Haraway, D., (1991), *Simians, Cyborgs, and Women*. New York: Routledge.

Latour, B., (1993), *We Have Never Been Modern*, trans. C. Porter. London: Harvester Wheatsheaf.

Levi-Strauss, C., (1992), *Tristes Tropiques*, trans. J. and D. Weightman. London: Penguin (Original work published in 1955).

Perloff, M., (1999), *Wittgenstein's Ladder: poetic strangeness of the language and the ordinary*. Chicago: University of Chicago Press.

Pound, E., (1996), *Machine Art and Other Writings*, M. Ardizzone (ed.), Durham, NC: Duke University Press.

Rose, D., (1995), 'Active Ingredients'. In J. Sherry (ed.) *Contemporary Marketing and Consumer Behavior*, London: Sage.

Rybczynski, W., (2000), *One Good Turn: A Natural History of the Screwdriver and the Screw*. New York: Scribner.

Scarry, E., (1985), *The Body in Pain*. Oxford: Oxford University Press.

Schiffer, M.B., (1999), *The Material Life of Human Beings*. London: Routledge.

Wittgenstein, L., (1953), *Philosophical Investigations*. New York: Macmillan.

The mystery of the Assumption: mothers and measures

Heather Höpfl

'A mother is a continuous separation, a division of the very flesh. And consequently a division of language – and it has always been so', (Kristeva, 1983; Moi, 1986: 178).

The structure of the chapter advances what it attempts to demonstrate. It seeks to elevate in order to annul. Hence, there are a series of movements which produce subversions or perturbations within the text. The argument is always-already defeated by its inevitable trajectory. It is a stylistic conceit. The headings serve to order the text and render it more ordinary. There are five sections and five elevations. The chapter is symmetrical in design. The middle section is concerned with the theme of the conference where this chapter was originally presented: as a paper on the consumption of mass.

Consumption

The first assumption is that the body haunts the text and is based on the writings of the poet and grammarian Callimachus. The poet was the librarian of the Library of Alexandria and wrote in the third century BC. He had been born in Cyrene in Africa but studied in Athens. Ptolemy II appointed him as the librarian of the great library of Alexandria and he held this post for more than twenty years. It is thought that he wrote in the region of eight hundred books including a catalogue of the works in the library. Callimachus is considered to be the founder of a critical approach to Greek literature and many of his works demonstrate a sophisticated and elaborate construction. He seems to have been particularly concerned with the relationship between poetic form and content and with the reconciliation of the intellectual content of the poem with its emotional consequence.

Here the concern is with his Hymn to Demeter which invokes Demeter as a personification of the earth, as the goddess of plenty, as a figure of authority and as an avenger of violations. It is also with the form of the poem and the intentions of the poet. In his commentary on The Hymn to Demeter, Hopkinson says of Callimachus that he, 'guides us ... into a subjective and highly literary story ... (where) he lurks apart behind the insubstantial voice, and we are left with a poem *in vacuo*, a narrative whose obvious emotion and subjectivity have no definable referent. This is a disconcerting effect ... '. (Hopkinson, 1984: 3). This suggests a structure which is haunted by his presence, like a murmuring which is on the edge of memory, always already there.

The story of the hymn runs as follows. In ancient times, the Pelasgians made a grove in honour of Demeter. The grove was so dense that an arrow could hardly penetrate its foliage. The grove was a locus amoenus, was idyllic. But, as Hopkinson comments, the scene 'is already undermined by a violence latent in the language and imagery' (Hopkinson, 1984: 5) so that water 'boils up' from the ditches and the goddess is described as 'madly fond' of her grove. The peace of the grove is soon to be ruptured by the arrival of Erysichthon and twenty of his retainers who rush into the grove and attack the largest tree, a huge poplar of supernatural size. Hearing the sounds of the axe and the shriek of the tree, Demeter disguises herself as her former priestess, Nicippe and three times warns Erysichthon that he will incur the goddess's wrath if he continues. Erysichthon is not to be deterred and responds with a speech of 'verbal violence' (Hopkinson, 1984: 7) in which he arrogantly explains that his purpose in taking the tree is to provide a roof for his banqueting-hall. Demeter is speechless with anger and assumes her own form. She towers to heaven and terrifies the servants who flee in dread. Her punishment is severe. She punishes him with a hunger that is wild and insatiable, which wracks his body with desire.

> At once she cast on him a dreadful hunger, burning and powerful, and he
> was tortured by the great disease. Poor wretch! Whatever
> he ate he desired as much again'
>
> (*lines: 67,68*)

She condemns him to consume and consume and consume. He can neither cease consuming nor be satisfied with his consumption. His mother and sisters, his old nurse and the serving maids, all weep for him. His mother recalls him at the breast.

> His mother wept; and his two
> Sisters and the breast which had nursed him and the
> Many tends of slave-girls all uttered heavy groans'
>
> (*lines: 95,96*)

His father shares his despair. The story does not tell Erysichthon's fate. The last section of the poem details the festival of Thesmophoria and of a fertility ritual involving a sacred basket drawn on a cart by four white horses, followed by women who are barefoot and bareheaded. This procession of women proceeds to the goddess's temple. There are even special instructions for women who are pregnant or sick who accompany the procession as far as they are able. The poem ends with a prayer for the city and Demeter's blessings.

61

On issues of form, it is interesting to consider that in writing hymns, Callimachus attempted to produce a new genre of poetic writing in which intellect and emotion co-exist and produce what Hopkinson has called 'a sophisticated dissonance' (Hopkinson, 1884: 13). The order of the hymns is unusual in that Callimachus presents a symmetrical arrangement of two short, two long and two short poems. The first pair is masculine, the second pair mixed and the third pair feminine. The short poems are mimetic, the long middle sections are epic and the last two poems are written in a Doric dialect which Hopkinson relates to their unheroic subject matter. However, he concedes that there may be no good reason, other than experimentation and a fondness for dialect, which prompts the 'feminine' poems to be written in this way. On the other hand, given that Callimachus is seeking to experiment with the relationship between intellect and the effects of emotion, it could be a softening of the verse away from the epic style of the middle section into the feminine and vernacular closing poems.

On issues of content, this is the story of vengeance. Demeter, the mother, Goddess of agriculture, fertility and growth, takes revenge on the youth who violates her sacred grove and condemns him to insatiable consumption. His punishment is that he will never be satisfied. He will consume endlessly but never be replete. Worse, the more he eats the hungrier he will become and eventually he will be reduced to eating trash and filth by the roadside. This is a terrifying metaphor of relentless quest without satisfaction, of continual consumption, of hunger without relief. Clearly, there are innumerable ways in which this allegory might serve as a cautionary tale of contemporary life. One might draw ecological parallels as readily as one might individual ones. However, the purpose of the story in the context in which it is presented here is to place an emphasis on Demeter as the mother. The name itself, Demeter, is from the Greek word for mother, meter, metros and is used here in contrast to the word, meter, metron, meaning measure. So one might compare, for example, metronome, metronomos as measure/law with metropolis, mother/city. In other words, the first assumption of this chapter is that it is possible to distinguish between metros and metron, between mother and measure, between body and law, between experience and its regulation. The metropolis is the mother city, the place of the mother, the womb, the locus amoenus. It is the place of polity of process and order. *Polis* is normally rendered city or city state yet, as Heidegger (1959) points out, the term polis means more than this, it is 'the place, the there, wherein and as which the historical being-there **is**' (Heidegger, 1959: 152). It is a coincident word that brings together the body and the law, mother and order: metropolis. Hence, the first *aufhebung* of the construction of this paper is the metropolis.

And he has found his way
To the resonance of the word,
And to wind-swift all-understanding,
And to the courage of rule over cities.

(*From lines 352–555, Sophocles, Antigone*)

Mass

The second assumption of this chapter is that the body is subject to the law. It concerns the relationship between the order and form of the Mass and how this stands in relation to the vernacular. So, it is possible to speak of the Ordinary of the Mass as the form and structure of the order of service. St Justin Martyr in the second century identifies the basic outline of the eucharistic celebration in a letter to the pagan emperor Antoninus Pius, in around 155 AD, as involving a gathering together, readings, a homily and prayers which are called liturgy of the Word and the presentation of bread and wine, the consecratory thanksgiving and communion, the liturgy of the Eucharist. 'The liturgy of the Word and the liturgy of the Eucharist together form one single act of worship, the Eucharistic table set for us is the table both of the Word of God and of the Body of the Lord' (Libreria Editrice Vaticana, 1994: 290). Hence, the elements of the Mass become a symbol of coincidence of body and law. However, outside of this is the ordering of the service itself: the anterior structuring which regulates the playing out of the ritual. This might be seen in the relationship between the Ordinary and the Vernacular (Höpfl, 2000) where the Ordinary, as for example in the Ordinary of the Mass, regulates the Vernacular, the language of slaves. The Ordinary of the Mass is the authoritative, sanctioned order of service and as such it specifies (L. *denotare*: to mark out for another) the sequence, content, order and form of the service. Widening the context, the Ordinary is the principal means of ordering. The ordinary is an ordering.

In contrast, the Vernacular is the language of the home born slave, the slave born into slavery, born in the master's house. This is the language of the *verna* not the *servus* and the case ending is feminine. The Ordinary regulates and structures the Vernacular, appropriates it, translates it into a more 'appropriate' language, defines, that is to say 'finalizes' (L. *(de)finire*, to finalize, to state exactly what a thing is) its meaning. So the Ordinary functions to regulate the experiences which are expressed in the Vernacular and to order them. In this sense, one might say that one submits to an ordering *in order* to render the body ordinary. It is the Ordinary that is authoritative and the Vernacular is inadmissible, that is to say, it cannot be 'sent in' without authorization. Hence, the documents of the Vatican II say of liturgical matters, 'In accordance with the centuries-old tradition of the Latin rite, the Latin language is to be retained by clerics in reciting the Divine Office. But in individual cases the ordinary *has the power of granting the use of* a vernacular translation ... . The vernacular version, however, must be the one that is drawn up according to the provision of Article 36. The competent superior has the power to grant the use of the vernacular in the celebration ... *The version, however, must be an approved one*', [italics added] (Abbott, 1967: 167).

Not only is the Ordinary authoritative but it also directs. It is the pro*ject*ion of the Ordinary into the future that determines ob*ject*ives and is the means of their achievement, the tra*ject*ory (L. *iacere*, to throw, to cast). It is *in the service* of such throwings and castings that the ordering takes place. And, here it seems appropriate to remain with the notion of projection and future states – business objectives, career objectives, indeed, any purposive move towards futurity – in order to identify the movement and direction which is described by such projection. In Ordinary language this is what is now frequently termed 'the mission' of the organization, the life plan of the individual, the career. The mission *sends*. It is directed into the future (L. *mittere*, to send). Hence, to send out a message, to *transmit*, to *commit*, to *admit, remit, permit* is to send something out. In other words, there is a direction of the mission. So 'the Mass' is a verbal substantive from the past participle of mittere. It is the evocation of a sending and, as such, a movement away from or towards another place. So, in the world of business, it has become quite *ordinary* to speak in terms of a mission and objectives in the same breath. The *mission* is the *message* (L. *mittere*) which is sent ahead of the strategy as its annunciation. It announces the trajectory of the Ordinary which regulates its very direction, form and content. The third assumption then is that the law has a mission and that this mission is to regulate the body. The second *aufhebung* is the Mass.

Clever indeed, mastering
The ways of skill beyond all hope,
He sometimes accomplishes evil,
Sometimes achieves brave deeds.
He wends his way between the laws of the earth
And the adjured justice of the gods.
Rising high above his place,
He who for the sake of adventure takes
The nonessent for the essent loses
His place in the end.

(From lines 359–373, Sophocles, Antigone)

The Consumption of mass

The third assumption is that if the body resists subjection, the law will erect a more compliant body. If then one *takes on* this specific interpretation of the notion of Mass, it is necessary *to take* account of how this relates to Consumption. In brief, the emphasis on the words *to take* provide this association and *take* it further into a discussion of the Assumption if this does not *presume* too much. All these terms, consumption, assumption, presumption, have their origins in the Latin *sumere* meaning to take. Hence, *to consume* is to take away, to use up, to take in, to waste away, to exhaust. Now the Mass as transmission, as a sending works in this way. There is an authoritative version of an ordering, the structure and content, and this is the transmission of the Ordinary. In other words, the transmission is a construction. However, for the purposes of this chapter, I would prefer here to use the term *erection*. There are a number of reasons for the choice of this terminology. First, the root of the word erection is the Latin *e-regere* meaning *to direct*. Second, there is the more straightforward association of the word with something built, erected. Third, there is the more supplemental idea of the erection of categories as, in the argument presented here, a male preoccupation and this latter consideration will be discussed further below. The erections *direct* the transmission of the structure and the content. Therefore, the erections are the means of achieving the ordering. The erection is the means by which the Ordinary is effected. Erections are authoritative because they lay claim to an anterior authority and create the world by verbal fiat and if, in saying this, I reify the erection, it is to transgress the way in which the erection reifies me.

Erections direct the transmission of the Ordinary and, given that this means that they establish an authorized sequence, they establish the Ordinary in the way that we encounter it as the commonplace. However, this is *metron* not *metros*. It is *meter* as Measure not *meter* as Mother. The Mother cannot be *admitted* within the regulatory function of the Measure. The law regulates the body and its trajectory seeks to finalise experience. In an illustration of this, in 1484 Pope Innocent VIII brought out an extraordinary *(note: extra – Ordinary)* Papal Bull, Summa Desiderantes, which seems to have resulted from a period of unusual male sexual anxiety and impotence which had been brought on by a fear of witchcraft. In the shamanistic tradition, magic was generally the province of men and such men were consulted on ways of appeasing the spirits or remedying wrongs. In this way, men with magical powers were regarded as able to work magic, to learn to read omens, and to be able to explain the unknown. Women who were supposed to have magical power, by contrast, tended to be healers and midwives but women were regarded as much more sinister, full of a primitive magic. Witches were believed to have considerable malevolent power as a result of copulating with devils. Their power was transmitted in secret and in an unwritten form. Witches then, possessed a knowledge that men could not regulate and this was seen as unruly. Since they did not get this knowledge or power from men but shared it between themselves, so it was argued, they must have got it from the devils.

The Pope com*mission*ed (sent out) two Dominican monks, Jacob Sprenger and Heinrich Kramer to investigate the practices of witchcraft and to report. They were commissioned to investigate the 'prevalence of the witch organisation' in Northern Germany and were granted 'an exceptional authorisation, by Letters Apostolic requiring the Bishop of Strasburg (sic) ... not only to take all steps to publish and proclaim the Bull' and to offer every assistance in the inquisition, (Summers, 1928, xiv). Apart from the impact on men's potency of the activities of witches, the chief claim against witches seems to have been that they were thought to collaborate with each other in secret organizations and to share their knowledge and skills. Sprenger's *Malleus Malificarum* was the result of the investigation and it is, in effect, a handbook designed for inquisitors to use in investigations of witchcraft. The *Malleus* was to be placed 'on the bench of every judge and the desk of every magistrate' (Summers, 1928: xiv) and imposed a duty on European jurisprudence for three centuries to combat the society of witches. The Malleus speaks of women in the following terms, 'All wickedness is but little to the wickedness of a woman .... What else is woman but a foe to friendship, an unescapable punishment, a necessary evil, a natural temptation, a desirable calamity, a domestic danger, a delectable detriment, an evil of nature, painted with fair colours' (Summers, 1928: 43). And, more damning, 'When a woman thinks alone, she thinks evil'. 'Women are intellectually like children ... she is more carnal than a man .... She is an imperfect animal, she always deceives', 'a woman is beautiful to look at, contaminating to the touch, and deadly to keep'. (Summers, 1928: 43, 44). The book concentrates most of its length on the 'maleficia' which women are supposed to inflict on men to rob them of their potency. Consider the proposition put forward by Sprenger in the Malleus for the etymology of the word 'feminus'.

Sprenger claims that 'when a woman weeps, she labours to deceive a man ... and all this is indicated by the etymology of the word; for Femina comes from Fe and Minus (that is to say Faithless) since she is ever weaker to hold and to preserve the faith' (Summers, 1928: 44). In fact, femina comes from a Sanskrit word meaning, 'to suckle'. But, worse is to come. After a series of cautionary tales about women's refusal to act as they are commanded and their contrariness, after a denunciation of women as the cause of worldly suffering, after an expression of a desire for a world without women, Sprenger comes to his point. 'All witchcraft', he concludes, 'comes from carnal lust, which is in women insatiable'. What can never be satisfied is 'the mouth of the womb' (Summers, 1928: 47). Indeed, 'the word woman is used to mean the lust of the flesh' (Summers, 1928: 43). Here it is women who are seen as insatiable, full of endless lust, demanding and desiring, intent on taking away the potency of men. These men, these two Dominicans, could not *permit* women to be *admitted* to the Faith on equal terms precisely because they took away men's power and because they lacked *commitment*. Women, therefore, had to *submit* to regulation by the Ordinary of this text, to conform to a trajectory and way of casting which laid down an ordering for them. The text established an ordering in which women were *subjected, thrown out, cast down, and rejected*. All these terms suggest that women were ordered out by the text. In these movements, the need for the restoration of the body to the text begins to emerge as a male concern. Hence, it could be argued that the bringing together of the body and the law in the elements of the Mass constitute a metaphysical reconciliation which is subjected to an ordering and consequently safe and reassuring. Women, as a cipher for the body, cannot be admitted unless they subject themselves to the constructions that are imposed on them. Women must conform themselves to the power of the erection and this applies on all levels of association. This then is the third assumption: that the law can erect its own body. The third *aufhebung* then, is the Erection.

Everywhere journeying, inexperienced and without issue,
He comes to nothingness.
Through no flight can he resist
The one assault of death,
Even if he has succeeded in cleverly evading
Painful sickness.

(*From lines 359–373, Sophocles, Antigone*)

The Assumption

The fourth assumption is an equation of assumption and *aufhebung*. The assumption of the Blessed Virgin Mary bodily into heaven is simultaneously an elevation and a cancellation: *Aufhebung*. So, where does this lead in relation to the prevailing Assumption of the paper. Here the argument follows another line of Catholic thinking because it provides a further perspective on the relationship between Measure and Mother. The cult of the Blessed Virgin Mary in Christendom began around the eleventh century and flourished in the Middle Ages. However, it was not until 1953 that the Catholic Church at the prompting of the Society of Jesus (the Jesuits) arrived at the dogma of the Assumption, the official teaching of the Church on the bodily assumption of Our Lady into Heaven. As the Catechism says,
   'Finally the Immaculate Virgin, preserved free from all stain of original sin, when the course of her earthly life was finished, was taken up body and soul into heavenly glory, and exalted by the Lord as Queen over all things, so that she might be the more fully conformed to her Son, the Lord of lords and conqueror of sin and death' (Libreria Editrice Vaticana, 1994: 208, Lumen Gentium, 59).
   Mary is the Virgin Mother of God, the sexless Mother who cannot damage the potency, the power of God and here one must assume that this is a God who has made man in his image. Mary does not damage men's potency because she is their construction and held safe within it. Mary is the immaculate model of Motherhood without body. When she is assumed into heaven, the Assumption, she is taken in and women are taken in by this extraordinary construction. This is not a real woman of flesh and blood. She is without desire, without the lust that apparently consumes ordinary women. She is the icon of a woman robbed of her power and conciliated to the desires of men. The men of the Church protect their erections by this movement. She is assumed so that she 'might be more fully conformed to her Son' (see above, Lumen Gentium, 59). This is a dogma of the Church. In other words, it is an authoritative statement about an ordering and about regulation. It is the regulating out of bodily experience and physicality by the metaphysics of ordering. Lumen Gentium says, 'we also see Mary by her prayers imploring the gift of the Spirit, who had already *overshadowed* her in the Annunciation' (Libreria Editrice Vaticana, 1994: 207). Her physical body is already overshadowed by its incorporation

into metaphysics. So, Mary is held up as a model of obedience and 'mother to us *in the order of* grace' (Libreria Editrice Vaticana, 1994: 208). Her submission stands as an emblem for the *incorporation* of the body into the text. She stands within the order of grace as in the sequence of order. This is metros rendered metron. She is the mother made into measure. She is conciliated into the ordering and deprived of her physical being. The trick of the Assumption, which seeks to persuade that the bodily assumption (into Heaven) is achieved by sinlessness, obedience and submission, is that there is no body. This is a story which is erection from start to finish. Mary's physicality is regulated by metaphysics so that she 'might be more fully conformed to her Son' (see above, Lumen Gentium, 59). Hence, the fourth assumption is that the law likes to pretend it has a body. The fourth *aufhebung* is the Blessed Virgin Mary.

There is little evidence that the popularity of feminine and maternal (religious) imagery in the high Middle Ages reflects an increased respect for actual women by men. Saints' lives might romanticise mothers, but there was in the general society not mystique of mother hood ... the males who popularised maternal and feminine imagery were those who had renounced the family and the company of women; the 'society' out of which their language comes is a substitute for (and implicitly a critique of) the world, (Bynum, 1984: 143/144).

Reproduction

The fifth assumption is that the primary function of the law is to ensure reproduction. In the context of this paper, this reproduction is of the measure not the mother. It is metron not metros. In recent years, there has been an obsession with metrics. This section of the paper deals with the *metra*, which is Greek for uterus, and seeks to explore the contest for reproduction which is being played out between metros and metron. However, I need to move from Greek to Latin for this etymology because the commonplace of the matrix in contemporary organizations suggests that it is more appropriate to use not the Greek word metra but the Latin, matrix. I have developed the argument about the matrix elsewhere (Höpfl, 1999, 2000) but it is necessary to represent these ideas in order to draw together the strands of the argument presented here. The *matrix*, formerly the term used to apply to a female breeding animal and not used to apply to women, in late Latin came to be the term used for the human uterus (Simpson, 1964; Hoad, 1986). Hence, in terms of the thrust of the law, here represented by the phallogocentric discourse, the matrix is appropriated by the male logos. The capture of the matrix and its conversion into a space of regulation is easily demonstrated by recourse to any contemporary use of the notion of a matrix as the ordering principle for ideas, locations, positions and so forth. The mastery of the matrix is achieved by the force of the erection and, in the assumption above, in the construction of the mother as a Virgin Mother.

This movement, in effect, renders the uterus impotent. Embodied reproduction is then replaced by the reproduction of text and the fertility of the site is surrendered to the fertility of words and regulation. So, the matrix is regulated so that its cells show location and defining characteristics on the basis of power. This is the power to authorize and regulate. In the substitution of words for the natural products of the matrix, the space is regulated, and the reproduction of homologues guaranteed. Men, here used to refer to both men and women in the service of the organization, reproduce themselves in their own image and give birth only to sons.

A woman can do battle with the mother, seize phallic power and become a man but in so doing, she renders all relationships with men homomorphic. However, to do otherwise or to seek to be other/different requires the patronage of men. Like the Virgin Mary in the Doctrine of the Assumption, honoured yet disavowed, emblems of the body are honoured yet disavowed by organizations so that the representation of the body within the regulation of the law is a travesty. In other words, the Virgin Mother, as representation, is the Law and, as Eagleton argues, 'The law is male, but hegemony is a woman; this transvestite law, which decks itself out in female drapery is in danger of having its phallus exposed', (Eagleton, 1990: 58). This is apparent in the familiar ways in which organizations seek to create the *feminine* in notions of care and satisfaction: customer care, client satisfaction, and emotional intelligence. The university as metropolis is metros and not metron: order by measurement. So, the organization constructs itself in diagrams and charts, texts and metrics which seek to uphold or hold up (*aufheben*) the representation of the body within the construction but which inevitably achieves a cancellation. It is little wonder, then that notions of quality and care, and the ubiquitous valorization of staff have more in them of melancholy than of matter. These are Eagleton's transvestite manifestations of the law attempting to present themselves as concerns of the body. The fifth assumption is that the law takes over reproduction. The *aufhebung* is of the Matrix. The matrix presented in Figure 1 is intended to be ironic. It is an *aufhebung*: elevation and

DEFINITION	ASSUMPTION	AUFHEBUNG
Consumption	the body haunts the text	Metropolis
Mass	the body is subject to the law	Mass
The Consumption of Mass	if the body resists subjection the law will erect a more compliant body	Erection
The Assumption	the equation of assumption and Aufhebung	BVM
Reproduction	the primary function of the law is to ensure reproduction	Matrix

Figure 1

cancellation. By giving attention to and raising up this textual matrix its meaning is cancelled and, as erection, it cannot be sustained. It is intended to render problematic the nature of definition and location that characterize the cells of the matrix. Hence, it appears to give definition and location within a structure which provides the vehicle for its reproduction. It is formal and appears to render intelligible those things which, admittedly, still within the text bear their own ambivalence. Hence, there is a movement in the chapter between form and content, between the body and the law and between regulation and experience. There is an attempt to characterize and locate, and an attempt to take on certain positions, assumptions. However, the play of the chapter is in the simultaneity of elevation and cancellation. The argument seeks to erect a series of such emblems in order to cancel them: the metropolis as mother/order; the Mass as law/body; the erection as order/disorder and as male/female; the Blessed Virgin Mary as mother/not mother; the matrix as embodied reproduction/textual reproduction.

Bitte nicht stören! *(Please do not disturb)*

The movements of the argument presented here seek, like the writings of Callimachus, to move between the intellectual concerns which dominate its structuring and the emotional counterpart which always-already haunts the text. The chapter is subject to its own masculine metaphysics which always wants to resist the contamination of the text by the intrusion of the body. Indeed, which *will* only permit the body to enter as representation *can* only permit the body to enter as representation. At the heart of the chapter is the contest between metros and metron, between mother and measure. So much of life is subject to scrutiny by a range of metrics which serve to monitor performance, experience, satisfaction. We consume and consume and consume but are never satisfied yet we constantly monitor ourselves to see if we are both satisfying and satisfied. Of course, we are not and we see the travesty of all this relentless monitoring. If the reader will permit one further etymology, it is that of monition. We monitor because we want to check whether we are performing adequately and *to monitor* comes from the Latin, *monere*, meaning, to warn. Ironically, in this regulatory way of thinking, metron is always the measure of how far we fall short of the mother, of metros. In other words, it is precisely in the melancholy of the lack, of the distance from the ideal or the erected sublime, that the monitoring takes place. This would suggest that the obsessive concern with monitoring is a measure of how far we have moved from our humanity although I want to avoid what Eagleton says, is 'a fantasy of mother and father in one, of love and law commingled' (Eagleton, 1990: 263). However, in the context of what I have tried to do with these ideas, the mother might be seen as the possibility of the 'ideal of compassionate community, of altruism and natural affection, ... which represents a threat to rationalism ... (but where) the political consequences ... are ambivalent', (Eagleton, 1990: 60) where the outcomes are not ambivalent but *ambivalence*. This, of course, is very disturbing: *'please do not disturb'*.

In organizational terms, the concerns in this chapter relate to workplaces where measure takes clear precedence over mother (again, as a cipher for body, experience), where the body is always subject to the law, that is to say, where the needs of the organization take precedence over the needs of the person or collectivity, where the organization requires compliant bodies regulated by structures which limit their capabilities, where feminine qualities are representational and masculine, where the primary function of the organization is reproduction. I cannot be too *explicit* since I am already *complicit*. Indeed, I am already implicated (Latin, *implicare*, to entangle) by my production of these ideas as text. 'The problem is that as soon as the insurgent 'substance' speaks, it is necessarily caught up in the kind of discourse *allowed by* and *submitted to* by the Law' (Moi, 1986: 10, italics added). So I am left with a dilemma. Should I become a homologue and conform myself to the order of the text and its associated metrics? Should I attempt the romantic ideal of restoring the mother? Should I perhaps invoke Demeter as a warning? Or, and perhaps the option I like best, as an expression of the impossibility of expressing my otherness, should I stay mum ... *oder vielleicht Mutter?*

'The love of God and for God resides in the gap: the broken space made explicit by sin on the one side, the beyond on the other. Discontinuity, lack of arbitrariness: topography of the sign, of the symbolic relation that posits my otherness as impossible. Love, here, is only for the impossible', (Kristeva, 1983; Moi, 1986: 184).

References

Abbott, W.M., (1967), *The Documents of Vatican II*, London: Geoffrey Chapman.

Andrews, E.A., (1875), *A Copious and Critical Latin-English Lexicon founded on the Larger Latin-German Lexicon of William Freund*, London: Sampson Low, Marston, Low and Searle.

Bynum, C.W., (1984), *Jesus as Mother, Studies in the Spirituality of the High Middle Ages*, Berkeley: University of California Press.

Concise Oxford Dictionary, Fifth Edition, (1974) London: BCA.

Docherty, T., (1987), *On Modern Authority*, Brighton: The Harvester Press.

Eagleton, T., (1990), *The Ideology of the Aesthetic*, Oxford: Blackwell.

Hart, K., (1989), *The Trespass of the Sign*, Cambridge: Cambridge University Press.

Heidegger, M., (1959), *An Introduction to Metaphysics*, New Haven: Yale University Press.

Hoad, T.F., (1986), *The Concise Oxford Dictionary of English Etymology*, Oxford: Oxford University Press.

Höpfl, H., (1999), *Strategic Quest and the Search for the Primal Mother*, a paper presented in the Gender Stream, EGOS Conference, Warwick, July 1999.

Höpfl, H., (2000), *On Being Moved*, Studies in Cultures, Organisations and Societies (in press).

Hopkinson, N., (1984), *Callimachus, Hymn to Demeter*, Cambridge: Cambridge University Press.

Irigaray, L., (1985), *Speculum of the Other Woman*, trans G Gill, Ithaca: Cornell University Press.

Kristeva, J., (1990), *Abjection, melancholia and love: the work of Julia Kristeva*, Fletcher, J. and A. Benjamin (eds), London: Routledge.

Kristeva, J., (1984a), *Revolution in Poetic Language*, New York: Columbia University Press.

Kristeva, J., (1984b), *Desire in Language. A Semiotic Approach to Literature and Art*, trans., Gora, T.S., Jardine, A. and Roudiez, L., Oxford: Basil Blackwell.

Kristeva, J., (1983), *Stabat Mater*, in reprinted in Moi, T. (ed.) 1986, *The Kristeva Reader*, Oxford: Blackwell.

Kristeva, J., (1982), *Powers of Horror, An Essay on Abjection*, New York: Columbia University Press.

Libreria Editrice Vaticana, (1994), *The Catechism of the Catholic Church* (authorized English translation in Canada), Ottowa: Canadian Conference of Catholic Bishops Publication Services.

Moi, T., (ed.) (1986), *The Kristeva Reader*, Oxford: Blackwell.

Oliver, K., (1993), *Reading Kristeva*, Bloomington: Indiana University Press.

Oliver, K., (ed.) (1993), *Ethics, Politics and Difference in Julia Kristeva's Writing*, New York: Routledge.

Simpson, D.P., (1964), *Cassell's New Latin-English, English-Latin Dictionary*, London: Cassell.

Summers, M., (1928), *Malleus Maleficarum*, London: The Hogarth Press.

Todorov, T., (1981), *Introduction to Poetics*, Brighton: The Harvester Press.

Warner, M., (1976), *Alone of All Her Sex*. The Myth and Cult of the Virgin Mary, New York: Knopf.

Sound, technics, energy: (consumption)

Rob Beeston

Understand? We hope you enjoy this listening experience. Pleasure is our business (Autechre Music Systems from Gescom Transcendental, 1994)

Lots of stuff happens with mass. Lots of stuff happens with a mass like electronic sound. Or a more and less specific mass like Autechre. Or Surgeon, System Error or Plastikman (the shakers and movers herein). Sounds get worked over and over from knob to knob. Over and over gets worked into perfectly pleasurable bass lines. Pleasure gets side-tracked by continuous plastic projections that out-run the bass lines. Lots of stuff happening with electronic sound. And lots of stuff happens again with electronic sound. When something happens to the happening. When over and over, and pleasurable bass lines, and plastic sounds happen again. When what gets produced simultaneously gets consumed.

When what gets produced makes connections with other productions, mass happens again. Following the connections of a composition and its mass products – its machines, operators, and sounds as they work over and over to pleasure bass lines and plasticate sounds – tracks them as they happen again. As they produce and are produced. As they consume and are consumed. As their exchanges make more of composition materials than materials of production-alone. As they become pleasures, pains, rushes, writer's block, unknown hours. Nudging materials into felt action and on to romances of knob twiddling, machine alterity, and limit philosophies of Underground sound. To begin telling of more *creative, poetic, affective* stuff that happens with materials. With a material mass like electronic sound.

Symmetry of cuts and bruises, or, balance (Surgeon, 1998)[1]

Allow materials both to produce and consume and they remake meanings. (Give and take.) The tracks which make and remake the meanings of electronic composition run out towards materials like machines/people/sounds. Producing and consuming each other. Tracks comprised of materials. Materials confined by their own materiality and the materiality of their relations in exchange (Munro, 1997). Tracks comprised of meaningful materials – materials full of meaning – being partially emptied out in exchange as

© The Editorial Board of The Sociological Review 2001. Published by Blackwell Publishers, 108 Cowley Road, Oxford OX4 1JF, UK and 350 Main Street, Malden, MA 02148, USA.

machines, people and sounds remake each other. (Give and take.)[2] Privileging neither biological materials (humanism), mechanical materials (technological determinism), nor acoustic materials (music theory).

Tracking mass – balancing its production with its consumption – entrusts none of the materials with the status of subject over object and none with the status of object over subject. On balance the operator subjects the machine to organic exchange and makes it an object (the operator subjects the machine to its *organic* confines). Simultaneously, the machine subjects the operator to mechanical exchange and makes *it* an object (the machine subjects the operator to its *mechanical* confines). And further still, the material confines of sound – the materialisation of 'x' frequencies above and below the pitch of the fundamental – subject both machine and operator to acoustic exchange and make *them* objects within the confines of fundamental tonality. Then knobs get twiddled and mouses get clicked and sounds get subjected to biological/mechanical exchange. People/machines/sounds simultaneously subjecting and objecting in material exchange along mass-tracks, the tracks of mass in mutual exchange.

Materials moved in exchanging relations balance more of a symmetry than do production-codes alone (codes which guarantee the [re]production of mass when exchanged). Thinking symmetrically, the translation of meaning – of its guaranteed [re]production – balances out as the meaning of translation – of movement in exchange.[3] The translation of machines and software. Of people that use machines and software by twiddling knobs and mouse-clicking to trim soundwaves. Of waves of sound that get fed back in and twiddled and clicked. All these operating tracks – and more – when thought symmetrically, exchange mass. The tracks mobilise mass. The tracks – symmetrically and recursively speaking – *are* mass. Mass made mobile. Exchanged and exchanging. Producing and consuming. Problematizing production-alone, and problematizing the production of consumption-alone. Because on balance, what produces is also produced, what consumes is also consumed.

Symmetrical takes on mass-tracks – on mass relations in mutual exchange – hang around the tensions and reverberations of [re]production work. Energy. Waiting on production work – hanging around – yields consumption. The movement of works of production. The movement that makes subjects and objects somewhat strange. And waiting on consumption work yields production. The stabilization of works of consumption. The stabilization that allows something of their recognition and naming. Thus, waiting symmetrically on production/consumption yields both *incision* – the cut of a groove – and *contusion* – the diffuse refrain of repetition. Balance. Balance places surgical precision within imprecision to maintain the rhythm-proper which simultaneously posits and passes the material. A rhythm rhyming in the unresolveable dialectic of both position and passage. Specific materials in felt-action. To problematize the inert a-rhythmia of both production-alone and the production of consumption-alone.

Tracing machine-/people-/sound-tracks – masses grazed and bruised with oblique angles to balance the incision of direct cuts – sets up this rhythmic exchange. Waiting yields the tensions and energies and reverberations – rhythm – of mass in exchange. Tensions which – should they not be allowed to collapse – might say something more true to form-experience. Hanging around uses the operating tracks of electronic synthesisers and sequencers to detail and layer form-after-force. It analyses and synthesises, divides and sequences. To ride the rhythm and to write the rhythm with a groove that's ridden and written out from synthesisers and sequencers. The rhythmic forces which nudge materials into felt action and on to romances of knob twiddling, machine alterity, and limit philosophies of Underground sound. Rhythm and touch.

Synthesising force, or, basic tonal vocabulary (Surgeon, 1997)

The [Novation] BassStation[4] features all the classic elements of analogue [...] synthesis [...] You start with sound which contains more than you need and remove parts of it until you are left with the required timbre and shape. (Novation, 1994: BassStation User Manual)[5]

There's a starting sound. A waveshape of variable type which establishes the basic sound range to be worked in. Parameter settings establish the range of frequencies and harmonics to be subjected to further analysis and synthesis by 'filtering' – 'removing the harmonics you don't need'. Rhythm-hacking. Gene splicing sound. Going deeper into the break (Eshun, 1998: 68). BassStation operations generate rhythm sequences not by programming/composing *with* sound but by programming the genus of sound itself. Basic tonal vocabulary (Surgeon, 1997).[6] Waveform specifications, frequency cut-offs and filter controls strip and tweak harmonic orders to order. Custom-blending tone colour. A mass-customization of wave-form – of material forms registering soundwave operations – that alienate structures to generate alien textures. Textures that grab the imagination. Textures mixed-up in the hold-up of the electronic text. From knob to knob.[7]

The SuperNova's Synthesis Engine features three completely independent oscillators. [Their] waveforms can be combined in the Mixer Section allowing the creation of very fat and complex timbres. (Novation, 1998a: 'SuperNova – Coming Soon'□)

Once filtered to remove unwanted harmonics (subtractive synthesis) each customized waveform can be 'combined in the Mixer Section'.[8] To specify 'very fat and complex timbres'. Timbres with frequencies spread wide over the low end of the spectrum, creating a highly resonant 'squelch' sound. Bass.[9]

From the analogue sound modelling of the BassStation through the SuperBassStation and to the SuperNova, the search is on for 'the perfect bass', 'killer bass' (Future Music, 1998: cover). What Novation call fat timbres. What Thomas (1998: 94) calls 'phatt bass'. Fat with a 'ph'. With a sonorous rasp.[10] 'The bass that ate the Earth'. The same bass detailing that excites the consumption of mass produced machines. Like Emu's *Planet Phatt* synthe-siser.[11] Like the Keyfax *Phat Boy*.[12] Or the Aphex *Type C2 Aural Exciter*, with *Big Bottom*.[13] The 'bottom end that endangers your woofers' (Novation, 1998b: 71). Combining analogue waveforms with particular harmonics to drive sound down into the low end of the frequency spectrum. Bass.[14]

Bass operations rumble the senses 'until they bristle like a spike' (Eshun, 1998: 71). The rumbling of something like a rush. Coming up on bass ops. What Eshun (1998: 71) – in his antidote to post-corporeal ideas on trans-humanism and virtuality – calls 'hyperembodiment via the Technics SL1200'.[15] Hyperembodiment via the sensuality of dedicated bass operations. Materials registering the exchanges of bass operations. Twitching power level lights, prickling skin, renegade soundwaves.[16] Subsonics are detected initially as a tell-tale prickle at the surface. Primed in the rumble and then in the rhythm-breeze of the bass-reflection. A prickle with a rate of replication that primes widespread shivers 'down' the distributed spine of the composite wave-form. Goosebumping wave-form. Skin up. [We hope you enjoy this listening experience. (Autechre/Gescom, 1994).][17]

> Modulation Section: this section allows you to set up modulations (automatic changes) to the pitch timbre of the [sound].[18] This gives the sound more 'life', by making it more interesting to the ear'. (Novation, 1994: BassStation User Manual)

The oscillating waveform of the BassStation can be set to change automatically as the sound continues. It changes by altering the degree of oscillation around the fundamental pitch. Steadily increasing the oscillation takes the sound through a series of basic tonal increments, generating a sense of movement through the unfolding of pitch timbre. Maximum pitch settings mean maximum projection. The generation of timbres that stand far out in frequency space. Modulation.[19]

The path of a single sound pitching up-out-and-around grabs the imagination as it streaks around in an energetic display of timbrel and spatial mobility. Warping wave-form out this way and that before wrenching it out along another vector, shifting it up a gear and pitching it forward with an attack velocity that runs over into the distortion zone of a far reaching frequency space. A space which is variably dis/connected from the base pitch of the sound-track. Escape velocity. Or, tracking deep space modulation in its roving timbrel 'plasticity', as a 'glob' of sound-space debris (Plastikman, 1993a, 1993b), as a pitch- 'plasmatik', an advanced 'plastique', wave-warped 'goo' (Plastikman, 1994a, 1994b, 1994c). A wave-warp operation which distracts out to the pitch sensitivities of machines/people/sounds. [We hope you enjoy this listening experience. Pleasure is our business.]

More sound (1), knobs and deconstruction

Setting the scene through particular operations of electronic synthesis – detail, bass, modulation – begins a move toward more force-fed tales of electronic composition. As dedicated synthesiser operations force the exchange of machines/people/sounds they begin offering more creative, poetic, affective tales of form. Material forms which begin promising more than their own terms, more energy than the inert terms of description-alone. Potential. Or, the unknown promised on the basis of what is known.

The poetics of the unknown is what motivates – en-forces – a symmetrical take on the wave-forms of electronic sound. And the sound synthesiser is tracked as it en-forces more creative, poetic, affective tales of form precisely because its operational interface does so with a direct appeal to the logic of potential energy. The interface en-forces a basic tonal vocabulary according to the operational logics of what electronic engineering calls *rotary potentiometry*. What elsewhere gets called *knob twiddling* (Mike and Rich, 1996).

A rotary potentiometer is a resistance device. It coils potential energy around a given force maintaining a resistance between the two. The rotary knob when relaxed – known energy – contains within itself a tensile potential – unknown energy. Rotating the knob engages the potential, releasing an unknown energy out of a known mass – the potential coiled within the machinic knob. And rotary potentiometers litter the interface of sound machines of mass contusion – the BassStation, SuperBasstation, and the SuperNova. They litter the interface with potential.[20]

When balanced in its material exchanges – when en-forced, *imagined* – the proliferation of knob-detail energises the potential which makes more of electronic sound's wave-form than simply machines, people and sounds – known masses – and picks up what they become as they exchange – partially unknown masses. Forced beyond position-alone. A force with which Derrida (1982) – in exchange with Michel Leiris – balances the knowability of Philosophy. Philosophy's wave-form. Its limit. And with which System Error (1998) soundtrack Derrida on the way to more rhythmic tales of form.

Tympan (Derrida, 1982)

Two terms from Derrida (xix–xx): 'hierarchy' and 'envelopment'. Hierarchy: the partial forms coiled within the limit of complete ones. And envelopment: the continual swallowing of the limit as the exchange makes more of form. Jam Derrida together with the BassStation and knob twiddling balances the limit of the sound-track's basic tonal vocabularies by engaging the energy coiled within the the the filter, resonance, and LFO control knobs. It balances complete forms with incomplete ones (hierarchy). And when the potential coiled within the potentiometer is en-forced by the potential coiled within the operator and the sound the limit of 'machines', 'people', 'sounds' is balanced. Their production codes re-written (envelopment).[21]

For each known mass there is an unknown tension. A resonance which envelops its own limit. There is always more (Cooper and Law, 1995: 268) to that which is always less. Inert division and division's energy. Both together, if the rhythm of sound is to be tracked without getting caught in narrative, descriptive categories-alone. Inert categories which are just as easily made of 'energy' as they are of 'inertia'. The energetic *in* the inert. The unknown in the known: 'awaiting only an imperceptible click to set it off like the ribbon of steel tightly wound on itself' (Leiris in Derrida, xii). The unknown in the known: awaiting only an imperceptible rotation to set it off like the 'wirewound rheostat' of the rotary potentiometer (Ohmite Manufacturing Company, 1998: 7). The potential at the edge of the actual. Force. Or, the reverberations of something and nothing. Derrida's soundtrack.

Nothing (System Error, 1997)[22]

The album is called Nothing because that's essentially what it was derived from. We wanted to reveal the hidden voice of sampling technology and play the samplers rather than the samples. Using no input signals at all, we just sampled nothing and looked really closely at it. We tried to listen to what the machines had to say. The album grew out of an interest in the surplus value of technology. For us the surplus value lay in the normally unwanted hums, glitches, crackles, software faults and associated background noises. We found ways to exploit these 'faults', encouraging the machines to crash and output data in ways not considered by the designers.

From warm tones moving in impossible ways, to ice cold glacial soundscapes, Nothing is an evocative, hypnotic and sensual trip into the heart of the machine.

Rotary potentiometry engages the potential at the edge of the actual. What System Error call Nothing. At the edge of the machines. Or – from the other side – at the edge of potential. System Error work at the edge of the unwritten chapter in the user manual. The chapter at the edge of mass production. They rotate the knobs and the dials out of the user manual. Out of mass production. Making more of the samplers tracks than a production code alone allows. Potential. Or as they call it, 'surplus value'. Evaluating the surplus regions of the machine-track. The ones that are 'mute without external input'. The normally 'unwanted hums and glitches' and the 'faults' and 'crashes' of mass production. The system errors.

An error works at the edges of a system of mass production. Its work extends the limit of mass into that which a fully functioning mass silences. Error – a potential in any functioning system – draws from that which is *dys*functional, that which contributes nothing to the functioning of a system. It works at the edge of the machine, at the edge of Nothing. And yet Nothing – over the edge of the machine – is also, according to System Error, 'an evocative, sensual trip into the heart of the machine'. Nothing is at the heart of

Something. Coiled within it. Powered with it. Force. A hierarchy continually being enveloped. Error contributes Nothing – it makes *Nothing* a vital contribution – to the functioning of a system. Error appropriates Nothing. And Something touches something-of-Nothing. Force.

Attending to error – or making error – appropriates its contusions of mass and extends the operational remit of masses like samplers and synthesisers. It makes more of the machine-track than a production code alone would allow. It makes voice from muteness. Something from Nothing. It systematises error. En-forcing it. Moving form further towards System Error's terminology of 'sensuality', 'hypnotics', 'tripping'. The terminology of those forces of form which begin to rhyme. *Intensification*. Intensification to the im/material.

Form is becoming force is becoming intense when the edge of form hears more than its own resonance.

Once sound is synthesised and sampled it has to be arranged in conjunction with other sounds. To begin telling more of the experience of sound. From synthesis to sequencing. Layering the groove. Operations which stack vertically the horizontal manoeuvres of synthesis. Which stack and matt the horizontal *forces* of synthesis. And a layering which animates force to a more delirous level and kick starts the romance with limit philosophies of Underground sound.

Sequencing force, or, passage in/passage out (Plastikman, 1998a, 1998b)[23]

[With the Notron Sequencer[24]] different parts of a multi-layered sound [...] can be independently treated then faded in and out [...]. This way you can have several combinations of sounds fully under your control to record. (Latronic, 1998: Notron Midi Controller User Notes)

During sequencing, multiple dedicated operations – syntheses – are arranged one above the other. Dedications stack as layered sequences. And the distinctive timbrel qualities worked over and over in synthesis form the basis of organization in sequencing.[25] Varese (1936: 26), presciently: 'the role of color or timbre would be completely changed from being incidental, anecdotal, sensual or picturesque; it would become an agent of delineation [...] These [delineated timbrel] zones would be felt as isolated, and the hitherto unobtainable *non-blending* [...] would become possible' (emphasis added).[26]

The tracks of the sequencer trace mass as a complex of detailing-displacing-modulating horizontal energies exchanging with a complex of stopping-starting-fading vertically stacked energies. Energies running as independent layers which stop-start-fade in relation to other independent layers. Or, 'independent treatments' – layers – which become 'combinations of sound' – groove. Layer/groove: 'when overlapping patterns of rhythm interlock, when beats synchromesh until they generate an automotion effect which pushes you along from behind until you're funky like a train' (Eshun, 1998: 82). Locomotion (Plastikman, 1998c).

Funk and groove – the 'combination of sounds' – are made from 'independent treatments' – synthesised layers. Layers of alien sounds fall in to the groove. They collect. And the sequencer's logic of layer-becoming-groove holds open the reverse path. Independent treatments made from combinations of sound. Groove falls out as alien layers. They distract. Layer and groove fall in-and-out. Collection and distraction. Sequencer logic tracks independents to dependents via this two-way passage. Passage in, passage out (Plastikman, 1998a, 1998b). Tracking a passage in brings mass together in the combination of sounds. Hearing the groove and getting funky. Tracking a passage out takes mass apart as independent treatments. Hearing the layers and alienating the sound. And tracking a passage in alongside a passage that tracks out – polyphonics – brings mass together whilst at the same time taking it apart. Hearing the groove in the layers to feed the funk and the layers in the groove to alienate the sound. The funky alien. The Plastikman. Funkin' and groovin' with that other-worldly return of gaze.[27]

The Plastikman[28]

In the sequence-track passage in/out exchanges the grooving of machines/people/sounds with their layering in basic tonal vocabularies. The collecting funk and groove distracts with the synthesis of *that* sound. Of that sensual, lacerating, bass-whipped alien sound that sparks the imagination. And distracting tonal vocabularies collect. In the funk of interlocking patterns a-float on the combining energies of the groove-line. Passage in, passage out. Groove gets funky with the visceral sensation of primed and alienated layers. Smak (Plastikman, 1993c). And layers alienate sounds with a collected groove-line whose funky motion is irresistible. Locomotion (Plastikman, 1998c).

'Smakked' by bass-whipped layers with a partial connection to the 'locomotive' rhythm of the groove. The speed of hearing:

Head and shoulders rock the groove-line. The nod *in* the rock paces the bass-line. Fingers labour the percussion pattern. Imagination drifts with the punctuated delay-space of a massive reverb. Feet walk the alternations of the kick-drum. Level lights twitch. Groove collects the fingers as the percussion pattern over-works co-ordination. The rock slipstreams the groove, loses drag and lightens up, as a click-pop-delay lashes out. [Rush.] Right side heel-toe rocks a half alternation before getting tangled like the fingers did and the nod is about to. Feet, hands and head roll into the rock of the shoulders as the groove attracts. Shiver rides out. Whilst the imagination wonders how far out the reverb stretches (cf. Locomotion and Consumed: Plastikman, 1998c, 1998d).

Speed-hearing. With groove the layers are never far away, with layers the groove is never far away. Because distractions buzz the groove-line to interfere with the inertia of layer and groove apart (inertia-alone) without collapsing the two and shifting the imbalance to the inertia of 'intensity' – alone (of layer and groove mixing up as one 'blend'). The funky alien with Deleuze/Guattari (1988): passage in/out hears sequenced sound in more than one place but less than many. In more than one place but less than all over the place. In more than the inertia-alone of layer or groove apart but less than the 'energy' – alone of layer and groove mixing up as one. The funky alien: funkin' and groovin' and catching your eye with that knowing, off-world gaze, that intense stare, freezing the moment. A double operation of collective focus with distributed distraction. The speed of hearing. [We hope you enjoy this listening experience.]

> [...] when you want to make a sequence travel twice as fast or half as slow as its neighbours; simply double or half the Ratio [...]. (Latronic, 1998: Notron MIDI Controller User Notes)

Once assigned to independent channels, dedicated sequences can be variably manipulated. Altering the Ratio control makes a sequence travel at a different speed to its neighbours. Varese (1936: 25): '[Non-blending is] the movement of sound masses, [of shifting planes of sound] which will seem to be projected onto other planes, moving at different speeds and different angles'.

Sound masses are the primed syntheses layered into the groove of the sequence-track on the basis of their timbrel distributions. The non-blending that alienates the funk and funks the alien. The switch-passaging that can't be told in one place at one time (Moser and Law, 1997). Or, the more-than-material which speeds the material. Making materials not only impossible to tell in one place at one time, but impossible to *hear* in one place at one time. [Locomotion .../... Smak!] The speed of hearing which makes, for Deleuze (1978), 'the impossible ear of non-pulsed time'. An ear which radiates out of regular, 'pulsed' time because it's made from wave-forms of 'non-pulsed', irregular times. Irregular times and places which – if the notion of time sorted by objects rather than objects sorted by time is ridden out- make the groove/layer 'polytemporal'. Of different times and places.[29]

Dilating Douglas (1966), different times and places make for a contusion of 'matter out of place' *and* time. And matter out of place and time interferes with simple wave-form to trip out with force and form. Materials in more than one place and less than all over the place. Because they're never far away from each/other. Distributed listening and peripheral hearing. Delirium. The edge of form which hears more than its own resonance. Force and form (Surgeon, 1999) becoming intensification. The speed-trip of hearing. The rock slipstreaming the groove, losing drag and lightening up as a click-pop-delay lashes the power level lights and the imagination wonders how far out the reverb stretches. The double moves of the funky alien. [Locomotion .../... Smak!]][30]

More sound (2), melody and indifference

The basic tonal vocabularies which begin telling something of the force of form now matt and stack their energies with the passage in/passage out of distributed listening and peripheral hearing. The delirium of combining energies, whilst materially specific, becomes necessarily difficult to contain, their experience only *apprehended* by indirect means. Because, if this notion of 'intensity' at the layer/groove is of two or more terms *on the verge of each other*, then the terms of the intensities specific to one location are never far from the intensities specific to another. And the term 'composition' comes to fulfill its duplicitous function, meaning both the more prosaic notion of *composing sound* (as in, in the studio, with BassStations and groove/layers), and the more indirect *composition of energies* wherever the intensities peculiar to the materials of electronic sound may travel (as in, more-than-in the studio, with groove/layers, writer's blocks, rushes and limit philosophies of sound). Composition that is always in perspective but never clearly posited (Kristeva, 1984). Drifting from home on the thread of a tune (Deleuze and Guattari, 1988).

The energy of terms like layer and groove on the verge of each other is their resonance. Rhythm – always in touch – travels indiscriminately at this verge. From term to term. It rides material refrains and strikes a chord. Indifference. Indifferent rhythm that is different according to its material composition. Different indifference. Melody (Genet, 1943). Tuning in-and-out from within different materials. A poetic with an earthly tie (Genet, 1943). The extra- within the terrestrial (Genet, 1951). Taking heed-taking leave, listening hard-hearing echoes. A melodic account of im/materiality.

Melody is the energy of a term hearing more than its own resonance, catching something of its opposition as indifference urges it beyond its identity on the way to a term it verges upon. Melody is the phase-sound of oppositions resonating. Of a term on its way to another by way of all that it is-not. The other term is not its opposition. The other term is its compliment. [Layer-groove.] The opposition is all the term is-not, which includes the compliment and is triggered by it, but is *more* than it. [Layer/groove.] The 'more' of both terms – as they verge – is the oppositional energy-surge of a delirious resonance. [The rush of layer/groove.]

To ride this energy rush is to travel with the terms which compliment their oppositions. The rush travels with pleasure on the verge of pain, desire on the verge of terror. The verge of their indifference is the brilliance of the rush of oppositions. The wince of pain never far from the pleasure of a big grin. Enter tinnitus (COH, 1999). The desire of production never far from the terror of destruction. The fun equation (Speedy J, 1995). Terms posited and passed. The rush is all both are-not, which, beyond the complimentary term, can only be expressed as *a specifically affected generality*. A delirium of layer-groove, pleasure-pain. A perspective more than a position. The resonance of oppositions triggered on the way to compliments. Identity-opposition-compliment. The resonance of the verge. Burning white-hot (Lyotard, 1993). Spinning (Noto, 1997). Of the 'mikro' spinning its way to the 'makro' (0 and Noto, 1997). Of a layer spinning its way to a groove, a block to a flow. And of pleasure on its way to pain – the business of melody, *amplified* to a felt intensity:

[We hope you enjoy this listening experience.] Pleasure-pain. The strobe-extra-brilliance that melts the eyes. [Warning!] The distortion that sweats the harmony of the sub-woofer. [Wow and flutter.] The deafening charm of rotary potential. [Enter tinnitus.] The elegant recoil of a dissonant bass-whip. The rhythmic breeze of a pummelling bass-reflection. The petrified agonies of composition, antagonizing the melody of the stand-off (writers' block). Writers' block: 'a brilliance that can be expressed only by the confrontation of the two terms that cancel each other out' (Genet, 1943: 145). Pleasure-pain, block-flow. The petrified agonies of perfecting a work. Pleasure-pain. Standing-off in a frozen moment. Never far from each other. An intense stare from within the exchange of a material gaze, with time 'forgotten' amidst the indifference of force (Lyotard, 1993). Writer's block *with unknown hours*. A frozen moment at the verge. A blast!

The frozen moment is served not by the encounter itself, but by its melody (Genet, 1943). More than material (less than immaterial). Melody is composed of more than health warnings, manufacturer's specifications, and the frustrations of petrified hours. More than these at the verge of their oppositions. Melody travels with danger-safety, frustration-excitement. Melody is material style. The style of materials intensified to the verge of pleasure-pain. Moment-force. The elegance of terms in confrontation and cancellation. Deafening charm, the breeze of pummelling, elegant laceration. Poetics from within specifics. The sheen of the prose which rides and writes the rhythm of force. Which *composes* more than writes (Boulez, 1985: 103). The form in the content written up as style. Style, the *diagonal relationship* of form and content (Boulez, 1985: 94). Writer's block with stylized hours. Indifferent *to* but different *with* content/form. The energy verge of intensified terms. [Where sonic miracles happen (Autechre/Gescom, 1993.)]

Indebted to the materials it meets, melody is an excitation of force (Lyotard, 1993) which 'puts in perspective but never posits' the delirious moment of a rush, writer's block, unknown hours. The moment where the pleasured look of pain verges on the pained look of pleasure [enter tinnitus] is a hi-energy moment of delirious indifference. Because with intensity there is no 'corporal over-pleasure' which seduces prematurely (Irigaray, 1977). Which confines place and sensation. Which misses the missing of the point of intensity's force (Derrida, 1982). Because melodic intensities tune in-and-out of place and position from within material exchanges. Because on balance – the balance of exchange – the maker is also *made*, the dancer *danced*, the listener *listened to*. Making, dancing and listening – stylized and amplified – tune in-out of their definition and placement. And the energy of composition rides the verge of terms like layer and groove, and block and flow. The composition tracked by the moves of the funky alien. [We hope you enjoy this listening experience.]

More sound (3): undergrounds and romances

The funky plastic alien. A material mass. Materials in more than one place and time – tones, bass, modulation – but less than all over place and time – the groove-line. The funky alien moves to the melody of terms hearing more than their own resonance on the way to the terms they verge upon. It is what happens *on the way* to a verging term, when a term powers into something of its identical opposition, that switches the melody of composition on – that spins it out – to the more-than-material, the distributed field of possibilities. The field of pure force whose power, poiesis, possibility *jump-cuts* the hit of a hi-energy moment across the material and the immaterial, the near and the far.

The melodies which the funky alien plays are melodies neither of materiality nor immateriality, near nor far, but of a third term (Lee, 1998) – a spinning diagonal verge – which gives rise to both. A term which coils immateriality within materiality, near within far. A term which radiates many melodious, indirect names. Intensity, speed, passaging. Delirium. A blast, a rush, a poetic with an earthly tie. A lyrical account, frozen moment or in/different style. Spin-style. Terms which contain many practices, and practices with which compositions like those of Plastikman *et al.* routinely engage something of the melody of their funky alien. Eshun (1998): the music is theorizing itself quite well. So where Philosophy can't go, send Autechre, System Error or Plastikman (Serres, 1995 with the funky alien). Their melodic figuratives of spin and their poetics.[31]

Composites like Autechre, Plastikman and System Error constantly theorize the verge of their own terms. Their obtuse operations which don't find such easy expression on the pages of the magazines. Like the poetics of delirium. The delirium of tripping out in the groove/layer. And, notably, like the poetics of *secrecy*. [Sub rosa.] Top secret kit lists and classified machine modifications (Plastikman the self-confessed retentive circuit board tinkerer).[32] Faceless and identity elusive artists (last count Plastikman owned up to at least sixteen other recording names).[33] And alien sounds of unknown origin (what Eshun calls UAO's, unidentified audio objects).[34] Operations which poeticize the regions over the edge of mass production and off the pages of the magazines. Regions which appropriate errors of identification – the verge of the artist or of a sound's origin. And regions which appropriate errors of function – the verge of a broken circuit board or a hacked rhythm or a software glitch or a happy accident of re-routing. Displacements of material placements. The melody of that which is never far from here.

These are practices which radiate many terms and many other practices. Practices couched in variable and unspecifiable discourses that are often less than full of meaning. Meaning never *posited* but always *in perspective* (Kristeva, 1984). Meaning emptied out as a delirious limit that none of the operatives can quite figure out. That none can figure out as anything other than some kind of creative aspiration, an ideal. An attitude, implicit philosophy or way of life. A poetic. A poetic field which jump-cuts near with far, a knob twiddle with a trip in the groove/layer with an ear piercing pleasure-pain, to here, on the verge of a grand philosophy, heard echoing within the finest knob twiddle or the most intimate writer's rush. What sometimes circulates as an 'Underground', an implicit philosophy of sound and energy.

An Underground is always troubled by the placement of composition, of its machines/people/sounds. In more structural analyses of electronic sound-tracks an underground – invariably conflated and located with Club Cultures – typically figures as 'the place to be', the coolest place to hang out with electronic sounds (see Thornton, 1995; Poschardt, 1998). But once there, an Underground is never there, hanging out. An Underground-proper – as a vehicle for thinking melody – is troubled by thoughts on composition based on production codes alone, on tactics which produce specific locations for 'machines', 'people' and 'sounds' and prescribe their functions, relations and limits accordingly. Corporal over-pleasures. An Underground thinks something of melody's indifference by concealing itself – by withdrawing from its placement – as soon as an advancement is made. It withdraws from the prescription of its material operating tracks – its machines/people/sounds – *according* to these placements. The melody of that which is never far from here. [Where sonic miracles happen.]

An Underground-proper is never *that* cool place. It's always more than a place. Always cooler than cool. Yet it's not all over the place. Stone cold. It emerges from particular material relations. Its rhythm always in touch. It emerges from the places where electronic sound is bound by production codes – studios, clubs, galleries, bodies, sound waves, stereos, BBC2, headphones, decks, games, genre asthmatics, 'cool' (as in, not white-hot), the underground (as in, definite article, small 'u'), wherever – and withdraws into what these places become as their materials exchange. A poetic with an earthly tie. As the maker in the studio is also *made*, as the dancer in the club is also *danced*, the listener at the stereo *listened to*. As sites of production exchange with sites of consumption at the edge of mass.

Refusing the code takes something of composition away. Spirits it away. Under the cover of its poetics. Poetics which make more than materials, mass, places, production. More than the labelling of a composite like 'Techno' but less than the unnameable-unthinkable. Poetics like those of the straining delirium of the groove/layer. Trip-time. Poetics like those which cloak the blueprints of classified machine modifications and top secret kit lists. Poetics like those which imagine sounds of unknown origin. And poetics like those which enchant identity by refusing and confusing it. Melodies which resist collapse, collection, completion, figuring and total understanding. Melodies which resist obsessive knowledge. [Fuck off trainspotter (Autechre, 1995).]

The poetic of an Underground is preserved knowing. Energy. In reserve. The 'becoming visible' of that which is not yet known. The poetics of regions over the edge of mass production. [Where sonic miracles happen.] Preserved knowing prompts at least the possibility of more voice in the machines, more cool in the place, more sound than a production code alone allows. Creative energy. *Knowing* there's more. Poetics probe the knowing of a potential but never reach a *knowledge* of it. Poetics probe the knowing of a cooler place to hang out but never find out where it is. The knowing of more sound but without the knowledge that might finally pin it down to a sound, a machine, a lifestyle, a scene, an origin myth or record collection. In perspective, never posited. Preserved knowing. [Fuck off trainspotter.]

Poetics spirit sound away while placing material clues. Sound in more than one place but less than all over the place with more than materials but less than immaterials. The delirium of the groove/layer. The secrecy of circuit boards, hacked sounds and confused authorship. Probe-heads for Deleuze/Guattari (1988). Or secrets secreted from concretes. Terrestrial melodies. Or elsewhere:

Ninja Tunes[35] and Jedi Knights.[36] Not knowing where or why or how but knowing *that*. Knowing that there is a where, a why and a how but never quite reaching them. Only imagining them. Mythologizing them. Like the shadow world of Ninja stealth and the absent presence of the Jedi Force. Like limit philosophies of Underground sound.[37] Mythologizing the immateriality and the displacement of material placements. Poetics with an earthly tie. Or, rigorous romance.

Flexistentialism (Ninja Cuts, 1997)[38]

Step into the realm of Ninja: Subways and swords, cloaks and daggers. Shadows fade silently across the sound-scape [...] Weapons of wax, solid steel and diamond tipped blades that cut like quick-silver through the groove [...] Cross faders of the lost ark, cutting paths for future flexporation of the Funk. Ninja is the spark of silence that lies deep within the core of your inner speaker stack [...] *Nuff cheez. Go eat some beatz* (emphasis added).

Romance, myth, immateriality. Mythologizing the DJ turntable. As a weapon of wax and steel with its diamond tipped blade-runner. Its mixer that moves between turntable sounds as a cross fader of the Lost Ark in pursuit of the 'future Funk', Ninja Tune's Holy Grail, its Underground. A creative aspiration, an ideal. An attitude, implicit philosophy or way of life. What Ninja Tune probe as 'the spark of silence that lies deep within the core of your inner speaker stack'. Before dragging the romance back, recognizing its pure immaterial indulgence, and checking it with the understated rush of the materials from which the romance unfurls: 'nuff cheez, go eat some beatz'. A romance rescued just in time (?) by the realities of the Beat. Machines/people/sounds. Powering the immaterial with the material. Switched on.

Are friends electrik? (Plastikman, 1998f)

Recorded during the exile for those who disappeared.

Electrifying a connection with absent friends. Friends in Detroit made absent by Plastikman's being exiled to his native Canada for illegal work activities in the US. The immaterial powers with the material. Into felt presence. Connection, rhythm, feeling. Felt presence. Jump-cutting the force-feel of electronic sound's material creativity to make immaterial connections. Jump-

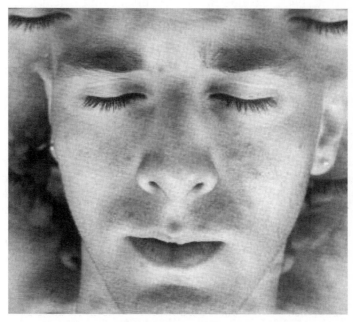

Richie Hawtin/Plastikman:
'From our minds to yours' (Plus 8 Records maxim).

cutting the near and far via the extending force-feel of sound's material presence. Its electricity. Its material hum. The splitting which constitutes the force-feel of both before and after the fact of presence. Making 'friends electrik' – through electronic music – when they 'disappear'. Customizing a poetic. 'Personalizing' its Underground sensibilities. The jump-cutting of a connection whose general character – its force-feel – depends on the specific machines/people/sounds involved in the exchange. Materials limit-ed by the real time materiality of fundamental tonality, technical capability, and Plastikman's mates. A different indifference. A rhythm in touch. Riding out from time, place and materiality. A qualified Underground. (One of many testing the elasticity of the verge. Because poetry only stretches so far from reality before it snaps.)

More sound (4), reflections and delicacy

The poetics of system errors and machine alterities, of groove/layers and funky aliens, of ninja tunes and jedi knights, of Underground sounds and electrik friends – imagine the 'more' of potential but needs the 'less' of the mass-actual to generate the friction necessary for the speeds of its poiesis. Because intensities – hearing more than their own resonance – track beyond the inert account of materials without resorting to a poetry cut off from the terrestrial world (Genet, 1943). To ride the rhythm of intensity is to trip out in this oblique line-space which is more than material and less than immaterial. To hold a phasing vision of immateriality's reflection within the material. A phasing sound space of layers echoing within the groove. The poetic of an Underground of electronic sound is this straining gaze. The vision of an Underworld obtained by effort (Genet, 1943).

An Underground is a poetic which escapes the inert. *And perfumes it*. A danger to the practical understanding of materials (Genet, 1951). Of machine specifications, health warnings, time spent composing. Its romance and myth become modes of escape and danger. Disregarding *commodified* escape – ie, the 'incarceration' of an effort-less underground – the romance of an Underground-proper works hard in this phasing line-space. The effort of holding two terms – inertia and the inert's energy – on the verge of each other is the effort taken to avert both a poetic fancy and a prosaic mundanity.[39] Its poetry – that of the highly valued, hi-energy moment of a rush, a writer's block, a phasing groove/layer – is delicate and obtained by effort. Delicate and elusive because a poetic blast needs a prosaic charge, and the two are never far from each other, easily lost to each other. The poetic of a rush lost to its come-down, the prosaic of a block spontaneously flashed with inspiration (Beeston, forthcoming). The verge. That the modes of 'escaping' the inert in search of 'danger' may be romance and myth matters little if *pains* are taken to track the rigour of their style (Genet, 1949). Rigorous romance. [Nuff cheez, go eat some beatz.][40]

Elements of romance are at the heart of material intensities. They are the regions of immateriality over the edge of mass which co-define materiality. The potential – the system errors, the preserved knowing – which intensifies material experience. Moment-force. Holding on – with teeth gritted – to the oblique line-space of delirium and secrecy. More sound. [Fuck off trainspotter.] The sensibility of an Underground is thus one which holds elements of idealism close to realism.[41] The poetic style of materials. Far in near and not reducible to either term. More than near less than far. Lee's third term. Boulez's diagonal. Noto's spin. The double moves of the funky alien dance this trip-space. This one within the other. Groove within layer. Romance within rigour. Style within content. Genet (1943): an 'internal astronomy' of materiality.

A million miles to earth, from within (1994)[42]

Terrestrial melody unfolds a rigorous romance from an internal astronomy. To track something of the melodic forces of electronic sound is to track the more-than-material which speeds the material. The transgressions of intensity take heed whilst taking leave of the terms in exchange. To track them is to hold a phasing space of the terms in confrontation. For while intensities disrespect identity, neither do they respect disparity. The rhythm of terms which touch is the luminescence of this phasing of more and less, near and far. A delirium of layer and groove. A secrecy of known and unknown machine modifications. More and less, far and near. The potential from within the actual.

The phasing of an internal astronomy is a poetic intensity. A spinning, oblique line-space. Of cuts and bruises. The intense line-space between the funk and the alien. [Where sonic miracles happen.] Between the machine and the operator and the sound. Between the micro-attentions of the rotary potentiometer and the macro-politics of cultures investing in Underground sensibilities. The delirious line-space which insists on the manageability of the global and the awe-some reach of the local. The poetic intensities that lie between the production of electronic sound and the consumption of bass.

Understand? We hope you enjoy this listening experience. Pleasure is our business. (Autechre Music Systems from Gescom Trascendental, 1994)

Acknowledgements

Day/night: Bob Cooper, Lee Crofts, Joanna Latimer, John Law, Nick Lee, Tiago Moreira, Rolland Munro. Night/day: adrian, andi, bobby @ hia, carsten @ noton, del, illi, jay @ pulse, liz, sooz, steve, tiago-a-go-go, tim.

Rob Beeston

Notes

1 Surgeon (and Certain Beyond Reasonable Doubt): variably dis/associated with Birmingham's Techno scene (resident DJ at House of God) and with industrial/noise influenced Techno and electronic drone tonalism.

2 Exchange: an idea returned to throughout, greatly informed by Rolland Munro's (1997) development of the term and Bob Cooper's (1996, 1997) discussions of 'symmetry' and 'sending on'.

3 Movement in exchange: or, 'the drift of repetition/alterity' (Derrida, 1972), 'the gain of again' (Cooper, 1993), 'betrayal in translation' (Law, 1997), 'the movement of moments of undecideability' (Munro, 1996), and, culturally closer to electronic composition, 'the means from an end' (Thaemlitz, 1998).

4 Novation BassStation: Analogue waveform synthesiser with digital controllers to stabilise tuning and parameter settings, and MIDI interface to integrate it with extended digital architectures. Keyboard or rack mounted.

5 Unless referenced otherwise all subsequent quotations are taken from the source which heads each section.

6 Basic tonal vocabulary: or, elements of tone, the mathematical exploration of tonality charted by Helmholtz (1862). The breaking down of simple notes into variable harmonic orders; positioning basic tonal elements in relation to vibrations above the pitch of the fundamental to create variable timbre (tone colour).

7 A mix up that can fractionate a sound source with variable degrees of complexity. Autechre (1998: 90) significantly complicating the process: 'microphones were positioned around a structure with a resonant frequency of 100 Hz. Electrical equipment inside the structure provided a constant tone of 50 Hz. Water channelling equipment was also used. Signals from the two microphones were passed through five parallel resonators, all tuned with intervals divisible by 25 Hz. Each resonator was filtered and the output mixed down to two channels and reversed'. Or, less technically: 'You can put things through and back into other things [...] and put those things into other things and perhaps sample other bits and sequence the samples, and then filter those bits and put them back into the computer and use a program to mutate them and then put them into a different machine until it spins you out' (Autechre, 1998: 91).

8 Whilst filtering the harmonics of a waveform is often referred to as 'subtractive synthesis', the combination of waveforms through the mixing facility talked of here is *not* 'additive synthesis'. Additive synthesis adds together tone partials to build up the details of a waveform, changing its spectral character. Mixing waveforms however, simply combines already formed waveforms to yield their sum total. Additive synthesis alters the waveshape itself to yield more than the sum of its parts. See Risset and Wessel (1982).

9 'The science of squelch: an understanding of filter resonance is essential for producing good bass [...]. The resonance control on your synth [...] emphasises the frequency just inside the filter cutoff. You can use this [...] to add welly to the frequency of your choice. The higher the resonance the louder the boost, until eventually the resonance self oscillates, producing a constant tone at the cutoff frequency. By changing the cutoff you can change the pitch of this sinewave, from an incredibly high pitched whine to a sub-sonic vibration' (Thomas, 1998: 92).

10 Translating the 'f' of fat into a 'ph' and adding an extra 't' at the end is a technique often used to engage the physical sensation of low end bass frequencies with its onomatopoeia in the text. Emphasising syllables to excite the sonority of the word. Or, 'language drag[ging] its flabby arse after sound' (Eshun, 1998: 71).

11 Emu Planet Phatt Swing System: analogue waveform synthesiser with digital controllers and MIDI interface.

12 Keyfax Phat Boy: analogue synthesiser with MIDI controllers. The gendering of machines like the Phat Boy and the phallogocentrics (Irigaray, 1977) of practices like fiddling and knob twiddling are energetic issues, particularly when the same machines and practices track out to notions of creativity, sensuality and distributed pleasure. Space restrictions mean discussion

90

remains implicit throughout, explicit in a wider Phd project. Acknowledgement: Joanna Latimer, sooz, bobby @ hia.

13 Aphex 104 Type C2 Aural Exciter with Big Bottom: analogue sound enhancer with digital controllers and MIDI interface.

14 Dedication to bass-quality works with the emphasis on particular sound qualities noted elsewhere. An emphasis on sound and texture that has emerged to parallel traditional emphases on music and structure. See: Reynolds (1999) with 'two-step breakbeat mutations'; Oliver (1998) with dance music technologies; Toop (1995: 202) with Kraftwerk; Eno (1986) with pop musics.

15 Technics SL1200: direct drive turntable (almost a club standard).

16 Dedicated bass: 'my house was shakin', my walls vibratin'. Renegade soundwave, renegade soundwave ...' (Renegade Soundwave, 1994).

17 Autechre (1992) on being asked who their music is for: 'for those who get goosebumps listening to their favourite track'.

18 Modulation as automatic change: the alternate rise and fall of the oscillating waveform around the set pitch. The degree of rise and fall is set by parameter modification – 'envelope', 'LFO', 'pulse width' – and determines the 'trajectory' of the modulation as it progresses in the sound envelope.

19 Unfolding timbre: what Risset (1985) calls 'interpolation between different timbres'. Strictly speaking this is an effect achieved through 'Frequency Modulation Synthesis' (Chowning, 1971, 1973) which synthesises tone partials to imitate an existing timbre, then re-synthesises them to extend it out towards another. (Piano sound transforms into chime sound.) A digital sound technique – relying on the analysis and synthesis of complex microstructures – whose degree of control cannot be achieved with the primarily analogue synthesis of the BassStation. Less sophisticated transformations of sound can, however, be achieved with analogue modulation.

20 Autechre (1998: 92): '[The Clavia Nord Lead Synthesiser is] a handy machine. I like everything about it. It allows you to create from very basic elements [...] and one of the reasons it's so lush is 'cos *it's covered in knobs*' (emphasis added).

21 In Tympan, Derrida exchanges narrative with Michel Leiris' Persephone. Persephone is the wife of Hades, and Queen of the Underworld. Leiris talks of Persephone as he appeals to the potential energy of beauty coiled within various forms, asking for the coil of potential 'not to be confused with the always more or less lenitive character of that which has been dulled' (xiii), that which has not been energised. For potential energy – the unknown and intangible – inhabits this underworld of which Persephone is Queen. It is a 'shadow world' which Blanchot (1982) locates under the 'veil of no'. The intangible negative to the simple presence of positive. It can never be comprehended – only apprehended – for it is always surpassing the limits of its own mass, always enveloping itself. It is because of this always [re]limit-ed vision that Derrida synaesthetically suggests 'the tympanum [the limit] squints' (xv). It is only partially 'sighted'. It can never form a complete picture. For its potential is differentially engaged with each exchange. All it can do is watch as potential unfolds in the moment of exchanging relations before its very [partially sighted] 'eyes'.

22 System Error: a collaboration between Bobby Bird of the Higher Intelligence Agency and Brian Duffy, a sound/visual artist.

23 Plastikman (or States of Mind, CyberSonik, Circuit Breaker, Fuse, From Within, Richie Hawtin, etc.[see note 42]): variably dis/associated with 'Detroit Techno', concentrated drum and percussion arrangements, 'acidic' sound modulations, and more recently, with the use of delay effects to extend sound-form and increase the spatial properties of layered sound arrangements.

24 Latronic Notron MIDI Controller: a digital central controller which manages MIDI information inputs from other MIDI interfaced machines to regulate and arrange multiple sound sources.

25 The Notron is similar to other sequencing systems – like MIT's Csound – which maintain the arrangement of discrete sound layers as a dedicated operation. Csound divides its control routines into 'orchestra' and 'score': 'an orchestra is really a computer programme that can produce sound [synthesis] while a score is a body of data which that program can react to [arrangement of sequences]' (Vercoe, 1994: 0. Preface to Csound Manual).

26 Varese's prescient interest in timbrally delineated zones in music is evident throughout works such as Ameriques, Integrales, Iionisation, and Hyperprism, and the language of 'sound masses', 'sound objects', 'sound planes' and 'contrasts in pure sound' he used to describe their composition (see Oullette, 1966). His Poem Electronique – commissioned by Philips in collaboration with Le Corbusier and Xennakis for the 1958 World's Fair in Brussels – is however Varese's most elaborate demonstration of the delineation of sound space. Using one hundred and fifty loudspeakers grouped into timbrally distinct zones to create dedicated sound paths, and controlled by (then) elaborate central mechanisms, this project made available for the first time the technology which Varese believed would realize his dream of non-blended sound masses mapping an acoustic space.

27 Passage in/out of the groove/layer: the movement between 'dependents that groove' and 'independents that layer' maps a spatiality contained by the groove, whose co-ordinates are simultaneously plotted and populated by layers. A recursive architecture of sound. Plastikman's characteristic 'layered-Techno-grooves' trade on such a spatiality: 'I like to be able to step in between a kick [drum] and a hi-hat and see a space around me [...] There's really a lot of space there, but there's also a lot going in. My new phrase to describe my style is 'complex minimalism' (Plastikman [Richie Hawtin], 1996: 65). 'It gets a groove going' (Fuse [Richie Hawtin], 1993: track 11).

28 Plastikman designed by Dominic Ayre (originally for a clothing company), and, so the story goes, strategically spray-painted around Detroit, USA (circa. 1992/3) to provide a clandestine route map to the early Plastikman parties.

29 Time sorted by objects: see Serres (1995), Latour (1992). A notion clarified by Bob Cooper's observation that it is *us* that pass rather than time.

30 The distribution of a form which is never far from what it is not – its potential – is what Irigaray (1977: 31) calls a feminising 'nearness'. Nearness forces form from its purely centred, rational identity. A force which *potentially* – but not necessarily – tracks the distance between heavily gendered machine practices like knob twiddling the Phat Boy, and notions of creativity, sensuality and distributed pleasure. Gendered machine practices not far from – ie, near to – less gendered ones. The machine not far from how it could be otherwise. Bobby Bird of the Higher Intelligence Agency/System Error: 'it [the machine]'s just a tool to make something else with' (fieldnotes).

31 Self-theorizing electronic musics: the 'intellectual' record label is perhaps the most recent home for the translation of self-philosophizing musics. What Shapiro (1998: 57) calls 'Electronica's cerebral smart boy ghetto['s]' (sic: note 14). See: Noton (1998: 'archive for sound and not-sound'), Sub Rosa (1998: some time allies of William S. Burroughs, Marcel Duchamp, Thomas Pynchon), and perhaps most explicitly and indebtedly, Mille Plateaux: '[...] the music goes beyond itself, this is the search for the forces of the minoritorial, that the label MILLE PLATEAUX is part of. In a letter Gilles Deleuze welcomed the existence of such a label' (Szepanski, 1996).

32 Autechre (1998: 91): 'I don't want to give anyone a kit list 'cos we're a bit anal [...] and we like to keep it a secret'. Plastikman (1996: 67): 'I don't give out equipment lists'. Plastikman (1998e: 108): 'Oh ... there is one other thing [but] I can't tell you. It's just my favourite bit of kit and I'm not going to tell anyone what it is.'

33 As of November 1998 Plastikman has used approximately sixteen other names to record under, most of which only became connected with his more prominent monikers – CyberSonik, Fuse, Plastikman, Richie Hawtin – when they were posted on his web site (see M_nus, 1998). Eshun (1998: 106) calls these 'heteronyms': parallel identities which disperse the artist and refuse the ground-base from which pseudonyms always maintain the ultimate knowability of identity.

34 Schafer (1977): uses the term 'schizophony' to refer to the state of sound production whereby sounds are 'split' from their sources and their origins not easily identified. Russolo (1916: 56), in an early Futurist manifesto, similarly indicated the use of sound 'freed from the necessities that produce it'.

35 Ninja Tune Records: music division of the multi-media umbrella Hexstatic. Their limit-brokering slogan, 'fuck dance let's art', is an initiative that trades on stealth tactics to make

more of electronic sound than body music that bombs the dance floor. Most recently Ninja Tune's Coldcut – with their Hexstatic collective – have been probing the limits of sound with interactive visuals, evolving the concept of 'Video Jockeying' which enables the live mixing of audio-visual material. Their VJamm software puts this capability on the desktop (see Ninja Tune, 1998).

36 Jedi Knights (or, Global Communication, Link, Pulusha, Reload, Tom Middleton/Mark Pritchard): variably dis/associated with ambient 'chill' and sci-fi aesthetics. The 'Jedi Knight' moniker borrows the limit-philosophy of Star Wars as it wrestles the spirituality of 'The Force' and its 'Dark Side'.

37 Preserving an Underground: a composite philosophy that trips out to many other cultures. Surfing, climbing, snowboarding, mountain biking, martial arts, 'extreme sports', computer hacking, grafitti writing, etc etc, trip out with similar concepts of intensity, creativity, community, fun, drive, dedication, progression, edge, spirituality. For a notably figurative, Eastern influenced, expression in skate[board] culture see Powell Peralta's (1988), film, *Bones III: The search for Animal Chin*.

38 Ninja Cuts (1997): compilation album from Ninja Tune. 'The joy of dex: 18 uncompromising positions to improve your stealth.'

39 Efforts after energy: commodified undergrounds often implicate the 'new' or the 'fast' – 'the cutting edge' – in the generation of energy. But the relative ease with which 'novelty' and 'speed' are apprehended beyond their familiarity and collapse shouldn't be confused with the energy of holding two terms on the verge of each other. Inert categories are just as easily made of 'speed' and 'novelty' as they are of the slow and the old. Or, terms are just as difficult to hold on the verge of each other when they are new and fast as when they are old and slow. See: Heidegger (1959) on the 're-call' of [old and slow] terms as a 're-coil' of their 'essential' energies. Acknowledgement: Rolland Munro.

40 Efforts after energy: to remember and hold something of a hi-energy moment it's often necessary to attempt either its re-creation, or to anticipate the conditions which may bring about its onset and prepare some means by which it – or more likely a dense trigger-motif – might be recorded. Both the re-creation and the anticipation of hi-energy moments are delicate, unpredictable, and effortful tasks. They often occur spontaneously in materials which appear far removed from those the energy is associated with or desired from. Inspired connections and in/difference. For this reason direct and effort-ful provocation often benefits from in-direct relaxation. Stop writing and go do something else. [Click!] Tension being never far from relaxation when thinking energetically.

41 Sartre (1952) says this of Genet.

42 From Within: collaboration between Richie Hawtin (Plastikman) and Pete Namlook (Fax Records).

References

Autechre (1998), Quoted in T. Marcus (1998), Unique sounds special: fifth elements. *Future Music: Making Music with Technology*, Issue 78 (July), 90–94.

Autechre (1993), BassCadet. On Autechre (1993), *Incunabula*, track 5. Warp Records.

Autechre (1992), Sleeve notes. *Artificial intelligence: electronic listening music from Warp*. Warp Records.

Autechre/Gescom (1994). Sleeve notes. *BassCadet EP*. Warp Records.

Autechre/Gescom (1993). Sleeve notes. *Incunabula*. Warp Records.

Boulez, P., (1985), *Orientations: collected writings*. London: Faber and Faber.

Blanchot, M., (1982), *The space of literature*. London, USA: University of Nebraska.

Chowning, J., (1971), The simulation of moving sound sources. Reprinted in *Computer Music Journal*, 1 (3): 48–52, 1977.

Chowning, J., (1973), The synthesis of complex audio spectra by means of frequency modulation.

Reprinted in C. Roads and J. Strawn (eds) *Foundations of computer music* (1985), Cambridge: MIT Press.

COH (1999), *Enter tinnitus*. Germany: Noton/Rastermusic.

Cooper, R., (1993), Technologies of representation. In P. Ahonen (ed.). *Tracing the semiotic boundaries of politics*. Berlin: Mouton de Gruyton.

Cooper, R., (1996), Samuel Butler, cyborganisation and the principle of symmetry. *Internet Document*. Accessed 05 March 1998 at *http://www.keele.ac.uk/depts/stt/staff/rc/pubs-RC2.htm*.

Cooper, R., (1997), Millenium notes for social theory. *Sociological Review*, 45 (4): 390–403.

Cooper, R. and Law, J., (1995), Organisation: distal and proximal views. In *Research in the sociology of organisations*, 13, 237–274.

Deleuze, G., (1971), Deleuze 14/12/71: The nature of flows. *Internet Document*. Accessed 27 December 1997 at http://www.imaginet.fr/deleuze/TXT/ENG/141271.html

Deleuze, G., (1977), Gilles Deleuze: Seminar session on music – 03 May 1977. *Internet Document*. Accessed 28 August 1998 at http://www.imaginet.fr/deleuze/TXT/ENG/030577.html

Deleuze, G., (1978), Deleuze: Conference presentation on musical time – IRCAM, 1978. *Internet Document*. Accessed 22 July 1998 at http://www.imaginet.fr/deleuze/TXT/ENG/IRCAMeng.htm

Deleuze, G. and Guattari, F., (1988), *A thousand plateaus: capitalism and schizophrenia*. London: Athlone.

Derrida, J., (1982), Tympan. In *Margins of Philosophy*. London: Harvester Wheatsheaf.

Douglas, M., (1966), Purity and danger: an analysis of the concepts of pollution and taboo. London: Routledge.

Eno, B., (1986), Aurora musicalis, *Art Forum* 24 (10): 26–36.

Eshun, K., (1998), *More brilliant than the sun: adventures in sonic fiction*. London: Quartet Books.

From Within (1994), A million miles to earth. On *Pete Namlook and Richie Hawtin*. Fax Records.

Fuse (1993), Logikal nonsense. On *Dimension intrusion*, track 11. Warp Records.

Future Music: Making Music with Technology (1998), Bass special: big bottom – killer bass sounds made easy. *Issue 70* (June).

Genet, J., (1943), *Our lady of the flowers*. London: Panther.

Genet, J., (1949), *The thief's journal*. London: Penguin.

Genet, J., (1951), *Miracle of the Rose*. London: Penguin.

Helmholtz, H.L.F. (1862, 1875), *On the sensations of tone as a physiological basis for the theory of music*. London: Longman Green, and Co.

Holmes, T.B., (1985), *Electronic and experimental music*. New York: Charles Scribner's Sons.

Irigaray, L., (1977), *The sex which is not one*. London: Athlone.

Kristeva, J., (1984), *Revolution in poetic language*. New York: Columbia.

Latour, B., (1992), *We have never been modern*. London: Harvester Wheatsheaf.

Latronic (1998), Notron MIDI Controller User Notes. *E-Mail Document*. Received 10 September 1998 from concourse@compuserve.com

Law, J., (1997), Traduction Trahison. *Internet Document*. Accessed 14 February 1998 at http://www.keele.ac.uk/depts/so/staff/jl/pubs-jl2.htm

Lee, N., (1998), Two speeds: how are real stabilities possible. In R. Chia (ed.). *Organised worlds: explorations in technology and organisation with Robert Cooper*. London: Routledge.

M_nus (1998), Richie Hawtin discography. *Internet Document*. Accessed 06 October 1998 at http://www.m-nus.com/projects/richie hawtin/discography.html

Mathews, M., (1958), MUSIC 1. In M., Mathews (1969), *The technology of computer music*. Cambridge, Mass.: MIT Press.

Mike and Rich (1996), *Expert knob twiddlers*. Rephlex Records.

Mills, J., (1993), *Waveform transmission, Volume 1*. Pow Wow Records.

Moser, I. and Law, J., (1997), Good passages, bad passages. In J. Law and J. Hassard (eds). *Actor Network Theory and After*. London: Blackwell.

Munro, R., (1996), A consumption view of self: extension, exchange and identity. In S. Edgell, K. Hetherington and A, Warde (eds). *Consumption Matters*. Oxford: Blackwell.

Munro, R., (1997), Power, conduct and accountability: re-distributing discretion and the new technologies of managing. Paper presented at the *5th Interdisciplinary Perspectives on Accounting Conference*, University of Manchester, 7–9 July 1997.

Ninja Cuts (1997), *Flexistentialism: 24 uncompromising tracks to improve your stealth*. Ninja Tune.

Ninja Tune (1998), Coldcut hd. *Internet Document*. Accessed 23 October 1998 at http://www.ninjatune.net/coldcut/home.iphtml

Noton (1998), *Internet Document*. Accessed 24 October 1998 at http://www.rastermusic.com

Novation (1994), BassStation User Manual. *Internet Document*. Accessed 09 September 1998 at http://www.novationusa.com/bskm

Novation (1996), SuperBassStation User Manual. *Internet Document*. Accessed 09 September 1998 at http://www.novationusa.com/sbskm

Novation (1998a), SuperNova – coming soon. *Internet Document*. Accessed 09 September 1998 at http://www.novationusa.com/sbs

Novation (1998b), SuperNova: polyphonic synthesiser. In *Future Music: Making Music with Technology, Issue 76* (November), 71.

Ohmite Manufacturing Company (1998), *Component selector 4000A*. Illinois, USA: Ohmite Manufacturing Company.

Oliver, T., (1998), Making more of your music: the basics. *Future Music: Making Music with Technology*, Issue 68 (April), 80–85.

Ouellette, F., (1966), *Edgard Varese*. London: Calder and Boyars.

Plastikman (1993a), Plasticity. On *Sheet One*, track 2. Novamute Records.

Plastikman (1993b), Glob. On *Sheet One*, track 6. Novamute Records.

Plastikman (1993c), Smak. On *Sheet One*, track 10. Novamute Records.

Plastikman (1994a), Plasmatik. On *Musik*, track 7. Novamute Records.

Plastikman (1994b), Plastique. On *Musik*, track 2. Novamute Records.

Plastikman (1994c), Goo. On *Musik*, track 8. Novamute Records.

Plastikman (1996), Quoted in Minimalist manoeuvres: how Richie Hawtin stripped Techno bare. In C. Kempster (ed.). *History of House*. London: Sanctuary Publishing.

Plastikman (1998a), Passage [in]. On *Consumed*, track 03. Novamute Records.

Plastikman (1998b), Passage [out]. On *Consumed*, track 11. Novamute Records.

Plastikman (1998c), Locomotion. On *Consumed*, track 8. Novamute Records.

Plastikman (1998d), Consumed. On *Consumed*, track 3. Novamute Records.

Plastikman (1998e), Quoted in D. Scott (1998), Plastik fantastik. *Future Music: Making Music with Technology*, Issue 76 (November), 107–110.

Plastikman (1998f), Are friends electrik?. On *Artifakts (bc)*, track 7. Novamute Records.

Poschardt, U., (1998), *DJ Culture*. London: Quartet.

Renegade Soundwave (1994), *Renegade soundwave*. London: Mute Records.

Risset, J-C., (1985), Digital techniques and sound structure in music. In C. Roads (ed.) *Composers and the computer*. California: William Kaufman, Inc.

Risset, J-C. and Wessel, D.L., (1982), Exploration of timbre by analysis and synthesis. In D. Deutsch (ed.). *The psychology of music*. London: Academic Press.

Rose, T., (1994), Give me a (break) beat! Sampling and repetition in rap production. In G. Bender and T. Druckrey (eds). *Culture on the brink: ideologies of technology*. Seattle: Bat Press.

Russolo, L., (1916), The art of noises. New acoustical pleasures. In L. Russolo (1986), *The art of noises (monographs in musicology no. 6)*. New York: Pendragon Press.

Sartre, J-P (1952), *Saint Genet: Comedian and Martyr*. London: W.H. Allen.

Schafer, R.M.(1977), *The tuning of the world*. Alfred A. Knopf.

Serres, M., (1987), *Statues*. Paris: Francois Bourin.

Serres, M with Latour, B., (1995), *Conversations on Science, Culture and Time*. Ann Arbor: University of Michigan Press.

Shapiro, P., (1998), Review of Restgeraeusch Volume 2 and Modulation and Transformation 3. In *The Wire: Adventures in Modern Music, Issue 168 (February)*, 57.

Speedy, J., (1995), *G-spot*. Toronto: Plus 8.

Sub Rosa (1998), *Internet Document*. Accessed 10 October 1998 at http://www.subrosa.be/

Surgeon (1997), *Basic tonal vocabulary*. Dynamic Tension Records.

Surgeon (1998), *Balance.* Dynamic Tension Records.

Surgeon (1999), *Force and form.* Berlin: Tresor.

System Error (1998), *Nothing.* Headphone.

Szepanski, A., (1996), In the beginning is the storm. Sleeve notes in *In memoriam: Gilles Deleuze.* Germany: Mille Plateaux Records.

Thaemlitz, T., (1998), *Means from an end.* Germany: Mille Plateaux Records.

Thomas, M., (1998), Bass is the place. *Future Music: Making Music with Technology,* Issue 70 (June), 92–95.

Thornton, S., (1995), *Club cultures: music, media and subcultural capital.* London: Polity.

Toop, D., (1995), *Ocean of sound: aether talk, ambient sound and imaginary worlds.* London: Serpents Tail.

Varese, E., (1936), The liberation of sound. In B. Boretz and E.T. Cone (eds). *Perspectives on American composers.* New York: W.W. Norton and Company Inc.

Vercoe, B., (1994), Preface to the Csound manual. In *Csound Manual: a manual for the audio processing system and supporting programs with tutorials.* Cambridge: MIT Press. Internet Document. Accessed 09 September 1998 at http://www.leeds.ac.uk/music/MAN/Csound/title.html

Part 2: Mass and Community

Introduction to Part 2

At the heart of the twentieth century is a tension in thinking about mass. On the one side is the *attraction* of mass, the manifestation of plenty in the production of millions of cars and homes and the fabrication of millions of almost identical goods to fill those cars and homes. On the other, a *repulsion* of mass, a disdain, disquiet, even fear, of community made vivid in images of holocaust – mass exterminations in the death camps; a policy of attrition that destroyed millions in the first world war trenches; and the genocide from dropping the atomic bomb on Japanese cities.

These two features, the necessity of mass markets and the retreat from mass organisation, are brought alongside each other in one of Heidegger's few cryptic comments about National Socialism:

> Agriculture is now motorized food industry – in essence the same as the manufacturing of corpses in gas chambers and extermination camps, the same as blockading and starving of nations, the same as the manufacture of hydrogen bombs. (Heidegger, original manuscript quoted by Bernstein, 1991: 130)

As Bernstein remarks, Heidegger's 'cool' comparison of motorised agriculture and mass extermination is not some grotesque lapse, it is a necessary consequence of the very way that Heidegger characterises our 'enframing' in technology.[1]

Zygmunt Bauman, in his chapter, contrasts the unruly, unlimited indiscrimination of mass pictured in early images of hell, where 'bodies were pressed, stuffed into each other' with the modern shape of damnation as the impossibility to fulfil the duty of individuality: 'the modern hell, the mass, is the punishment for the failure to perform that duty'. He goes on, however, to argue against the common and snobbish assumption that the consumption of mass-produced goods is the result of a general failure even to attempt individuation. Instead, a 'phantom community' of the shopping mall has emerged out of our best efforts to be individual and avoid the horror of 'common taste'. The problem today is that individuality is tormented by uncertainty; false consciousness becomes the nightmare that 'infuses the pre-modern dreams of redemption and modern dreams of emancipation alike'. For Bauman, the 'mark of the mass is deception' and, compensating for the absence of community, we are ready to believe in the healing powers of goods.

Mass has come to replace community, and purchasing patterns have come to replace genuine individuality, because Euro-American moderns have a tendency to mistake community for mass and belonging for unfreedom. It is the goods' promise that *we* are choosing *them* out of our freedom and distinctive taste that has us endlessly acting out autonomy, individuality and self assertion (so sorely lacking in daily life) in the 'outer space' of the shopping malls (spaces that reassure us that loneliness is a common state for each to overcome). In concluding, Bauman develops these insights to identify a novel twist on belonging that he calls the 'peg community'. Just as brands, bestsellers and hit movies are pegs to hang our individual, 'discriminating' selves on, so paedophiles, the tragic deaths of the famous, or a hike in petrol prices, help us peg up our bafflement into the shapes of community, concern and mutuality – at least for a week or so at a time.

Rolland Munro's intricately woven text reflects the complex material relations of the social. In picking up the motif of *communal* forms of mass – such as the chorus – he questions contemporary treatments of community and belonging as something imaginary and deceptive and takes the view that we become what we are (however momentarily) through 'extension'. As such, we are always moving in and out of a maze of cultural interconnections by altering our different prosthetic attachments. Yet in spite of this deep commitment to materials, Euro-Americans live their daily lives on the basis of a *forgetfulness* of this fact. To think of ourselves *as* individual is to be in the habit of forgetting how we are materialized in extension. In response, throughout his chapter, Munro 'forgets' to forget.

Drawing on an ethnography by Dan Rose, he re-imagines community as 'cathected' to objects. In the case of West Chester, the object is the horse; there is no single community, rather massive sets of interconnections around this object. War as a consumption of mass is more puzzling, unless the virtual object to which armies are cathected is death. In the light of the scathing critique of attrition in *Oh! What a Lovely War!*, Munro notices an officer class cathected to the horse, instead of the trenches, and draws attention to the lethal function of rhythm to let us forget. As the tempo of a ride increases, the rhythm of men dying moves towards oblivion.

While the previous two chapters explore and extend Euro-American debates about community, **Jane Parish**'s ethnographic research allows for a comparison between ethnically English and ethnically African-Caribbean communities in Liverpool, England. While all Parish's informants are aware that being part of a community carries the risk of becoming a victim of crime, their responses differ markedly and involve distinct vocabularies and practices of visualizing 'mass'.

Out of these two usages of 'mass', one quasi-scientific, one quasi-magical, two distinct ontologies of community arise. Her ethnically English informants assess their susceptibility to crime by seeing themselves as individuals against a backdrop of a large *number* of others. The world of crime and risk involves a world of statistics made up only of individual data-points (person or crime-event) admidst the overall patterns of masses of data. Risk is assessed by guessing one's position relative to the most notable feature of the presumed data-set – the average. Whatever events might exist in the gulf between the very small (person or crime-event) and the very large (data-set) can only be accounted for by 'luck'. Parish's work with African-Caribbean informants reveals quite a different approach to the assessment of risk, one that is intimately connected with people's daily rounds and frequent haunts. It is so connected with the materiality of daily life that each person's deliberate distribution of certain materials in the local area is understood to allow for the management of risk.

When the material grounds of a national identity are removed, when a revolution displaces a dominant group and disperses them around the globe, can that identity persist? **Doug Stuart** examines the use of the internet by the global community of Rhodesians, white Africans without a country. He argues that their nationality is not just a work of imagination. The internet, so often understood as a flight from materiality has come to compose the material grounds of the Rhodesian identity. Yet, as Bauman in his chapter has captured the contrast: 'If *Gemeinschaften* augured restful tranquillity of arrival, peg communities portend the arduous perpetuity of travel'. As a virtual community, the spectre of Rhodesia offers itself as a giant peg on which to collect the dispersal of white discontent, but with none of the duty, obligation, or reciprocity that make more durable social bonds so arduous.

Notes

1 To Bernstein, writing in *The New Constellation* (Polity, 1991: 131) and concerned with the question of Heidegger's so-called 'silence', this lack of discrimination represents exactly a *failure* of thinking. In contrast, Zygmunt Bauman has pointed to matters which suggest a complicity, for example, between the holocaust and systems of mass administration (and rejected attempts to valorise the holocaust as a 'one-off monster').

On mass, individuals, and peg communities

Zygmunt Bauman

You have seen many paintings of 'great historical events' recorded for posterity or invented by posterity; events that claim their place in history because they changed its course, broke the routine in which history sinks and suffocates. The paintings are many and different, human figures in paintings come in many shapes and colours, the dresses they wear and the weapons they wield differ; and yet in one respect all the paintings are strikingly similar: in each painting there are a few people with name and face, and many without either.

The few in question have finely-featured or coarsely-set, but always distinctive, unmistakably distinct eyes, cheeks, brows, hair, limbs, bodies; you won't forget them – you would know them if you met them again. And each one of them stands, sits or lies in a unique place of the canvass; you cannot move him elsewhere, let alone wipe out, without destroying the composition of the picture together with its narrative and sense. The many, on the other hand, could be, for all you know, clones or xerox copies of each other. There is pretty little to go by if you wish to tell one from another, or for that matter any one of them from all the rest. These or their faces are all alike – if the painter bothered to paint them, that is. And none has a place clearly of his own and his alone; you can move them around, erase some, add others – nothing will change the message, just as nothing will transform the occasion preserved or imagined in the painting into another. The few are *individuals*; the many are the *mass*.

Or, as Elias Canetti would prefer, a *crowd*. Canetti surveys symbols – entities which 'do not consist of men' yet 'recall the crowd' and so stand for the crowd 'in myth, dream, speech and song'. One of such symbols is sand. What makes it recall the crowd is 'the smallness and the sameness of its parts. This is one quality, not two, for grains of sand are felt to be the same only because they are so small'. Another symbol is the sea. What makes the sea into an apt metaphor of the crowd is the sinister might of the waves which, if broken down, disintegrates into pitiable feebleness, impotence of drops. 'Their smallness and singleness makes them seem powerless .... They only begin to count again when they can no longer be counted'.[1] In portentousness of the waves the inconspicousness and the insignificance of drops is avenged.

On sand, though, Wislawa Szymborska, the great poet and a Nobel Laureate, had the following to say:

We call it a grain of sand,
but it calls itself neither grain nor sand.
It does just fine without a name,
whether general, particular,
Permanent, passing,
incorrect or apt.[2]

The grains of sand know nothing of having no face or bearing no name. If they happen to be human sand-grains, they would be amazed if told that they are faceless and nameless. What made the human grains into quicksand and the drops into wave was that they all, each one of them, were moved by the craving of face and the thirst for name. The painters of historical *tableaux*, by denying them faces and names other than that of the crowd, suggested that they failed: that through numbers they won't get what they singly lack, that no wave would make a drop unique and no sand would make a grain singular; that, on the contrary, falling into sea or flying into sand-dune means to forfeit the face and to surrender the right to name.

It was the modern drive to individuality that construed the mass, this alter-ego of the individual. Individuality was a shaky business, punctuated by pitfalls to fall in and rocks to stumble on, calling for constant vigilance and struggle, seeking in vain a trustworthy, let alone foolproof, guarantee, never ultimately victorious and complete, forever 'until further notice'. Being an individual meant striving to be an individual; it had no other meaning, and so being an individual was a recipe for a life full of strain, anxiety and fear. There was a bottomless sea of anonymity and quicksands of facelessness lying in wait but a few inches away, always eager to suck the escapees back, devour them and dissolve. The mass was the modern individual's hell. The salvation (in modern vocabulary, the emancipation) of the moderns sentenced to lifelong individuality lay in the escape from the mass.

At the threshold of the modern era the imagery of hell changed beyond recognition. Gone was the neatly parcelled, geometrically elegant Dante's inferno, spacious enough to offer everyone of the damned a place made to the measure of their guilt and diversified enough to suit every failure and cater for every sin. As Piero Camporesi finds out in his unsurpassed study of the early modern images of damnation and salvation, 'the great invention of the Baroque hell lay in the restoration of disorder, in the return to an infernal chaos'. The early modern hell was:

Enforced cohabitation, overcrowding and intolerable promiscuity .... The bodies were pressed, stuffed into each other, stretched until they interpenetrated and permeated one another in a superfluous, gigantic poultice of mixed, dirty, infected and foul flesh.

But there was something more than overcrowding which made hell into the hell it was. Indiscrimination was perhaps yet more frightening than the lack of space. Camporesi quotes Tomasso Buffa, a Dominican preacher of Gregory XVI pontificate:

> ... inside the tombs the corpses of persons standing are not normally placed in a pile on top of those of the wretched and the poor, since everlasting sepulchres and precious urns usually divide the honourable bones of the great from the ignoble ashes of the poor. But in hell the damned are not treated like this: down there the rich and the poor, the great and the humble, the noble and the plebeian, the scholar and the ignorant will be thrown together, in confusion ...[3]

These and suchlike news hardly brought consolation for the poor, the plebeian and the ignorant. But they filled with horror the hearts and minds of the rich, the great and the scholars. The modern shape of damnation was the impossibility to fulfil the duty of individuality; the modern hell, the mass, is the punishment for the failure to perform that duty. As modern times put the concern with eternity on a side burner and anaesthetised the pains of the flesh, fears of this-worldly quicksands of the mass came to replace the horrors of other-worldly eternal fire.

Emancipation, that modern substitute for salvation, deliverance and redemption, has been problematized as the triumph of individuality over mass; by those, of course, who have made their faces visible and their names audible and have accomplished that feat by making face and name a privilege of the few. As long as the mass remained, no emancipation was confident and secure; but were the mass miraculously to disappear, emancipation would be as meaningless as in its time the salvation would have been without hell. For better or worse, the hope of individuality and the fate of the mass were tied in a wedlock no human action or imagination could separate. People sentenced to individuality need the mass to know how to serve their sentence. The mass is a fall-out of the individualist explosion, the profane cinders of the sacred individualist fire.

Easy to say: I wish to be saved. The real trick is how to be sure that, indeed, I have been. Following prescriptions and avoiding proscriptions is not enough to reassure. Misreadings of signs are as likely, if not more, as correct readings. Once the certainty of piety and goodness was but a hair-breadth away from the sin of pride; similarly, the joy of individuality is forever contaminated with the horror of common taste (to wit, tastelessness). Individuality is now suspect, like once piety was and, like piety, tormented by uncertainty. 'False consciousness' was not Gyorgy Lukacs' invention. It is the nightmare which infuses the premodern dreams of redemption and modern dreams of emancipation alike. It was a private horror long before it could be re-cast as the stigma of the feared mass.

It is part of the image of the mass that it is devoid of individuality. But it is also crucial that mass is unaware of its deprivation; people form a mass in so far as they are duped, or self-cheating to believe that the part of the body above the neck is indeed a face, and the sounds they keep emitting form a name. The mark of the mass is deception – induced or self-inflicted. The individuals who self-constitute through constituting the mass cannot do it otherwise than by making the mass the natural home of their own inner demons. The yarn of which the image of the mass is woven is not just the refusal of individuality, but the refusal (or inability) to admit that refusal.

In her analysis of Walter Benjamin's copious notes and sketches for the unfinished *Arkaden* project, Susan Buck-Morss points out that the mass of consumers produced by the capitalist market was seen there as a 'dreaming collective' in a double sense: it was 'unawake' since immersed in the dream-world, but also (perhaps most importantly) 'because it was unconscious of itself, composed of atomized individuals, consumers who imagined their commodity-dreams to be uniquely personal'.[4] By this description, the urge of individuality is in the consumer mass extinguished well before it is fulfilled; it is dreamed to have-been-already satisfied inside the dream-world, and so its 'awakening' power peters out. Not enough energy is left in that urge to prompt the dreamers to pierce through the tissue of dreams and so to reveal the dream-like nature of ostensible emancipation. The soporifics supplied by the consumer market not only facilitate falling asleep, but effectively prevent awakening. The problem of the mass (the consuming mass in particular) is the difference between genuine and putative individuality; 'mass' means a 'false individuality' standing in the way of the true one.

In Benjamin's rendering of the problem, individuality is 'false' in as far as it keeps the individuals in their atomized condition which is not followed up by formation of collectivities; only commonality of fate and prospects reforged into communal solidarity of action could lead to genuine emancipation. The major charge held by Benjamin against consumer society is (in Buck-Morss' rendition) that it engendered identities and conformities in people's lives, but not social solidarity, no new level of collective *consciousness* concerning their commonality, and thus 'no way of waking up from the dream in which they were enveloped'. In a mass, people are doubly duped: first they are duped into believing that they have indeed reached the modality of the self-assertive and self-constituting individuals which modern society presents to them as their ideal state and teaches them to desire – while in fact the apparently self-asserting routines are manipulated, pre-fabricated and scripted in advance; second, they are duped into accepting the mode of self-constitution which effectively prevents them from calling the bluff of 'atomised individuality' and so indefinitely postpones the act of emancipation that could be only achieved collectively.

Mass is a gaseous substance, an aggregate of atoms with little mutual attraction. The atoms are similar – but similarity does not make community. Similarity refers to the traits which every element of the aggregate carries alone and on its own, while community refers to the space between the elements – the links and bonds which make the elements mutually complementary and indispensable to each other. The kind of togetherness specific to the mass reinforces the atomization of the elements. In mass, the dearth of individuality is accompanied by the dearth of community.

The consumer mass owes its remarkable capacity of self-perpetuation to the shaping-up of the practices of individualization. This shaping takes place in a way which allows the putative individual to be fully accommodated within the dreamworld of consumption; where the consumer mass denies people genuine individuality, it compensates for the loss and anaesthetises the pain with an offer of a substitute individuality, that of consumer choice and of self-constitution through consumer choices. Another capacity ought to be added, however, to grasp the secret of the astonishing resilience of the consumer mass: the capacity of compensating for the absence of community and so relieving the pain which that absence may cause, by offering substitutes. Most prominently here, I have in mind phantom communities, whose main distinguishing attribute is *inconsequential (uncommital) gregariousness*: the occasions to unload the sociating urge without lasting commitment, and so avoiding the sedimentation of durable bonds.

The shopping mall has come to serve social analysts as the archetypal site of phantom communities. The shopping mall is, indeed, the dream-world incarnate and the pattern for all other sanctuaries of consumption. In Harvie Ferguson's description, it 'represents itself as an entire *world*, self-sufficient and abundant'; it is 'ideally a building which absorbs and swallows the shopper.[5] It may swallow the shopper since it first cut the shoppers free from their daily entanglements: shopping mall is elsewhere, symbolically located in the middle of nowhere, at an exit from the anonymous dullness of the motorway. A shopping escapade is a journey in space and time, a visit to a place which from the perspective of quotidianity is an outer space, exempt from mundane measurements of proximity and distance and from the pitiless flow of time; an exterritorial and extemporal location. Once there, one can play the kind of games of choice, of power and of power of choice which are strictly out of bounds in the space temporarily left.

Periodical trips to the shopping mall are Bakhtin's carnivals where normal constraints are suspended and the steam accumulated in quotidianity can be unloaded without damage to daily routine but with notable psychological gain to the revellers; shopping trips, as carnivals, keep the revellers sane as they make quotidianity bearable and liveable. In the avatar of the shopper, one acts out the individuality, the self-assertion, the autonomy which are sorely lacking in daily life; acting them out in the 'outer space' of shopping malls makes their sense of absence in daily routine less harrowing – and in effect less noticeable. 'Go buy yourself something' has become by now a common counsel to people grieved by their impotence whenever they smart under the blows of indomitable and merciless fate which they neither control nor hope to overcome.

If one wants to be fit, one buys a season ticket to a fitness club. If one wants to be a self-asserting individual, one would be well advised to visit shopping malls regularly. But individuality is not the only art practised inside the vast exercise ranges of the shopping mall. Another is community. A phantom community, to be sure, but also a sanitized one, cleansed of cumbersome commitments, freed of all 'strings attached'. As the communities outside the shopping malls grow increasingly friable and transient, more a source of anxiety than safe havens for the seekers of security – the phantom communities inside the mall, brought together solely by the simultaneous practices of commodity cult and common (though not shared) desires, score reasonably well in comparison. What would give them an edge over competition (were the other communities strong enough to compete) is that they raise to the level of constitutional rule the kind of freedom which is much in demand in the consumer society but which the non-phantom communities would not tolerate: namely, freedom from long-term commitment, from giving 'hostages to fortune', from 'mortgaging the future'; more generally, from the obligations entered, deliberately or inadvertently, in the consequence of one's actions.

Non-phantom communities are networks of mutual obligations; the denser the network, the more 'closely-knit' they are. This kind of weaving technique agrees, however, no longer with the nature of the yarn; producing a durable canvass with consumers as the only weft and woof available would be a tall order. Long-term commitment goes against the grain of consumerism – of life shaped as a string of consumer choices. Any choice that ties a stretch of time longer than the brief moment of satisfaction limits further choices and jeopardizes future satisfactions. Equally out of place in the life of the consumer is the idea of self-limitation (not to mention self-abnegation), which the mutuality of obligations, that attribute of all social bonds, inevitably entails. 'Phantom communities' offered by the shopping mall are free from all the snags which make the other communities, however intensely they may be desired, into a mixture of blessing and curse, simultaneously an attractive and off-putting target and an entity notoriously fragile and vulnerable.

The shopping mall episodic communities without past or future seem to gratify the urge of sociation without demanding in exchange the commitments which the alumni of a consumer society view as a price too high to seriously contemplate; if you are lucky, you may be even offered that ultimate freedom from consequences embodied in the 'money back' guarantee. Gratification of the sociating urge may be exceedingly short-term, but the mission has been accomplished: the tension has been temporarily brought down to the bearable level. As for the managers of the shopping malls, the short-termism of the phantom remedy is, if anything, an asset: the quicker the effects wear off, the more often the patient will return for a new dosage of the medicine. As Lauren Langman observed, 'the longings for human connection, momentarily satisfied in mall-based illusions of community, become repressed and indeed denied'.[6] That is, what has been repressed (or rather unloaded) are the longings for a human connection different from one to be found and enjoyed during the moments of strolling between the shelves and show-cases in the crowd of other shoppers strolling between the shelves and show-cases.

107

It follows from what has been said so far that it is a grave if common mistake to theorize mass consumption as a denial or rejection of individuality and community. Unfortunately, this common mistake is unlikely to be eradicated, however powerful may be the arguments to the contrary. The image of the mass is the sediment of exorcist rites, the inner demon in exile – the demon of unfulfilment, of the task failed, of looming defeat. 'The mass' is what I am perpetually hovering on the brink – where I perhaps have already fallen without noticing, or may fall at any moment of lapsed vigilance. The tall order of individuality is unlikely ever to be fulfilled, at least to be fulfilled to a lasting satisfaction. If so, the gnawing suspicion of futility mixed with self-reprobation will always need an address and a postcode. Mass is not what the individuality is not – but what we all, in moments of sobriety, suspect our flaunted and proudly displayed individuality of being. Mass is the *individual's* nightmare, and an individual without nightmares is, almost, a contradiction in terms.

The truth of the mass is rather the opposite of common opinion: the 'consuming mass' is not a deceptive shelter conjured up by, or for, escapees from freedom. It is a phenomenon produced and daily reproduced out of the individuating efforts and sociating impulses. But – and here is the catch – all this takes place in a society which provides no clear guidance nor handy tools for either. The services rendered to these two well-nigh universal and never fading concerns are the glittering attractions and principal sources of the grip in which the actions and imagination of millions of people are held. They are sentenced to the life of individuals, while having been denied the comfort of communally set exam papers which would define the volume, and so also the limits, of their task. The supply of individuality and community (be them but phantom versions of both) is not a side-effect of the consumer mass; even less can it be dismissed as a mere commercial gimmick and promptly explained away by shrewd conspiracy or duplicitous merchandizers. In this kind of society here and now, the society which sets (or not, as the case may be) the tasks of our lives and supplies (or not) the tools of task-fulfilment, the only gangway to individuality and community wide enough to accommodate most of us has been delimited to the territory populated by the 'consuming mass'.

Ulrich Beck and Elisabeth Gernsheim-Beck pointed out a decade or so ago that we have entered the era in which neither estate nor class draw the individual's life-trajectory. In the era of estates, the place in society with all its accoutrements, privileges and duties, used to be by and large decided at birth and little was left to the discretion of the born except 'staying true to their kind'. To be sure, the idea of the 'individual' could be formed only at the estate's graveyard (according to OED, the word 'individual' meaning a separate and *distinctive* person came into use only in the course of the 17th Century, when estates were well on the way out). 'Individual' makes sense only as a task and a target; it comes into its own only when social placement no more precedes, but instead follows life. To speak of 'self-made individual' is to utter tautology. 'Individual' came into being once 'class' had come to replace the 'estate' as the mark of social identity; from that moment being an individual meant the expectation and the duty of self-constitution and self-assertion. Through classes, however, modern society supplied the individuals *de jure* (or, to be more precise, the individuals *de lege lata*, 'by the law that binds', though often *de mauvaise grâce*, 'against one's will') with Ordnance Survey maps entailing clearly marked itinerary. The trademark of the individual was the following of the map, taking right turns at the crossroads and avoiding cul-de-sacs.

A word of caution is, however, in order. In its classic phase, the modern condition was primarily a middle-class universe and a middle-class problem, since what has just been said about the task of 'self-classification' applied mostly, perhaps solely, to the middle class' – called 'middle' precisely for being suspended mid-way, between and betwixt the clearly marked poles of the 'upper' and 'lower' classes. Neither those at the top nor those at the bottom faced the task of self-determination: the first because they *need not* do anything to be what they were, the second because they could not do anything to become someone else. Only the people suspended in the middle needed 'self-plotting' in the space stretching between the hard, immobile poles. Sartre said that it was not enough to be a bourgeois; to be a bourgeois, one needed a 'whole life' of the bourgeois. Significantly, he said nothing of the sort about the proletarians, nobility or scions of hereditary fortunes. 'Self-individuation' was from the start, a life-philosophy extrapolated from the middle-class experience. But it turned into dominant philosophy as the carriers of that experience turned into the dominant pattern for modern men and women, and as their mode of life became the universal condition of modern society. In this sense, the story of modernity was indeed the story of gradual yet relentless *embourgeoisement spreading from the a-morphic middle in both polar dirertions*.

In the process, though, the class-society Ordnance Survey offices have been phased out: or sold out to the 'free market'. Maps have not fallen from use, but cartographers are now many and different and so are the maps they offer for sale; above all, old roads keep being blocked, diverted or falling into disrepair, and new roads keep being built, so that maps may mislead as easily as they may instruct. Besides, destinations worth the costs of travel lose their allure fast, often faster than it takes to reach them. Being an individual no more means marching steadily and resolutely from here to there, but being constantly on the move: travelling with no hope of arrival to anything but another half-way inn. While travelling with a slightest hope of arrival anywhere at all requires running, not walking. Hope and speed rise together; and together they fall.

Under the circumstances, one is tempted to paraphrase Voltaire: if the shopping malls did not exist, they would have to be invented. Identity tokens – the only ones that could be sensibly used by people in a hurry – must be not unlike the plastic cups thrust in the palms of marathon runners or *Tour de France* riders. Many kinds of stuff could be used in the never-ending process of individualization, but they all must share one feature: they must be easy to paste on and as easy to wash off. Identity kits must be as easy to take apart instantaneously as they must be quick to assemble: light cloaks on the shoulders should never solidify into iron casings. And whatever tokens are used in the construction of identity must be instantly, with no need to argue, recognizable as the carriers of intended meaning: to compose sonnets of your choice, you need the words with which all meaningful sentences are built. The writers of advertising slogans are quick to oblige: 'They are all unique. They are all individual. They all use Panthene'.

Elizabeth from the firm of the same name, the future Gloriana, was born a daughter of Henry the Eighth; a good enough reason, one would say, to rule England. Being the monarch *de jure* proved to be, however, not enough to make the high and mighty, even the dutiful servants, treat you as the monarch *de facto* should be treated. No one truly believed that this girl is anything but a bait for a royal-born man from abroad to come over and rule the country; she was a girl, was she not? – and that was that. Elizabeth tried to argue, but in vain. No one could treat seriously what she said, not because of what she said, but because whatever she said fell from the lips which ought to be seen, kissed perhaps, but not heard. It all changed, though; and changed overnight, instantaneously, without a word being spoken. Elizabeth sent her maid to the shops to buy jarfuls of paints (brand-name make-ups had to wait another couple of centuries to be invented – there was no point inventing them as long as but a few royal bloods were lumbered with individuality problems). She changed her hairstyle, topped it with a heavy headgear and covered her face with a thick-layer-upon-thick-layer of paint until she became a walking monument of royalty. The reincarnated Elizabeth entered the assembly hall full of pratting and laughing courtiers – and everyone, without further ado, fell silent, bowed and knelt. The wondrous transmogrification had been achieved; the individual was born through immaculate self-conception, with the help of a few gadgets available to any shopper.

The movie 'Elizabeth' is a smartly designed two-hour long commercial of commerciality; an advertisement of the blessings of advertising. We, the individuals *de lege lata*, sentenced to the sisyphean labour of self-construction, need examples as much as we have no use for leaders: we need other individuals like us, who can show us how to do it and reassure us that it can be done. Elisabeth-of-the-movie has been offered to us as such an example. Whatever she could do, we can do as well. And we do it, for better or worse, with the help of a little paint, scissors, shampoo, friend's advice or a teach-yourself handbook. Perhaps this was all a fairy tale; does this matter, though, if there is no other world to settle in except the fairy-tale one? Perhaps what happened in the film was a miracle; yet what used to be a miracle that few miracle-makers could manage, has become our routine duty. The choosers of self-identity cannot be choosers of worlds. And as long as no choice of worlds is on the cards, the miracle of individuality is available only by courtesy of the *consumer mass*, the mass of the consumers, consumers in their mass.

The late-modern individuals, like their forefather Sisyphus, are solitary creatures. 'Individualization' is, after all, about standing (or rather, running) on one's own feet. The impulse of sociation always means stretching to other people and reverberates in the longing for community – but in the individual's *de lege lata* impulse leads to a special kind of stretching and is echoed in dreams of a special kind of community. The succour, support and comfort the individuals seek and hope to get from huddling together may come only from the 'togetherness of loners'.

Individuals in the consumer mass, like the components of any other mass, are all alike (they form a mass because they resemble each other and are, in their similarity, exchangeable and disposable); but they are alike in being, all of them and each one of them, *individuals* who *individually* face up to *individual* problems. In the company of 'the others like me', the individuals of consumer society do not seek escape from their loneliness; they seek *reassurance* that loneliness is the right and proper state to be in, and that even if this condition is not all roses, it is at least common to all, a challenge everyone needs to face up to one time or another, handle and cope with *on his or her own*. 'Consumer mass' offers all the paraphernalia needed to construe the kind of togetherness that offers such reassurance. As much as a cauldron in which individualities are compounded and decomposed, the consumer mass is a tubful of communities in various stages of sedimentation or disintegration.

There are important services which the consumer mass, and only the consumer mass, may render to the loners seeking approval of their loneliness. First and foremost, with the authority drawn from the endorsement by the many, it translates for them the vague anxieties and unanchored fears into the tasks made to their muscles' and brains' measure: the tasks which can be confronted and dealt with individually. It slices the unease which cannot be singly fought into 'problems' which can. It gives a public-vocabulary name to otherwise ineffable worries, by the same token taming them and defusing, and it eliminates from public vocabulary the names of any worries which resist this kind of taming. Consumer mass is a translating device, but all translation is uni-directional: public issues belong to that foreign language which is to be translated fully (with the leftovers dumped onto rubbish heaps) into the vernacular of private struggles, victories and defeats. Few services the consumer mass renders can however stand in competition to the supply of fixtures needed to construe exactly the sort of communities that answers the individuals' *de lege lata* demand.

Such fixtures are pegs; and they serve the creation of peg communities. The 'pegs' are points on which the scattered and shifting attention and diffuse and drifting concerns of many individuals can be simultaneously, and for a time, hanged. Pegs, importantly, are not lockers. Those who use them can never lose or misplace the key and so cannot be stopped against their will the moment they decide that enough is enough and wish to leave; a tremendous advantage over those other, original or 'true' communities which lent the distant relatives their name: Ulrich Beck's 'zombies', dead yet still alive (though mainly in the communitarian propaganda disguised as nostalgia, in which – to recall Phil Cohen's juicy expression – the bewailed originals remind one more of prisons, orphanages and madhouses than sites of potential liberation).

111

Pegs come in many shapes and colours. A peg could be a brand name or a label one can wear 'to belong'. A best-seller or a box-office hit one can buy or see to 'stay in touch'. A star who conjures up a community of fans *ab nihilo* or a new product which makes into a community the scattered bunch of individuals who had no inkling of belonging together. A fitness regime, a diet, a cuisine which cuts a gathering of devotees out of the amorphous mass of consumers. An event which attracts crowds because it has been for a few days the talk of the town and stays the talk of the town for a few days longer because it has attracted crowds. A public scandal which fills all the front page headlines and so makes everyone simultaneously angry, or a public loss that fills all television screens and thereby makes everyone simultaneously sad.

There are big pegs, able to accommodate millions and alluring millions for that very reason; and there are smaller ones, which on the contrary derive their attraction from their limited capacity: they would not bear more than a few hundreds or a few thousands. Between themselves, pegs of all sizes cater for all sorts of needs. The boundaries encircling peg communities cut society in all possible directions and engross devotees drawn from all possible walks of life. The feverish construction and deconstruction of peg communities has definitely replaced (or merely, as some would say, cast into shade) the obstinate and obdurate reassertion of the structure built of estates, classes, genders, generations or races. Even the divisions bidding for the structural status could not hope for much were they to refrain from using the peg-communities' services.

In our civilization of spare-parts and disposables the pegs wear out quickly, and their wear and tear is all the faster the more coats and anoraks are hung on them. There are, to be sure, a few pegs which prove more resistant than others and measure their utility in years rather than days. But all of them have a life-expectation which seems small and insignificant when compared with the longevity of individual life. This is, basically, what makes them an entity qualitatively different from the *Gemeinshaften* in whose fading glory they bask and which they struggle to imitate. Before the trials and tribulation of the individual's life come to their (still, stubbornly, inevitable) end, one would need to use as many disposable and fast ageing pegs as disposable syringes or lighters and fast ageing computers or cars. If *Gemeinshaften* augured restful tranquility of arrival, peg communities portend the arduous perpetuity of travel. What an employee of the Marriage guidance council said about marriages, could be said of peg communities: they will continue to be terrifically popular, and more and more people will try to fit more and more of them into their lifetimes.

The popularity in question comes easy, as there is no competition in sight. The Hebrew slaves in Biblical Egypt had been told to go on making bricks while the supply of grass needed to hold them together was stopped. The individuals *de lege lata* are much in the same position. As long as we are all individuals *de jure* – yet bridging the gap separating us from the status of individual *de facto* remains a private matter – 'consumer mass', with its phantom individualization and spectral communities, need not worry about its future.

References

1. Elias Canetti, *Crowds and Power*, transl, by Carol Stewart, Penguin 1973, pp. 87, 101, 93.
2. Wislawa Szymborska, 'View with a Grain of Sand', in: *Noting Twide: selected poems*, transl. by Stanislaw Barańczak & Clare Cavanagh, Kraków, Wydawnictwo Literackie 1997, p. 247.
3. Piero Camporesi, *The Fear of Hell*, transl, by Lucinda Byatt, Pennsylvania State University Press 1991, pp. 8, 9, 122.
4. See Susan Buck-Morss, 'Dream World of Mass Culture: Walter Benjamin's Theory of Modernity and the Dialectics of Seeing', in: *Modernity and the Hegemony of Vision*, ed. by David Micjeal Levin, Berkeley, University of California Press 1993, pp. 318–9.
5. Harvie Ferguson, 'Watching the world go round: Atrium culture and the psychology of shopping', in: *Lifestyle Shopping: The Subject of Consumption*, ed. by Rob shields, London, Routledge 1992, pp. 29, 30.
6. Lauren Langman, 'Neon Cages: Shopping for subjectivity', in: *Lifestyle Shopping: Subject of Consumption*, ed. by Rob shields, London, Routledge 1992, p. 69.

The waiting of mass: endless displacement and the death of community

Rolland Munro

The real, then, is that which, sooner or later, information and reasoning would finally result in, and which is therefore independent of the vagaries of me and you. Thus, the very origin of the conception of reality shows that this conception essentially involves the notion of a COMMUNITY, without definite limits, and capable of a definite increase in knowledge.

(C.S. Peirce, *Collected Papers*, Vol. 5, para. 311, quoted by Weber, 1980: 43).

Introduction

The focus of this chapter is community, an indefinable spirit evoked from co-presence, hovering between sameness and difference and erasing boundaries between self and other. This spirit is understood to be elicited during rituals and ceremonies of belonging, including hunting and storytelling, gift-giving and feasts. Critically these occasions involve a *consumption of mass* – feelings of belonging to the whole. One need not be nostalgic here: the stoning of someone, for example, is a rite of consumption that is communal; it is murder when undertaken alone. Of course, identifying matters as ritual and ceremony is already to admit something more than effects which can be produced *en masse*, such as panic in a crowd, or hatred in a mob.

My emphasis takes as its motif the mass of chorus. It would seem helpful, ahead of this, to distinguish the kind of community arising out of a consumption of mass from a so-called 'culture of mass'. No analysis will be offered here about a conformance in individual taste which makes possible the *aggregate* consumption of burgers and training shoes in a society that sets store by choice. Yet the issues are complex. While other chapters in this volume also emphasise an antipathy between the concepts of the individual and society, Strathern (1991) hints that their precise relations lie within a process of *obviation* (Wagner, 1986). Just as a way of seeing 'forgets' its ground of being, so Strathern (1991: 79) suggests that 'sociality is a taken-for-granted background to human intention'.

Within a process of obviation, individuality and sociality might be understood thus as *mutually* contrasting tropes, rather than competing.[1] As social beings, in a Western context, we are called upon to display ourselves *as* individuals. The effect is that of individuality, but the 'cause' is social. As such, the sense of individuality enjoyed by Euro-Americans seems to require a 'forgetting' of the very forms of sociality that make Euro-Americans possible. If so, then a consumption of mass – a *return* to the whole – might seem to require 'double forgetting'.

These matters suggest notions of mass are best placed under erasure, rather than eliminated as unsociological. We are likely to 'forget' mass *because* it is an effect we are *already* consuming. If this is so, then we might try to give it presence by rendering mass 'strange'. At the risk of slowing the reader down, I try to achieve this effect in what follows by switching between different forms of mass, the community and the chorale.

The blankness of the wait

In Simmel's discussions of sociality, but also in Durkheim's treatment of solidarity, there are feelings of belonging, if not to the whole, at least to something 'more'. What is this 'more'? Before riding out in the highest Pinks of November in later sections of this chapter we should hesitate.

Do feelings of belonging and union not stem from a prior sense of individuality; an aloneness and estrangement that we would discard? Well, yes and no. If a sense of individual consciousness – what Derrida calls presence – is itself an effect of a 'forgetting' of mass, then this implies that any meeting between strangers can also entail a *reverse* effect: a response-ability (Latimer, 1999; cf Bauman, 1991) that flows as medium and outcome of the very coming into being of the phenomenology of mass.

Here is a key moment of 'waiting' in *A Servant's Tale*, Paula Fox's story of Luisa de la Cuevas, the daughter of a kitchen maid and the son of a wealthy plantation owner in the Caribbean island of San Pedro. Emigrating to New York in the thirties, Luisa chooses to become a servant and is now a single mother scraping by:

> When I first saw the old stone pile of an apartment house on Riverside drive with its great dusty windows, my heart sank. The lobby floor was marble, the mirrored walls reflected in their perpetual dusk the white hair of the doorman and his red face which grew redder as he told me to use the service elevator. I caught a glimpse of myself in the mirror as I walked toward the door that led to the elevator, the collar of Amy's coat under my cheek, my hair undone by the wind on the Drive. The doorman followed me and jabbed a bell and cursed someone named Henry. When the elevator doors clanged open, the doorman expostulated, 'What the hell you doing

down there, Henry? Playing with yourself? Take this woman up to Mr Clare's'.

Henry gave me a cold, bored glance. He was an old Negro with long horse teeth which held clenched between them an extinguished cigar. His fingers came through his cotton work gloves. He left me on the eighth floor, slamming the doors behind me. I stood in the service hall delaying the moment when the door must open, when I would have to cross a new threshold. An old firehose was coiled upon the wall. A neatly tied sack of garbage stood on the floor. I lifted my hand to knock. Before I had touched the door, it opened. Mr Clare stood there looking at me. A small, long-haired dog came to sit by his feet.

I wondered if the same look was on my face that I saw on his, a kind of blankness across which, like light stealing across a wall, the first pale expression of another person, a stranger played. The first moment of meeting seemed very long.

'Mrs Greer?' he said at last.

I nodded, gesturing slightly with the paper bag in which I carried my working clothes.

'You're not to come up that filthy old elevator again. I'll speak to the doorman. You've to come up the elevator we all use. Come in. You must be frozen, the Drive is hellish on cold mornings. I've got some hot coffee ready for you'.

How should this moment of 'blankness' be read? Is this a story of two individuals, Luisa and Mr Clare, bonding? Is the 'long' wait a prelude to a more true regard, one that will find its way between instant dismissal – Henry's 'cold hard glance' – and a premature judgement in which each is read for someone who has gone before.

Or is this moment of blankness an involuntary *return* to union? Brushing away her scrawled note of reference, Mr Clare declares 'it will all work out beautifully'. And it does. From that no-man's land – between the service elevator and Mr Clare's apartment – reflected in their wait – the long threshold of blankness – a mutuality develops that has Mr Clare sharing his earnings as a consultant for museums and helping Luisa survive her ex-husband's ravings about her exposing *his* son to a homosexual. Response-ability is the potential for persons to *turn* back from their unremitting magnification of self-presence, however temporarily, towards a consumption of mass.

The denial of mass

Can response-ability jump in scale? A rejection of any large scale 'consumption' of mass seems to be at the heart of Benedict Anderson's much admired critique *Imagined Communities*. Anderson holds the idea of a large community, such as a nation, to be 'imagined' because:

> ... even the members of the smallest nation will never know most of their fellow-members, meet them, or even hear of them, yet in the minds of each lives the image of their communion ... . Unfortunately it is this fraternity that makes it possible, over the past two centuries, for so many millions of people, not so much to kill, as to willingly die for such limited imaginings. (Anderson, 1983: 15–16)

The nub of Anderson's position is that communion takes place by knowing people and meeting them. Communion, in Anderson's view, is a transactional matter which – in a surface reading of Luisa's meeting with Mr Clare – takes place between *individual* persons.[2]

As such, there seem severe limits in scale to the common accord. And this is perhaps what is at the heart of Mrs Thatcher's much-quoted dictum: 'There is no such thing as society ... . There are individual men and women and there are families' (quoted by Strathern, 1992). This (common) denial of *mass* communion is very persuasive. (Its appeal to common sense perversely eliciting its own massive nodding of heads among scholars, who otherwise never meet). For the transactionally inclined, the notion of a consumption of mass represents, most likely, a contradiction in terms. Mass is exactly what Euro-Americans do *not* consume.

In the normal way of understanding things, therefore, mass lies quite outside matters like communion. Instead, mass appears as a necessary, if irritating, by-product from the process of *reduction:* attempts to make sense of the 'external' world. Mass is always the undigested residual of our making entities – 'things' – in order to obviate a Hericlitean sense of flux. *It is what reason cannot take in.* Like the frog's eye, our consumption is imagined as working off movement and difference, not mass and identity. But reduction – Reason – can be aimed at more than blocking out the 'buzzing, blooming confusion' that the pragmatist William James had in mind.

The enemy of reason is also its very ground of being. This is not only the community per se, but the community within, the 'inner' mass of cognition. As another pragmatist sees the difficulty:

> There is but one state of mind from which you can 'set out', namely, the very state of mind in which you actually find yourself at the time you do 'set out' – a state in which you are laden with an immense *mass* of cognition already formed, of which you cannot divest yourself if you would ... (C.S. Peirce, Collected Papers, Vol. 5, para. 416, quoted by Weber, 1980: 42, emphasis added).

Reason would have us find a point of origin and then set out step by step. But the difficulties for so setting out are set up by this very 'immense mass of cognition'. Peirce's insight is that this mass of cognition is itself on-going and indispensible.

This inability to divest ourselves of this immense mass of cognition brings us close to the condition which Heidegger (1962) marked as our 'thrownness' into the world. We wake up to reason long after our relations are embodied by language and materials. The question at hand is what exactly is this thrownness? And how is reason to be re-connected to a consumption of mass that is so sedimented and indispensible?

The landscape of consumption

The idea that the social could be stuck together by materials is most forcibly put forward by Mary Douglas and Baron Isherwoood in their seminal work on consumption. Arguing that 'any choice between goods is the result of, and contributes to, culture', Douglas and Isherwood (1980: 76) posit that goods are consumed because they are 'good to think'. For them, the consumption of goods ensures the circulation and recreation of culture. But, analytically, perhaps this works most obviously for a relatively closed society? What happens to consumption when societies are fragmented? How are *displays* of culture perpetuated over time and space when communities are no longer geographically or temporally contained?

As a cultural anthropologist, Dan Rose has tried to make sense of America by examining it as a local variant of the culture of contemporary world capitalism, a market economy that has penetrated to the remotest reaches of the planet.

> We all lead lives driven more or less by obscure market forces. The market – the *pricing* of goods, services, labor, communications, and of money – propagates an endless array of new products and innumerable possibilities for how we ought to lead our daily lives. (Rose, 1990: 158)

The pure product of these 'innumerable possibilities' is *displacement*. You can be 'more'! This is the insistent refrain today. As fast as it denies possibilities for belonging to any 'whole', contemporary world capitalism generates an ever-increasing range of possibilities for a display of self. Although Rose never quite says so, the lure of the market is to be who you wanna be.

Few would contest America's centrality to the imagination of contemporary culture. Strangely, then, we meet Rose not in Disneyland or MacDonald's, the haunt of other ethnographers of capitalism, but out with the hunt at Runnymede, a large tract of farmland in the bucolic countryside of West Chester, Pennsylvania. The Englishness of the scene, once owned by Quakers and others whose ancestors emigrated from the British Isles, is epitomized by the dress of tailored tweeds and the pack of 'superbly disciplined English foxhounds' all capped by the huntsman being British born.

True, dressed in her blue and red nylon Adidas windbreaker and old sneakers, the Master of Foxhounds cuts a different figure in her four-wheel drive pick-up. Injuries accumulated over forty years have ensured that Mrs Hannum can no longer ride and she blends in well with the ten or so other people who are there 'to drive along and *spectate'* (158). Noticeably, these stick to their vehicles and are described by Rose as working-class. It is as if all the solid permanence (and exclusiveness) of British country life – class divisions and all – has been zipped up and transported several thousand miles across the Atlantic.

It is this kind of displacement that precisely makes Rose's point about the 'ceaseless transformation' of contemporary capitalism:

> The here and now becomes ceaselessly transformed by its pure product which is *repeated displacement* – displacement not only of old goods, but of old beliefs, traditions, values and the imagined autonomy of our cultural histories substituted by marketable new ones. (p. 158, emphasis added)

The pure product is 'repeated displacement'. Yesterday's stuff – values as well as goods – is made anew. The hunt offers good sport, according to a newspaper cutting quoted by Rose, for those willing 'to cut themselves off from the active world of business and live, for a while at least, the lives of country gentlemen'.

Reinscribing the material world

The key to this endless displacement, in Rose's view is the movement of materials. A consumption of mass – on a very large scale – is still going on:

> Large corporations take naturally occurring materials [mass], fashion them into [mass] consumables, and through market allocations redistribute them in places far removed from sources of origin. (1990: 158)

None of this mutation and movement of mass is surprising. The bringing of 'things far' and making them 'near' is the exotic logic driving consumption and is as much as others have imagined it (cf Barthes, 1982: 19).

Moving this 'essential' process of consuming and circulating materials up to a different level, Rose continues:

> ... one of the most significant products of the culture of capitalism is *reality*, a sensibility continually formed and reformed within large companies. Inquiry into reality must thus be inquiry into reality formation and reality consumption; formation and the relentless production of consumption are processes which resemble nothing less than the refabrification of the

material world and the ceaseless production of its physical and symbolic uses. (158)

Reality and imagination are not, as Anderson (1988) anticipated, priors that could discriminate between the possibility of a community and its illusion. In the culture of capitalism, it is reality itself that becomes one of its main products.

As Rose argues, two familiar ideas – economic production and consumption – capture the two major phases in the never ending transformation of the material world and our mundane lives:

> Both phases have during the last four hundred years reinscribed local places anywhere we look. In early twentieth-century America the landscape of consumption (new consumption sites, really) became wrenched from the landscape of production as new suburbs were opened for commuting by rail and automobile and as factory and shop were left behind at the end of the working day. (159)

The re-inscription of the locality of Chester County, Pennsylvania into a landscape 'devoted to sustaining the sport of hunting fox' began in 1912, the hunt having been started by Mrs Hannum's grandfather, E.H. Harriman, one of the owners of extensive railroad holdings. Only 61 years old when he died, he had 'turned the corner from producer of great wealth to its consumer' and 'began to approach the leisure pursuits of a gentleman of enormous fortune' (165).

But not all Mrs Hannum's world is as it was imagined yesterday. To aid her efforts in perpetuating foxhunting at West Chester, Mrs Hannum has drawn upon the services of the form of *corporation* that helped make her grandfather rich. The complex business of ensuring the hunt's continuation – its future reality – is entrusted to a privately held company which Mrs Hannum has set up and in which she is Chairman of the Board. Ironically, this unusual form of displacement, the 'incorporation' of a community, is being used to ensure that hunting in Chester County does not fall victim to the process of endless displacement.

The stated strategy is to 'build a sociable community among large landowners whether or not they ride to hounds through lavish events and parties' (167). Against this project, there are competing forms of consumption (in the shape of problems of succession in three heirs with equal claims to acreage and the adjacency of a new city that is in the process of being built). The forces of the market, which once made possible this particular displacement – the use of 15,000 acres for the 'elaborate ritual' of hunting – now seem poised for 'pulling the hunt country apart' (167). As Rose remarks, executives running the growing businesses of the region would wish nothing more than to live in the large houses that make up the hunt country. Eating spaghetti in Shrewsbury, or chewing burgers alongside life-sized dining companions in the form of Pluto and Minnie Mouse, we have all become familiar with the process of endless displacement and can hardly be surprised that 'expert opinion' suggests that the corporate strategy of the Cheshire Hunt Conservancy may fail.

Cathected to an object

A ceaseless movement, then, of repeated displacement. Among the books in Mrs Hannum's library is *Foxhunting Formalities*, written by the great friend of her father and former owner of Runnymede, J. Stanley Reeve. As a source-book of 'quick competence for the cultural handyman' Rose (1990: 164) suggests that this is a genre of book given to 'the acquisition of instant tradition'.

As the following sample of the condescending quality of the how-to-do-it prose in *Foxhunting Formalities* indicates, U-do-it books disseminate helpful hints:

> Several one dollar bills are very handy to have in one's pocket, and a bit of small change is apt to be useful for telephoning, or to give a lad for opening a gate or taking out a rail. If one has a fall and one's horse gets away, by all means reward the groom who brings him back to you. (164)

Activities take on the air of requiring a 'know-how' in which, according to Peirce: 'The method must be such that the ultimate conclusion of *every man shall be the same*' (Peirce, quoted by Rose: 164, emphasis added). Custom – 'the way we do things round here' – stands always ready to slip its register from the descriptive to the normative. The lavish parties, the Pink of the hunting jacket, each becomes *de rigueur*. What gives the 'just-us' feeling becomes in time the just-ice; the freezing of the rules we live by.

As an ever-present brake on the process of endless displacement, culture often is caricatured as a 'drag' on change (Strathern, 1993). Yet as Rose observes about West Chester, the usual tropes of community are missing:

> ... there is no membership cadre in a community organization or commune either political, religious, secular, or corporate; they do not engage in collective action; despite the spatial contiguity there is no neighborhood focus where everyone owning horse farms can meet. (158)

To be sure, the spatial contiguity of the farm properties is made up of the rich and the very rich. No doubt, sanctions of expulsion and exclusion remain crucial, but the rich are not de facto a single community; some buy islands, others castles. Not everyone who is rich hunts.

This raises the question about how a hunting community can be perpetuated? How does the community not fall apart? Rose suggests that the community to which Mrs Hannum belongs is made up of networks of people who are 'cathected to an object'. That is:

... an object, in a conversational and material sense, organizes their interests and it is along the lines of their interests that they get to know one another, invite one another to dinner, or parties, or see one another, more or less regularly. (158)

This object in West Chester is the horse. What people have 'in common' is, most often the 'race track proved American thoroughbred'.[3]

But what interests me in this notion of communities being cathected to objects is this question: *who speaks?* Certainly, the title to speak in West Chester demands an 'intimate knowledge' of horses and the equestrian way of life. But there is something more. As Rose points out, what people share, the horse, is 'not necessarily enough to constitute friendship' (159). For example the man who married the owner of Runnymede is described by Mrs Hannum as 'the little twerp' and she describes, at great length, the huntsman as 'stupid' (159).

While the horse certainly offers a basis for daily discourse, the ability to 'pass on' this reality to others requires a 'voice' in that community. Community is divisive in the sense that others can either help include us within, or work to exclude us.[4]

The redistribution of discretion

But what could give 'voice', this right to speak? Here we might be tempted into thinking of knowledge communities being fragmented into a multiplicity of language games (Munro, 2001), but I want to stick with materials.

Much anthropology has focused around the ever-pressing question of who sleeps with whom. As such, a key object to which communities are assumed to be 'cathected' is the bed. Here kinship has its spokespersons for the exchange of women. 'How can I give my daughter to a man I know nothing about?' says Mr Wharton, brother to a QC and the inheritor of one of Anthony Trollope's Hertfordshire estates. Tradition, as Mary Douglas notes, lets the father, not the bride, speak.

Yet moving alongside the ceaseless circulation of goods is a *re-distribution* of the conversations determining titles to speak. Yes, one can think of the invention of the automobile as creating a 'mobile bed', and so impute changes in morality. But the key point in any specific shift in the circulation of materials is the accompanying change in *spokespersons*. In consequence of the availability of cars to the young, discretion over who sleeps with whom shifts *from* fathers *to* daughters.

From which it is perhaps a small step also to think about 'virtual objects' (Law, 1994) as doing more than bringing people together. If the objects to which we are cathected can alter local politics, so then might 'virtual objects'?[5] These too, like the horse, might also command a circulation of mass. We are soon back to wondering about those imaginary communities. And their 'limited imaginings'.

The chorus of mass

War, disease and famine, the three great consumers of mass, continue to take their toll, despite advances in consumer wealth, public health and liberal stealth. For example, although many infectious bacterial diseases such as pulmonary tuberculosis – formerly known as consumption – are no longer regarded as a killer disease, mass exterminations in the name of prevention are carried out on any herd of cattle suspected of carrying a disease such as tuberculosis.

Similarly, we might feel distant to those outbreaks of mass self-flagellation witnessed in the middle ages, but as Brown (1997) has documented in respect of the Gulf war, events of mass hysteria are still being recorded and bear some similitude to St. Vitus's Dance. A calumny, no doubt. But is it a calumny that its other name 'chorea' carries the Greek *khoreia* – as chorus?

Such an intuition over the events of the first world war might have occurred to Charles Chilton, deviser and producer of individualistic BBC radio programmes, when in 1958 he yielded to his grandmother's request for a photograph of his father's grave at Arras; unfortunately, only to find that his father had no grave. Instead his name was inscribed upon a wall together with 35,942 'officers and men of the British Army who fell in the battle of Arras and who have no known grave'. Chilton returned home with the following questions, which would not leave him. *What could have possibly happened to a man that rendered his burial impossible? What horror could have taken place that rendered the burial of 35,942 men impossible and all in one relatively small area?*

As Danchev (1991: 281) who interviewed Chilton in 1988 goes on to record, Chilton spun a web of reflection around soldier's songs of the period, some forty in all, seeking to catch the spirit of what did happen to the common man on the Western Front. With Chilton's active participation, this became the model and prime source for Joan Littlewood's Theatre Workshop production of *Oh! What a Lovely War*. Here is an extract from Philip French's review of the 1969 film version, together with some additional commentary by Alex Danchev:

Here the surviving Smith soldier goes into battle on the eve of the Armistice. Following a red guide tape to the attack start line, he finds himself alone in swirling smoke. A control sergeant ... escorts him through a blockhouse which lead into a conference hall where busy politicians are signing peace documents. Silently he follows the red tape around the room and out the other side to emerge on the Sussex Downs and joins his dead relatives, who are reclining on the grass beside the family's picknicking female survivors.

At this point the sound returns. Smith's small daughter asks the ever-present question, 'what did Daddy do in the war?' The slow sad Great War parody of Jerome Kern's 'They Wouldn't Believe Me' rises in answer on the soundtrack. The men dissolve into white crosses. The camera soars away into the sky to reveal the four living Smiths marooned in a sea of crosses, those neat, clean, anonymous, familiar rows of crosses, which gradually fill the screen. (Danchev, p. 286)

In the cinema, as Danchev adds, this effect is overwhelming. He goes on to say that Philip French was not alone in experiencing an infinite sense of waste, 'a feeling of impenetrable sadness, of unassuagable grief'.

A mass outburst, then, even if the spats of grief exhibit a temporal variance, depending on its electronic release (from the Paramount Cinema, Piccadilly to the local cinema in Scotland where I saw it almost thirty years ago). But what is secreted in this passage of Smith's, moving from the attack start line, through the peace conference and onto the South Downs? Why should the full horror of war penetrate only in the moment when the film drops Littlewood's 'clownerie' (a fusion of music hall, *commedia dell'arte*, and Brechtian epic theatre)?

Well, not because we feel for families like the Smiths that the men have died to save. Yes, the scene of a family picnic on green rolling hills is more Calvary than Eden, but by now our rejection of the family is near total.[6] It is not the 'fraternity' of a nation that is held to blame, as Benedict Anderson would have it, but the foolishness and blindness of the family that seems responsible – if not for the war itself at least for its continuation on a grand scale. During the film, it is the family who embody the adiaphoric (Bauman, 1991) values that have caused so many fathers, husbands and sons to die.

The men dissolve into white crosses. The lives of the men are emptied out. If they cannot live on in their families – and they cannot live where their horror cannot be believed – then there is nowhere. All that remains of the men who fell in the no-mans land of the Western Front are those 'neat, clean, anonymous, familiar rows of crosses'. And this blankness is all. There is no body on the cross, as with the effigies of Christ, to remind us of what has been sacrificed; nor even the blood – for the white cross is quite unlike the red of the Holy Roman Empire, filmed so evocatively by Eisenstein.

The secret of mass

So what is being secreted? I think, perhaps, the secret is number. We have to remember that all through *Oh! What a Lovely War*, we are in 'numbers'. The men slip into a music hall number at the drop of a hat. Rat-a-tat. With the rhythm of a gatling-gun, they get in line and join up in song; they are forever the chorus. Good-byee, they sing, good-byee. Wipe the darling tear from your eye-ee! Ho-ho and off we go-oh!

As the men empty into white crosses, this is the moment in the film that begins to add up the consequences of the tomfoolery. And what the incompetence of the officers – many of whom are still cathected to the horse – adds up to is 'mass murder'. This is the nub of it. Haig's notion was that 'we cannot hope to win until we have defeated the German army' (quoted in Danchev, p. 275). This not only made certain the holocaust of war, but turned it into a consumption of mass:

> There is no course open to us but to fight it out. Every position must be held to the last man: there must be no retirement. With our backs to the wall, and believing in the justice of our cause, each one of us must fight on to the end. (Haig's April 13th Order of the Day, quoted in Pat Barker's *The Eye in the Door*, Penguin, 1994, p. 6)

It was a *calculation* about the consumption of mass that made this particular war possible: we would win because *we* had more than *them*.

The reduction of mass in this final scene to the 'neat, clean, anonymous, familiar rows of crosses', had symbolic antecedents that might carry a very personal meaning for Charles Chilton. But something else carries to all of us. As the white crosses gradually fill the screen, there is something infinitely sad about a group of soldiers that are still in chorus when they are dead.

The death of mass

What is this chorus? Wherein lies its 'lethal function'? As Lyotard (1984: 22) notes, nursery rhymes and repetitive forms of contemporary music exhibit 'a surprising feature':

> ... as meter takes precedence over accent in the production of sound (spoken or not), time ceases to be a support for memory to become an immemorial beating that, in the absence of a noticeable separation between periods, prevents their being numbered and consigns them to oblivion.

Lyotard sees a 'congruence' between this lethal function of what he calls 'narrative knowledge' and the functions he cites earlier, namely criteria formation, the unification of areas of competence, and social regulation.

I find this insight by Lyotard perhaps the most striking idea in the whole of the *Postmodern Condition*. For it is not only the noticeable separations in time – the differences – which are consigned to oblivion. Up the tempo and we 'forget'. The blankness takes us – as material beings – with it. *Goodby-ee! Goodby-ee!* Up the tempo and there can be no meaning. No hold.

No. Hold! Let's restate that. Up the tempo and there's no 'wait'. The rhythmn consigns to oblivion everything that is going on *at a distance*. While the men wait, rotting in their trenches, the officers can exercise their horses safely behind the corrals of mud. At the trot. *Clip clop. Clip clop.*

In the abolition of memory, there may be no meaning*s*. More generally, this is to touch not only on obviation but understand the potential for disposal on a large scale. Out goes all that talk, all those discourses and ideas that have forever clouded 'the real' since language began. In the rhythm of daily sales bulletins and production numbers, building up to weekly and quarterly reports to the stock exchanges, the tempo of society is heightened towards an 'immemorial beating' in which the memory of ends beyond means is finally consigned to oblivion.

The harnessing of the lethal function of tempo does not mean though that meaning itself is abolished. Virtual objects – like profit – create a vacuum into which there may be also greater chances for the pure experience of meaning: belonging. Not a belonging *to* something, for this would require memory. But be-*longing*. Extension. A boy in his car. A man on his horse. A consumption of mass.

Breaking ranks

The community imagined by social theory is a leviathan that floats in the waters of an abstract consumption. It is all mass and no movement. It has little to say about the *motility* of Euro-Americans – their ability to cathect themselves to different objects and move between the 'lived categories' (Latimer, 1997) of performing community one moment and 'cutting' the figure of the individual the next (Munro, 1999b).

As I have discussed elsewhere, we are always in extension. Indeed, extension is all we are ever 'in' (Munro, 1996; Strathern, 1991). But the rhythm we deploy is not that of a spatial extension, *a la* Locke. This is certainly, in our visual blindness, where endless displacement will lead: the search for a magnification of self. Only cathect! One moment we indulge ourselves in a consumption of mass – when it is good to think of ourselves as members of a community; the next moment we exercise our 'right' to choose, to stick out *as* individuals. It is only with all-too-rare notions such as Goffman's 'role distance' that we approach the paradoxes of exercising traditional realities alongside our extolling of reality-as-choice.

There is also a wider range of goods to be considered than anticipated by many who have followed Mary Douglas's insights into consumption. As a form of extension, the current emphasis on a circulation of goods seems little more than a visual desert wherein we are left forever wandering. What the chorus offers is more a temporal extension, a movement across time. Getting in time is how we sing. *Goodby-ee!* There is no title needed to speak, other than to know the tune – and to be in time. *Clip, clop.* Thus, rather than treat communities as being imaginary – when could they not be? – I have drawn attention to the possibility of communities being cathected to virtual objects. A policy of attrition, the idea of winning, a calculation, each of these suggests possibilities for mass communion that are not to be dismissed by drawing hard lines between reality and imagination.

In our endless displacement, Euro-Americans 'forget' their material attachments. But not only this. We draw upon certain goods to help figure ourselves as part of communities. For a moment. Then in the next, to figure ourselves *as* individuals, we require more specific materials that can obviate this 'return to the whole'. This said, reality-as-choice is likely to be less a matter of creating your own destiny and more a matter of 'waiting'. Waiting to see if anyone accepts this reality you are helping bring about. Fail to produce the real and the justice is that you can be expelled from the 'just-us' effect. Perversely, it is in this exaggeration of self that we are now beginning to witness the greatest effects of a consumption of mass.

Notes

1 For example Thomas Kuhn (1970) stresses the role of community in science. However, in his psychologising of the moment of revolution, the figure who makes the 'Gestalt switch' is always an individual. For theory development, the insight then has to be returned to research communities, which either cohere or disperse. The 'great man' view of science obviates this return to community.

2 Anderson, in passing, admits possibilities raised by our hearing about particular people, a matter all the more crucial given recent phenomena such as the death of Diana.

3 Without difficulty one can think also of other 'partial' communities, cathected to different objects, such as music or paintings. Typically, many of these objects, such as the car, are further divided up into the racing car, rally cars, four-wheel drives, vintage cars and of course cars to steal, cars for joy-riding and cars to vandalise and crash.

4 Exclude us, that is, sometimes *as* an individual and sometimes *as* mass. For example, in respect of her earlier employers, the Millers, Luisa realizes that for all their efforts to make themselves comfortable with her presence, she holds some mystery for them:

> I surmised, had I been a Negro servant, they would have seen me as a flat surface. Not in their most private thoughts would they have considered me more than a dark-skinned vacancy. As it was, there was an odd, shifting equality between us; we were all working people together, except, of course, I didn't set them tasks. I sensed I must relinquish nothing of my secret life. (145–6)

> All too easily each of us is returned to being part of the mass, the blankness of a being nothing more than a background effect. For example, Luisa perceives that for her friend Ellen, a young black woman, acquiring a profession was a matter of the life or death of her spirit – 'that to be unknown was ordinary, but to be cancelled out as a creature undeserving of interest, was an unnatural death in life' (146).

5 Not everything is going in the general direction of democracy. See Munro (1999a) on the impact of individuated performance measurements on the distribution of discretion within organisations.

6 The motif of the picnic may be Hollywood, but the register is not. But why not move from clownerie into realism? Why not, as others have done using documentary sources, show the dead in their trenchs, rotting and eyeless? Or to show the horror of war, why not recreate reality a la

Spielberg, as in *Saving Private Ryan*? Well, sometimes titles suggest all and Spielberg's is still Hollywood; not so much a calumny as a liberal fairytale about the importance of saving one life.

References

Anderson, B., (1983), *Imagined communities: reflections on the origin and spread of nationalism*. London: Verso.

Barthes, R., (1982), Empire of Signs, translated by Richard Howard, New York: Hill and Wang.

Bauman, Z., (1991), The social manipulation of morality: moralising actors, adiaphorizing action. *Theory, Culture & Society*, 8: (1) 137–151.

Brown, S., (1997), In the wake of disaster: stress, hysteria and the event. In Kevin Hetherington and Rolland Munro (eds) *Ideas of Difference: social spaces and the labour of division*. Sociological Review Monograph. Oxford: Blackwells.

Callon, M., (1998), Introduction: the embeddedness of economic markets in economics. In Michel Callon (ed.) *The Laws of the Market*. Sociological Review Monograph: 1–57. Oxford: Blackwells.

Danchev, A., (1991), 'Bunking' and Debunking: the controversies of the 1960s. In Brian Bond (ed.) *The First World War and British Military History*. Oxford: Clarendon Press.

Douglas, M., (1966), *Purity and Danger: an analysis of the concepts of pollution and taboo*. London: Routledge.

Douglas, M., (1975), *Implicit Meanings: Essays in Anthropolog*. London: Routledge.

Douglas, M. and Baron Isherwood, (1980), *The World of Goods: towards an Anthropology of Consumption*, Harmondsworth: Penguin.

Friedman J., (1990), Being in the World: Globalization and Localization, *Theory, Culture & Society* 8 (4) p. 327.

Garfinkel, H., (1967), *Studies in Ethnomethodology*, Englewood Cliffs, N.J.: Prentice Hall.

Hughes-Freeland, F., ed. (1998), *Ritual, Performance, Media*, ASA Monographs 35, London: Routledge.

Kuhn, T., (1970), *The Structure of Scientific Revolutions*, 2nd Edition. Chicago: University of Chicago Press.

Latimer, J., (1997), Giving Patients a Future: the constituting of classes in an acute medical unit. *Sociology of Health and Illness*, 19(2): 160–185.

Latimer, J., (1999), The Dark at the Bottom of the Stair: participation and performance of older people in hospital. *Medical Anthropology Quarterly*, 13 (2): 186–213.

Law, J., (1994), *Organizing Modernity*. Oxford: Blackwells.

Lyotard, J-F., (1984), *The postmodern condition: a report on knowledge*, trans. G. Bennington, G. and B. Massumi. Manchester: Manchester University Press.

Munro, R., (1996), The Consumption View of Self: Extension, Exchange and Identity. In S. Edgell, K. Hetherington and A. Warde (eds) *Consumption Matters*. Sociological Review Monograph, pp. 248–273. Oxford: Blackwell Publisher.

Munro, R., (1999a), Power and Discretion: membership work in the time of technology', *Organization*, 6 (3): 1999, 429–450.

Munro, R., (1999b), The Cultural Performance of Control, *Organization Studies*, 20 (4): 619–639.

Munro, R., (2001), After Knowledge: the language of information'. In S. Linstead and R. Westwood (eds) *The Language of Organization*, London: Sage.

Peirce, C.S., (1931–5), *Collected Papers*, Vol. 5, eds Charles Hartshorne and Paul Weiss. Cambridge, Mass: Harvard University Press.

Rose, D., (1990), Quixote's Library and Pragmatic Discourse: toward understanding the culture of capitalism. *Anthropology Quarterly*, 63 (4): 155–168.

Shields, R., (1992), *Lifestyle Shopping: The Subject of Consumption*. London: Routledge.

Strathern, M., (1991), *Partial Connections*. Savage, Maryland: Rowman & Littlefield.

Strathern, M., (1992), *After nature*. Cambridge: Cambridge University Press.

Weber, S., (1980), Closure and Exclusion, *Diacritics*, June: 35–46.

Consuming averages: interpreting luck and the social mass

Jane Parish

Introduction

In this chapter I argue that ideas of mass loom large in communities' considerations of their vulnerability to crime. In this sense mass is consumed, but this consumption often becomes neglected with the employment of more static measurements in which mass is scaled according to an average, a self-organizing device (see Strathern, 1991). However, I argue in this chapter, the nature of risk cannot be determined by appealing to general averages only. Rather, I show how two Neighbourhood Watch Schemes conceive of their own specific 'average' in order to shape their own space around a 'middle', a concept which refers both to a unified social structure and to a movement of the in-between (Cooper, 1998). It is to the in-between movement of the 'middle' that actors refer to as good and bad luck in assessing their susceptibility to crime in their neighbourhood.

The research for this chapter stems from fieldwork carried out between 1995–1997 among two 'Neighbourhood Watch Schemes' in Toxteth, Liverpool 8. The 'Neighbourhood Watch Schemes' analysed in this chapter are located in two areas of inner-city Liverpool. The first meets in the Dingle, a predominantly white working-class area in one of the oldest areas of inner-city Liverpool being located alongside the waterfront. Interviews were conducted with men and women who were interviewed either in their homes or in groups in various social clubs and cafes.

The second 'Neighbourhood Watch Scheme' is based in the Granby/Abercromby District of Toxteth, an area which runs parallel to the Dingle, separated by a large boulevard. Research was conducted among African-Caribbean men and women and semi-structured interviews were conducted.

Residents in both neighbourhood schemes spend large amounts of time assessing whether the rates of burglary are higher during particular times of the year, for example, and the likelihood of being mugged along certain streets and in specific areas in Toxteth. Although no member of either group has actually been the victim of a crime, in one group, from the Dingle, generalizations flow from the horror stories of friends of friends. A specific incidence of mugging is enough to categorize a particular street as dangerous, although by far the worst areas of crime are those other than where the residents live. In the second group, residents concentrated on specific details about the mugging and why one specific person is the victim of mugging rather than another.

Do residents, in trying to average crimes, consume mass in different ways? How is the movement of mass conceptualized? Among the neighbourhood group in the Dingle this movement is called luck, a patterning that comes from nowhere and enables an association between unexpected and sudden events which do not add up. Among the second neighbourhood watch, transience characterizes events which are construed in very personal terms rather than, as Strathern points out, the 'abstract possibility of a common measure which dominates Euro-American thinking about division and comparison' (1997b: 52).

Averaging crime in an inner-city

Crime, like risk, is commonly assumed to be 'out there'. The main sources of data for these statistics are: (1) criminal statistics; (2) judicial statistics; (3) probation statistics and (4) prison statistics. How are crimes counted?

*In offences of violence against the person or sexual offenses with more than one victim: one offence per victim.
*With other offences, where several offences are committed 'in one incident' only the most serious is counted.
*If there is a 'continuous series of offences, where there is some special relationship, knowledge or position that exists between the offender and the person or the property offended against which enables the offender to repeat the offences, only one offence is counted for each continuous offence' (Coleman and Moynihan, 1996: 22).

A person who has committed several offences at the same time may be indicted for only one offence. Another offender who repeats the same crime on several different occasions will be tried each time for this offence. By working out laws or averages of rates of crime, it is possible to assess the incidents which might or might not happen in particularly areas. For example, recorded crime increased by 60% in Merseyside after 1974, while between 1983 and 1985 the rates of detection for burglary and car theft increased (Coleman and Moynihan, 1996). Risk can be measured because the rate of incidents of crime make this explicit.

The Dingle and Granby have a higher rate of social breakdown when compared with other areas. Residents in the Dingle were very fond of quoting averages to support this. An average is what 'experts think you should do' and this in turn is based, according to respondents, on 'really old laws', 'nature' and social ideas of how 'normal people behave'. In turn, the average can be broken down into different units according to relations between 'close kin' and more distant kin 'who you know, but not so well', 'neighbours' and 'strangers' (see Strathern, 1992; 1997a).

Society, however, is not about the relations between people. It is to do with the 'relations between institutions'. The family, however, is no longer an 'important institution'. It has no power outside the most immediate vicinity, 'the front door'. Crime takes place outside of 'the family home' or is brought into the home by 'external factors' such as 'unemployment and poor housing which are nothing to do with the family'. Mugging is to do with the 'breakdown of society' which is 'out of control'. It is made up of 'too many parts' which do not stick together. Kenny, aged forty-two, whose family had lived in the same street for forty years, compared how the average was used as a moral scale:

Once there were very strict ... I suppose rules ... lines ... Here, for example, there is the family ... work and the bingo. They each had areas in common ... People I worked with were also family. But today there is too much that separates us from all the other things that make up the world ... all different things ... we don't have here. We're behind ... the rest. It is all out of reach ... the world has got bigger ... us smaller ... There are statistics which describe us as scum. There is nothing we can do about it ... it is beyond our control ... makes us look bad when compared with everyone else.

Fatalism shows itself in recurring patterns that are picked up by outside agencies and reflected in statistics. Unemployment, homelessness, poverty and lack of education are common factors highlighted by people to account for where crime is statistically high and where people commit crime as a way of getting out of the trap they find themselves in, as opposed to in the suburbs where people have more access to a world beyond their doorsteps. A person living is the suburbs 'sees less crime', is exposed to less crime and therefore is less likely to commit it, but is more likely to report it because of this.

Actors in the Dingle often remarked on the relation between normality and familiarity, like Billy, aged thirty-two and an unemployed electrician:

It's weird really because here everyone still knows everyone else ... there is a sense that you don't really know what is going on. The other week, this scally ... drug dealer from round here was picked up by the bizzies (police). Everyone knew about him ... but not the scale of it all. It turns out that he was like the two-hundredth richest man in Britain, worth about £200 million ... Yet if you saw him in the street, you would always say hello. He was OK ... But now, I realize that I didn't know him at all ... In today's world people can hide things about themselves if they want, even here. In the suburbs up in Woollton, they wouldn't see this at all. They would not notice him unless he opened his mouth!

In the above case, danger is monitored in different ways, a kind of 'eyes in the back of your head' mentality that is contrasted with the idea that there are dangers which are 'simply out there'. This safety strategy rests on gathering information and a type of surveillance which is particular to the inner-city said Frank aged thirty-three and unemployed:

> We are all at risk here ... this is a fuck-off mean area [laughter]. We ... eat the wrong foods, drink and smoke, inhale polluted air ... need money to change all that. I can't do anything about it. Fuck it ... I don't really worry about these things ... Crime is like that. Its all statistics ... and I can't help where I live so I'm likely to be a victim of crime. But what I can do, what we can all do, is gather surveillance ... be on the look-out, trade information about the scallies here on the rob, find out about their thieving little ways before they have a chance to do anything ... We all know who they are. This sort of information makes a difference .... like fuck it's not ... in their fuck-off statistics.

Shaping and personalizing crime

In Granby, Toxteth, amongst residents interviewed, the world is controlled by objects that replicate the self-similar image of a person such that they are able to consume space and recurring happenings can be controlled by actors possessing particular materials. These happenings are made up of the many actions and events of everyday life. The following examples are evidence of the events that make up a person's week: breakfast; visit to the shops; meet with friends; travel on the bus; a visit to a church. It is often stressed how each event is repetitive. Detail is a key feature.

Detail is very important because out of the interaction of so-called simple events is derived very complex patterns and relations. The world is composed of very mobile relations between persons and things. Indeed, even the most concrete is composed of knowledge threaded through a number of persons, and persons are composed of knowledge and talk threaded through objects. In this way the totality relates neither to an individual or a group. Rather, the person is a kaleidoscope of scale shifts (Strathern, 1997a).

To prevent a mugging the image of the person is replicated through a number of self-similar parts. For one elderly man, in order to construct the image a few simple bits of a person, fragments of skin, a piece of hair or a fingernail are necessary. Stuck onto an object, for another interviewee, these bits have the power to alter the relationship, scattering and clustering of events in any person's life. The significance to the actor of each object lies in its composition and the ability of the actor to infuse the object with small parts of him or herself. Remoulding the object in a part of their image, the object extends that person's influence over daily interactions. It is like a cat's cradle.

The materials are the same and the same length, but threaded in an infinite number of patterns (see Haraway, 1997).

In some instances the object is not always worn about the person or kept among their belongings. Rather it might be placed on the high street or left outside a shop or community centre that many of the people will pass who see the actor daily. Through the object, the actor is able to influence in positive ways peoples' attitudes towards him. The image of the actor is felt in more than one place and is able to exert more influence among many more individuals (see Strathern, 1991; 1997a). In effect, his or her influence extends beyond the body to consume several different locations.

Not only are objects able to extend the influence of a person over the people that make up his or her life, but, according to two interviewees, if left in the neighbourhood are able to influence the actions of anyone who passes by. In this way it is possible to see how familiar objects are threaded through and make up the person and vice versa. Actors use particular objects to scale their influence, rather than to affect a scale change (Wagner, 1991). Any object represents an infinite number of routes which enclose a finite area, an actors neighbourhood. If a person is mugged by someone they know or in their own neighbourhood, it will be argued that they did not take necessary precautions. If they are mugged in an area other than one that they visit often, the mugging is not preventable. Rather, the mugging is explained in terms of the objects belonging to someone else, as extending their own influence over their victim. In spite of a perpetrator of crime and their victim having little to connect them, to the African-Caribbeans cited here, the crime will always be construed in personal terms, of what they do have in common rather than what they do not.

Averaging luck

Among African-Caribbeans in one Neighbourhood Watch Scheme, understanding the world depends upon the reiteration of a constant mass, the body. The body is the common denominator. It acts as a benchmark for generating social patterns, which in one way or another replicate an image of the person in many different places within touching distance. This is at odds with the following case-studies, from the Dingle, where making sense of crime depends on imagining a social structure, which is out of reach of the individual, and reducing it. Mugging there is not about the dynamic relations and irregular patterns between people, but about the relations of individuals to this abstract structure. It is the social structure that acts as a reference point for actors (Strathern, 1992). It is a structure that cannot be influenced by the actions of one person or even two or three. It is a structure that is made up of facts which represent a range of given possibilities in everyday life.

The social structure, argues interlocuters, gives off abbreviated statements which are abbreviations of the laws of nature, the fundamental bedrock of the universe. Thus, actors described how some people are simply more predisposed towards crime than others. It is in their nature. Logic dictates that crime takes place irrespective of whether a person knows the perpetrator or not. If you have never been the victim of crime or know anyone who has been the victim of a mugging, this is not to say that it will not happen. Statistics are based on crimes involving people 'you do not know'. These averages can affect whether you are attacked and will guide a person in their daily lives; whether to walk along this street or that one; whether to go out after dark; whether to go out on your own in certain parts of Liverpool.

Invariably, actors in the Dingle felt helpless as to whether they would be mugged or not. Mugging is a statistical average which they see as something which the individual can do little about. Statistics are explanatory in themselves. These are patterns which are repeatable at different scales. For example, an actor will often describe how the probability that a person will be mugged is far greater in Toxteth than in the suburbs of Liverpool. There are certain precautions that people can take to reduce the risk of mugging. For example, to walk about at night is to increase the risk of being mugged, compared to being out in the day time. However, statistic averages dictate that one in eight people will be mugged and sooner or later this will happen whatever precautions are taken. As Gerry, aged twenty eight, described:

> Society is like impossible to like imagine you know ... but it's big ... It doesn't change in size like ... and does all sorts of things and averages things out, divides them ... into categories. It's like a bank that contains all this secret knowledge about how society works ... society is straight down the line .... Regularity like produces I don't know ... time and motion ...

Laws of regularity dominate a persons perception of the world. Patterned interconnections of averages are constructed, based in laws of nature made to coincide by reference to an explicit measurement. Probability may be assessed, decided and scaled. If probability is small, and an event still occurs, this can be referred to its improbability, and its coincidence in relation to laws and numbers. Marie, aged thirty-three, illustrated this:

> Averages even things out, spread them around. I saw a friend of mine in the city centre who I had not seen in years ... like .... We were both in the same shop at the same time at the same counter ... you know .... How do you account for that? Its not about me'or her ... or the shop. It's about how it all adds up .... But some things mess it up ....

The higher the degree of improbability, the more the erratic smooths out over a greater range. If a crime happens twice, it is less likely to happen again. What does this say about the scale of unpredictability (Bachelard, 1940)? Abstract connections are generated which repeat the same patterns of ordering again and again (Strathern, 1991; 1995a). Structure averages and grades mass according to importance and size. Kate, aged thirty-five, described the way in which whole events are built up:

> Society is made up of these structures that like you cannot see ... and these structures are made up of things I can't see. I can't measure it ... it's big though ... . These structures exist for everyone and mean that we can say things like there is only a small chance that this or that will happen because you want your life to be the same ... no surprises ... where there's more crime ... babe ... well you're more likely to be the victim ... you cannot change this ... .

The risk of being mugged is determined by social structure, an invariant mass whose intrinsic properties work in an ordely fashion. Structure involves quantities and ways of measuring and weighing things. Luck, on the other hand, is used to refer to dramatic changes in patterns that defy the social structure which cannot encode this information because luck entails, explained John, aged forty, a jump that comes suddenly, from nowhere:

> Sometimes things happen which surprise you, there is no sign of where they come from, they are so small. The other day, I decided not to go to my usual shop for a paper ... I also had to get something for the wife. That shop was robbed ... when I would usually be in there. See? So a very small change ... led to me avoiding a very big thing. That's luck.

Luck does not move along a well defined path. It is a discontinuous movement, a movement of in-betweeness. Luck is about dramatic detours in scale which the average cannot measure nor account for. Luck generates patterns which disturb the regularity generated by social structure. Frank used the analogy of a video tuner in order to compare structure to a vertical patterning that is repeated over and over again:

> A television when you tune in your video makes vertical black and white lines. This is what I imagine this society is ... . Later the lines go all fuzzy like when the thieving poll tax was introduced (laughter) ... . This is like luck. It messes normal patterns up and surprises you, not always for the bad like ... you avoid your house being done over even though the house next door is robbed ... like that programme ... it disrupts the vertical!

Luck is a contextualization that establishes an association between spatially-disparate events which do not add up and therefore defy the notion of the average. It is an in-between context, a middle that displaces structural relations, a kind of temporary consumption of social mass (Cooper, 1998). Alan, a former bouncer, explained how luck is very specific to a person, but explains how general things do not add up:

I have a coin. It's been in my family for ever. Well, three generations. It can't stop events, like ... crime ... it can bring about things that I want, like money, or it will help my children and people in my family. It can even bring you money like ... well sometimes! ... . But it cannot help two people at the same time or two people who both want the same thing. It could not bring good fortune to the whole of the Dingle either. Its about ... my little world and how this world becomes bigger suddenly, or changes. It explains things that do not add up ... avoiding the police when you should be caught ... .

Lucky events are unexpected 'like suddenly getting loads of money or a really good job' and knowing that you do not have the means to get there because there is this imperceptible something which means it's possible. Rose, aged fifty, described this:

I'm unemployed. It would be great if I had a job, but it is not going to happen is it? My lad is unemployed and probably his lad will be unemployed ... . It's the same with my brother and my brother-in-law. I know what I want for myself and for them like ... . There is too much in between unemployment and having a good job, things like qualifications, knowing the right people, having money behind you ... . When I write off for a job, I go out to the post office and look for black cats, blackbirds, anything really ... . I think that they will bring me luck, land me the job without having to go through all the motions.

Rose draws attention to how the lucky individual does not have 'to go through all the motions'. Others defined luck as being in the right place at the right time, but without actually having to do anything to ensure this. Again, this is seen as not having to go through the motions, of skipping a jump. Jimmy, who had been unemployed for five years, tried to list the complex patterns that this involved, how luck may involve the same routines, but how suddenly, their importance assumes significance out of all proportion:

My neighbour is a lucky bastard. No matter what he does, he's always in the right place at the right time ... . The other night at the club, prize money totalled £1000. For £1 you can buy a ticket ... like a lottery ticket. At the end of the night, three numbers are called and a key is given to the three winners. One of these keys will open a chest in which the money collected from the tickets is put. For two months, no one has won. Last week he goes along for the first time since Christmas ... And of course he wins. How can you account for that? He got lucky just doing a normal thing and bingo, everything changes ... without doing it.

Luck often refers to relations which cannot be measured, said Karen, aged thirty. It refers to very, very small things that go unnoticed, but which when added up may cause very big unimaginative things to occur which lie outside the realm of probability. Jimmy continued:

> If I walk under a ladder, I might fall down and hurt myself. I might lose some money .... Something will go wrong that I cannot predict, that do not add up ... I avoid the ladder ... Everton win at home. That does not add up either. It's like dropping something which cannot be put exactly back together again .... Luck is like ... an invisible super-glue ... because it's going to work anyway in spite of how the world says things should be.

In the Dingle, actors identify large parts of the 'external' world which are separate from the person and whose internal composition depend on their relation to a mass structure that measures and weighs. It's 'the way things work' and enables the ordering of repeatable global/local patterns. Luck consumes the notion of a mass average. However, in the long run, luck 'does not matter' for luck refers to a personal context that emerges suddenly, that the social mass eventually overtakes. In other words, luck always runs out because contradiction is resolved by appealing to another order which as well as differentiating entities also ranks them (see also Strathern, 1997b).

Among African-Caribbeans belonging to the second Neighbourhood Watch Scheme no such idea of luck is apparent because there is nothing 'to stick it too' as one informant said. The external world is not bigger than the individual, but a constant size shaped and consumed by the body. It is the body which through the use of objects is able to extend its influence over others and not an inanimate abstract structure which instills regularity in the face of sudden and traumatic events.

Measuring the average

Points of comparison

Of the two Neighbourhood Watch Schemes, each consume and conceptualize mass in different ways. While the Dingle Neighbourhood Watch Scheme use the idea of a constant mass to measure the likelihood of crime, in Granby, among African-Caribbeans, personal relationships and tensions between kin, friends and work colleagues dominate their assessments of their susceptability to crime. It is the body which keeps its scale, like a fractal, irrespective of a magnification or a diminishing of knowledge (Strathern, 1991):

> The possibility remains that social and cultural phenomena might be collapsed along a number of axes to yield scale-retaining understandings of unsuspected elegance and force, the generalizing forms of concept and person that are neither singular nor plural [...]. Fractality, then, relates to,

converts to and reproduces the whole, something as different from a sum as it is from the individual part (Wagner, 1991: 162).

This of course undermines the taken-for-granted-assumption in Euro-American cultures that associated with the growth of the average comes a knowledge which is derived from comparison and valuation against others (see Strathern, 1997b). Furthermore, the fractal body undermines Simmel's concept of the social collective which only comes about through the suppression of individual difference and the adding and subtracting of social units:

> It is misleading to designate the level of a society that considers itself a unit and practically operates as a unit, as an average level. The 'average' would result from adding up the levels of the individuals and dividing the sum by their number. This procedure would involve a raising of the lowest individuals which actually is impossible. In reality, the level of a society is very close to that of its lowest components, since it must be possible for all to participate in it with identical valuation and effectiveness. The character of collective behaviour does not lie near the 'middle' but near the lower limits of its participants (cited in Cooper, 1987: 411).

Among residents in the Dingle, observed values cluster around their average as their knowledge of the world is derived from statistics which outweigh personal experiences. Statistics extend even to the perception of risk where, according to Beck (1992), a risk society is a stage of modernity that presumes a normative horizon of lost trust where humans are not capable of controlling the consequences of their own knowledge and risks are abstract, impersonal and unobservable (Gidden, 1991). Decision-making takes place in an environment of increasing uncertainty (Douglas, 1983,1992). Risk becomes ever likely as hitherto unacknowledged dangers become apparent. Disguised as objectified numbers and mathematical formulas, crime statistics, for example, are used by residents in the Dingle either to relate to an inflated perception of violent crime, or a low rate of certain types of crime as society randomly distributes risk, a strategy that becomes obvious in the platitude 'we are all at risk' (Furedi, 1997: 58).

Making risk impersonal

This different organization and scaling of knowledge has implications for what Giddens calls 'globalization', the mutual interlocking of presence and absence, and the interlocking of social events 'at distance' with local contextualities (1991: 21). The global becomes the 'infinitely recurring possibility of measurement – not the scales but the capacity to imagine them' (Strathern, 1995b: 179). In Granby, the global is shaped by the body and is influenced by its actions. There is no social mass which remains out of its reach. In the Dingle, the concept of mass comes to scale what respondents cannot touch like the abstract systems which, according to Luhmann, characterize the modern world. The reliance placed by actors upon a method of abstract scaling is not just a matter of trust about an independently given universe of events. The binary coding characteristic of the societal system, writes Luhnmann, possesses a highly specific form for contextualizing uncertain behaviour:

> It is only when a decision has been made on whether something is just or unjust, true or false, that the system can determine the consequences and make use of the security thus gained within the system. This is the only way it can learn, the only way it can create order, which then includes and excludes what is to continue to be possible in the system .... The progressive differentiation of binary coded function systems eliminates decision criteria external to the particular system (Luhmann, 1991: 79).

The reconstitution of the world is such that all 'disembedded' abstract systems interact with 'reembedded' contexts of actions to refigure personal relations themselves. In the Dingle, among respondents, we can see what Goffman calls civil inattention, the epitome of encounters in the anonymous city setting and characteristic of an infinite number of meetings that occur everyday. A stranger walks past another stranger on the way to work or to catch a bus. Their eyes meet and then they look away. Each actor recognizes the other as a potential acquaintance and then looks away in a movement of reassurance to a lack of hostile intent. A substratum of generalized trust brackets out most potentially disturbing happenings from the world of normal appearances (Giddens, 1991).

Yet residents in the Dingle and Granby use different models of abstraction to watch over their worlds. In the Dingle a whole host of potential and actual happenings are consigned to an impersonal social realm which is watched over, but with minimal carefulness.This uneventful character of everyday life is the result of different interpretations of normalcy which extends over contrasting notions of time and space which enframe the individuals life. In Granby, everything is watched over, so to speak. Potential tensions and conflicts are around every corner. Much attention is paid to even the smallest encounter which, in their eyes, not the systems, can have enormous repercussions. Movement is already incorporated into daily life and the unexpected, so to speak, is already anticipated such that there is no concept of luck to account for sudden improbability.

Conclusion

In the Dingle, actors attempt to assess their susceptibility to crime by referring to a social mass, conceptualized as a fixed middle ground which defines 'the average'. Averaging divides the world into categories and scales events which are out of reach of the individual who has no influence over their occurrence. In this process, good and bad luck is used to account for the probability of events which the social average defines as beyond comparison and comprehension. Luck refers to a movement, an inbetweeness, which defies the composition of an average, the 'middle' (see Cooper, 1998). By defining events as lucky or unlucky, the actor is able to look at this movement of the middle, the way things work, and the inbetweeness that cannot be resolved by appealing to an unified abstract structure (see Cooper, 1998).

While in the Dingle, respondents organize mass according to an objective, abstract criteria, among African-Caribbeans interviewed in Granby/Abercromby, large-scale knowledge that organize the social and material world in which they live is kept personal. There is no inanimate centrism which divides mass up, or social average by which to compare and contrast the incidents of crime in different places because there is no 'middle' which allows scaling and comparison. Furthermore, an attention to detail and the realization that very big problems can result from the smallest of social interactions means that jumps between different scales of knowledge can be made without having to appeal to the notion of luck. The unbelievable is already part of everyday life because it is the 'fractal' body which consumes the 'external' world and which, through the wearing of objects, is able to extend the wishes of the wearer over others who desire to cause him or her harm.

Bibliography

Bachelard, G., (1940), *The Philosophy of No. A philosophy of the new scientific mind*, New York: Orion Press

Beck, U., (1992), *Risk society. Towards a new Modernity*, London: Sage.

Coleman, C. and Moynihan, J., (1996), *Understanding crime data. Haunted by the dark figure*, Buckingham: Open University Press

Cooper, R., (1987), 'Information, Communication and Organisation: A Post-Structural Revision', in *The Journal of Mind and Behaviour*, 8 (3): 395–416.

Cooper, R., (1998), 'Assemblage Notes', in Chia, R. (ed.) *Organised Worlds: Explorations in Technology and Organisation with Robert Cooper*, London: Routledge.

Douglas, M. and Wildavasky, A., (1983), *Risk and Culture:An Essay on the Selection of Technological and Environment Dangers*, Berkeley: University of California Press

Douglas, M., (1992), *Risk and Blame:Essays in Cultural Theory*, London: Routledge

Furdei, F., (1997), *Culture of Fear. Risk-Taking and the Morality of Low Expectation*, London: Cassell.

Giddens, A., (1990), *The Consequences of Modernity*, Oxford: Polity.

Giddens, A., (1991), *Modernity and Self-Identity. Self and Society in the Late Modern Age*, Oxford: Polity

Haraway, D., (1997), Modest_Witness@ Second Millenium. London. FemaleMan_Meets_Onco Moiese, Routledge.

Luhmann, N., (1991), *Risk: A Sociological Perspective*, New York: Walter de Gruyter.

Strathern, M., (1991), *Partial Connections*. Savage, Maryland: Rowman and Littlefield.

Strathern, M., (1992), *Reproducing the Future. Essays on anthropology, kinship and the new reproductive technologies*, Manchester: Manchester University Press.

Strathern, M., (1995a), *The Relation: Issues In Complexity and Scale*, Cambridge: Pricky Pear.

Strathern, M., (1995b), 'Afterword Relocations', in Marilyn Strathern (ed.) *Shifting Contexts*. London: Routledge.

Strathern, M., (1997a), 'Cutting the Network', *Man* (N.S.) 2: 517–535.

Strathern, M., (1997b), 'Gender: division or comparison?', in Kevin Hetherington and Rolland Munro (eds) *Ideas of Difference*, Oxford: Blackwell.

Wagner, R., (1991), 'The Fractal Person', in M. Godlier and M. Strathern (eds) *Big Men and Great Men:Personifications of Power in Melanesia*, Cambridge: Cambridge University Press

Virtual masses and real minorities: imagining the nation across space and time: the case of Rhodesians on the world wide web

Doug Stuart

The plasticity of time and space offered by late twentieth century information technology has created possibilities for new forms of community and social identity. An enquiry into what is 'new' in these developments requires some critical reflection on the role of technology in the production and consumption of identities in modern societies.

This chapter critically reviews recent literature on the impact of new digital media, the Internet, and so called virtual reality on modern identities. Industrialisation has long eroded the importance of history and locality in modern collectivities. Yet, the same process has also created new networks, or webs, of interconnectivity. Colonialism was driven forward by railways and telegraphs, consumer society by motorways and cars. New telecommunication technologies are taking human interconnectivity forward at such a revolutionary pace that we are required to recast the sociological conundrum of the individual and society as rather a question of 'the net and the self' (Castells, 1996).

A particular focus of the chapter is on the question of nationalism and its relation to history and geography. This is explored in the second half of the chapter through a discussion of the use of the World Wide Web by 'Rhodesians' to foster their sense of national identity long after the passing of the Rhodesian State.

Virtuality and technology

As a relatively recent form of social organization the nation-state has frequently, if not always, presented itself as natural, with a timelessness that is deeply rooted in history. The manipulation and distortion of time and space necessary for the production of the nation-state has been evocatively described by Benedict Anderson (1983) as a form of 'imagining'. In this sense the production and consumption of nationhood has always involved a process of 'virtuality'. Images and products of nationhood, which we consume in everyday life, sustain the process through which this distortion of time and space is made possible.

Technology has played a critical part in the construction of this imagining from the beginning, as Anderson shows through his discussion on the role of the printing press in the construction of modern nationalism (1983). Very much earlier, Hobbes's (1651/1968: 81) arguments on the state, in 'Leviathan', begin with a discussion on how the 'Art of man ... can make an artificial animal, that great Leviathan, called a Common-Wealth, or State ... which is but an Artificiall Man'. Questions of artificiality and reality remain central to current debates on the role of technologies in the production of human identities.

The term 'virtual' implies on the one hand a sense of being 'not really there,' but more profoundly a temporary or imagined space to play out ideas and mirror reality. In this sense computers have 'virtual drives' meaning space created on hard disks to behave as if they were part of the built in memory system. Asserting that virtuality has always been a facet of human culture is not intended to downplay the possible significance of innovation. All technologies of virtuality brought something 'new', for example as Anderson (1983) argued, the printing press enabled the dominance of the novel as a key component in the production of modern nations. We can only grasp the potential importance of current developments from a perspective that emphasizes the creative imagination, and virtuality, inherent in human cultures.

Constructing Cyberia

The opportunities that the global mass communication system gives for individuals and groups to form networks enables them to produce and consume national cultures across historical and geographic spaces. In many accounts, the impact in particular of the Internet has been presented as so profound that spatial significances have been eradicated and that the digital revolution marks an 'end of geography'. Nothing more clearly epitomizes this claim than the notion that the Internet itself constitutes a super-geographical realm. This is the mythical sounding realm of Cyberia.

Telecommunication industries, it is argued, operate more like a nation then a tool, with an importance that transcends functional uses. For example, Mark Poster writing on Cyberdemocracy comments, 'The Internet is more like a social space than a thing so its effects are more like those of Germany than those of hammers'. (1997: 216) The argument here is that the failure to realize the importance of the Internet as a 'context' reproduces a modernist simplicity in which pre-conceived individuals are instruments of other (grand) narratives which are being read off at a level of theory.

In some recent accounts the Internet and digital media provides a technological front end for post-modernity itself. Whereas modernist science sought to represent reality accurately so it could control it, post-modern science changes reality so that our representations of it seem more real. David Holmes argues that in Virtual Reality, 'Truth is not determined as the adequacy of knowledge to reality'. (1997: 10) In other words, the simulated reality of Cyberia is itself a simulation. Indeed, Holmes claims that 'we can bring the real to us in whatever form we so desire and, in doing so, abolish the real' (1997: 11).

The reason for the collapsing of all spaces and temporalities in a 'Cyberian' utopia (literally no place) is the quality of new digital media themselves. Because they allow endless reproduction and consumption in contexts which may bear no relation to their production, Internet communications according to Holmes, become disembodied and come to have 'no more significance than a note in a bottle floating between continents' (1997: 37). In his view the meaning of such messages may fortuitously be grasped but will never become a basis for forming community or for the production of social knowledge.

Disembodiment of messages paradoxically is why the Internet is claimed as a liberatory medium undermining or dissolving old social divides.

> Participants in virtual communities can thus escape their own embodied identities and accordingly can escape any social inequalities and attitudes relating to various forms of embodiment. Race, gender or physical disability is indiscernible over the Internet. Any basis for enacting embodiment discrimination is removed, freeing access to participation and granting each participant equal status within the network. (Wilson, 1997: 149)

Predictably, however, such utopian promises serve also to disguise dis-empowerment and dis-association. The individual, far from becoming an active citizen through being able to play with identity in this way, becomes disconnected or abstracted 'from physical action and a sense of social and personal responsibility to others' (Wilson, 1997: 153).

Cyberia appears to stand for an embodiment of post-modern malaise. However, does the Internet disembody and fragment identity, and leave cultural meaning rootless and incapable of any kind of assembly or bricolage into new meanings? I use the Internet to check train times but surely I would soon stop doing so if there was no relationship between the knowledge it gives me and reality? In this sense, the Internet is very like a hammer and the transition from paper timetables to the electronic medium is relatively robust. Of course, not all Internet usage is so instrumental. If, however, people begin to use Internet technologies to perform daily household chores, such as programming the microwave, it is likely to become more so.

It is the manner in which the Internet affects the production of meanings that is less clear. The 'disembodiment' of textually based exchanges so central to these arguments is actually a function of the primitive stage of the Internet where most information was centred around various forms of e-mail. Some of the most profound and emotionally engaging ideas to be encountered are based in what is after all 'just text'. It is not that communications are limited to text that constrains their possibilities, but rather, the fact that the text is displayed in a limited way on a video screen. Charles Crook and David Webster argue convincingly that 'email exchanges are not conversational in the usual sense – the asynchronous exchange of discrete messages is not a convincing model of conversational discourse' (1997: 50) The implications of this they take to mean that e-mail based initiatives in undergraduate teaching are likely to be of limited success. Significantly, however, they conclude, 'there are other forms of mediation made possible by computers'. (1997: 51) Increasingly computers are being used to access and exchange a range of audio and visual material in increasingly sophisticated and interactive ways.

One of the problems with definitions of virtuality is that they tend to suggest a dichotomy with reality. In 'real life' some people are more able, or likely, than others to escape the confines of their gender and other social signifiers. It is not clear, therefore, that there is any quantifiable difference in the extent to which people are able to do so in 'virtual' realms, even when these are limited to text. Internet communication made with live pictures and sound may present new challenges, and possibilities, for hiding or changing gender, ethnicity and so on. It is improbable that meanings are necessarily disembodied just because they are on the Internet. Problematically, however, the embedding of cultural meanings on the Internet by means of images, music, video and all the other paraphernalia of the modern World Wide Web, cannot be taken to mean that a more meaningful basis is created for the production of communities.

The problem of opposing the 'virtual' and 'real' becomes most acute in relation to the impact of the Internet on Geography. According to Mike Holderness 'everyone who is on the Internet is in the same place' and as a result,

> Communities of communication can therefore be expected to form around common interests and not around common physical location: 'Ideography' replaces geography. (1998: 35–36)

It is not clear what is meant here by geography other than in a common-sense use to designate natural spaces. Geography like history is important because it marks sites (as history marks periods) of social struggle. In geography, we can trace the exercise of social power, the operations of class and the other constraints that govern peoples' lives.

Even in the simplistic sense, when geography equates to locality, it is not clear that the Internet replaces its importance. Most Internet usage is probably local, certainly the people I e-mail most frequently are probably people with whom I teach. We can think of the University as a community of 'Ideography' as many academics do have interests in common. However, the level of ideas seems to say little about the conditions either of work, or of the social processes operating in the geographical and historical production of the University. Constructed spaces are legitimate subjects for geography. If India is suitably studied as a geographical entity then so too are uses made of digital spaces.

The claim that geography has ended serves to encourage the study of the Internet as a separate and relatively autonomous field. The fundamental weakness of the problematic of studying telecommunications as if they are independent of all other social variables was grasped long before the Internet was fashionable object of study. Writing in New Left Review, in 1984, Jameson argued against the idea that technology was, 'in any way "the ultimately determining instance",' of either social life, or cultural production.

> ... our faulty representations of some immense communicational and computer network are themselves but a distorted figuration of something even deeper, namely the whole world system of present-day multinational capitalism (Jameson, 1984).

Jameson identifies the key issue of power as centred on that 'Leviathan' of our age, the pressures of globalization. Formulating the problem in this way usefully indicates, for example, that the essential problem of digital reproduction lies in the realm of copyright and branding. The ability to make digital copies, for example of musical works, that are identical to the original recording means that copies can become indistinguishable from the branded and expensive commercial product. This combined with a global unregulated distribution system poses massive problems for the music industry. Similarly, the erosion of traditional points of control in national boundaries poses more problems for commerce then it does for culture. More significantly if modern science is able to abolish 'reality' does this include the historical and sociological reality we inhabit, that is the globalized, market driven, class divided, unevenly developed system of capitalism that came to dominance at the end of the twentieth century?

The constitution of identities, or communities, on the Internet must be set in the frame of the problems of their formation in our time, not as independent variables relating only to Internet exchanges. Recognizing the agency of individuals participating in Internet exchanges is important, but this agency is to varying degrees also created and situated outside of the realm of the Internet. This may create problems for the use of the Internet as source for ethnographic research in itself. The same point could be made, for example, about the use of agony columns in women's magazines as guide to understanding social life.

Whatever the significance of the revolutions that have occurred in the realm of information technologies, there has been nothing to diminish C. Wright Mills' (1959) observation, that any sociology worth the name is historical sociology, and perhaps one should add 'geographical sociology'.

The troubled history of Rhodesia

Benedict Anderson's definition of nationalism as 'imagined community' was intended, in part, as a corrective to more reductionist accounts, which had failed to take sufficient account of the imaginative and creative process involved. There is nothing imaginary about nationalism, in the sense of its construction being a falsity. Anderson points out that all communities larger then those of 'face to face contact (and perhaps even these) are imagined' (Anderson, 1986: 89). This is a helpful starting point for considering Rhodesian nationalism, as it presents an extreme case of an imagined comradeship.

From its foundation, in the late nineteenth century, the Rhodesian state was a problematic construct. The handful of settlers and speculators were part of an outrageous and only quasi-legal experiment in venture capital. Although nominally part of the great expanding empire, British influence was initially limited to a charter licensing the mining activities of Cecil Rhodes's British South Africa Company. For the first decades of the extraordinarily brutal regime the government was the private company (Ranger, 1979). Its lasting legacy can be seen in the fact that the police force continued to be called the British South Africa Police until independence in 1980. The legitimization of a settler presence in the territory, a contravention of the charter, required an extraordinary media campaign and two wars, known by Zimbabweans as the First Chimurenga (Beach, 1979).

Despite the Rhodesian administration's control of state apparatus it had little success in extending its hegemony over the massive majority of the population, as evidenced by the scale and intensity of the civil war (Ranger, 1985). Not until the internal settlement of 1978, with the 'moderate' black leader Bishop Muzorewa, did it manage to co-opt even moderate black support. The bitter and prolonged war of independence, or second Chimurenga, saw large swathes of countryside where effectively the new Zimbabwean state was already in control long before final independence (Frederikse, 1982: 5).

At a level of national imagining the fact that old soldiers of the first Chimurenga lived to see the second being fought illustrates the transient nature of Rhodesian nationhood (Lan, 1985). In addition, colonial Rhodesian nationalism presents a by no means monolithic front. Only a few years before Ian Smith's declaration of Independence in 1965 Rhodesians had returned the moderate liberal Garfield Todd to power on a platform that envisaged a gradual transition to majority rule (Windrich, 1975).

It was the period known as the UDI (Unilateral Declaration of Independence) experience, when the Smith regime defied the British government and international community, which formed the focal point for the development of Rhodesian nationalism. Yet, this period lasted for only thirteen years. Furthermore the massive emigration of whites during UDI, and following independence illustrates the shallowness of the 'roots' of white Rhodesian nationalism, and put paid to the Smith regime's propaganda slogan of 'We're here to stay' (Frederikse, 1982).

This briefly is the setting against which the development of a revived Internet-based form of Rhodesian nationalism needs to be considered.

The lost tribe of Africa?

This is how one page describes the phenomena:

> INTERNET 'RESCUES' LOST TRIBE OF RHODESIANS
> Rhodesians are nothing if not resourceful. Their country might have been taken from them by politicians, but the spirit still roams the world, looking for a home. Taking advantage of late 20th century technology, they are creating a virtual country on computers around the world.
> They've logged in from more than 20 US states, from Canada's Yukon and from Port Elizabeth to Perth.
> Rhodesians are everywhere, and they've taken to the Internet with a vengeance. (H.Ref. 1)

How is it that decades after the ending of the UDI period, groups of people are elaborating a Rhodesian national identity, especially when the life stories of many reveal they were first generation settlers in the first place? Can this extreme case reveal anything about the formation of national identities? Does it provide any insights into how these processes are mediated by modern telecommunications?

The virtual imagining of Rhodesian identity appears to mirror image the reality. The historical Rhodesia consisted of minority rule (by about 3% of the population) in which the power of the state was in the hands of a group with little claim to national hegemony. Most definitions of nationhood stress that as a form of community it must contain what Anderson describes as 'deep horizontal comradeship' regardless of exploitation and inequality (1986: 89). At least members of nations need to share what Nira Yuval-Davis refers to as 'common destiny' (1997: 19). The extent to which this was true for most people in the territory of Rhodesia is highly questionable. The 'them and us' complex of nationhood in this instance was an internal division. Rhodesian nationalism was always racist.

The plasticity of time and space offered by new information technologies has created the possibility of a re-creation of Rhodesian nationalism. There is even a site that declares itself as the 'Government of Rhodesia in Exile'. The opening paragraph of the page describes the current state of Rhodesian's: 'Homeless, stateless, rudderless, brainless ...'. and urges a return to the good old days adding, 'If it cannot be done peacefully, we will return to the bush and wage a new Chimp-urenga, or Gorilla war'. (H.Ref. 2) The intended joke is meant to be offensive.

Flouting the conventions of what is perceived as politically correct 'pommie' 'yankee' or 'ozzie' society is a popular theme. Being a Rhodesian is construed as act of resistance. The 'them and us' becomes Rhodesians against the rest of the world. A site by the name of 'Rhodesians at War' encourages responses:

148   © The Editorial Board of The Sociological Review 2001

I invite you, and anybody you know who was there, to contribute, in an attempt to tell the story of how ordinary Rhodesians 'soldiered on' regardless.

I'd like your family snaps, the backyard braai, the fishing trip to the lake. Anything that says: 'We're bloody coping despite international attempts to cow us into submission!' (H.Ref. 3)

In this instance, Tom Nairn's observation that nationalism is a social neurosis the equivalent of infantilism in individuals may seem to have some truth (cited in Anderson, 1986). 'We promise to carry the Rhodesian spirit to our graves and we promise to spread the word of our 'Faith' to all we come in contact with' writes a correspondent in Australia who bemoans leaving Rhodesia in 1978 at age 16 before he had a chance to fight in the war.

I feel as though we are part of this Rhodesian global community and can help each other in the process, this adds to our purpose of existence and who knows where this might lead: to another Rhodesia where we can all be together again perhaps? (H.Ref. 4)

Sentiments like these are not easily or usefully disassociated with the concept of nationalism despite their problematic formulation.

The theme of the lost tribe has a particular significance. A popular Rhodesian myth concerned the building of Great Zimbabwe (an impressive group of ruins from which the modern country takes it name) by either the queen of Sheba or a lost tribe of Israel. Against all historical evidence Rhodesians denied that local Shona people's ancestors could ever have built such an impressive structure. In some way this established a prior claim to the land and implied that African were just as much interlopers as white settlers. The notion of being specially chosen by God and that Rhodesian independence marked a resistance to communist, atheistic, immoral and decadent Western social and political developments was a popular theme of Rhodesian propaganda. It too finds expression on the Internet in images of Rhodesia cradled in caring hands with the slogan 'God's Own Country'. (H.Ref. 5) (see Figure 1.)

As though carved out of its African context, the disembodied image of Rhodesia is both cradled and offered for consumption. In much the same way the historical Rhodesia is stripped of its brief and violent context to be both preserved and presented in a celebration of braais (barbecues), fishing and hunting tales, and old photographs.

This exemplifies Adorno's observation, 'that people never quite fully believe what they pretend to believe and therefore overdo their own beliefs' (Adorno, 1994: 122). It is the very irrationality of identifying with a nationalism that is based in the historical quirk of the few years of white rule, which interrupted the transition from colonialism to independence in Zimbabwe, that makes it attractive. Consuming the image of Rhodesia confers an identity on those

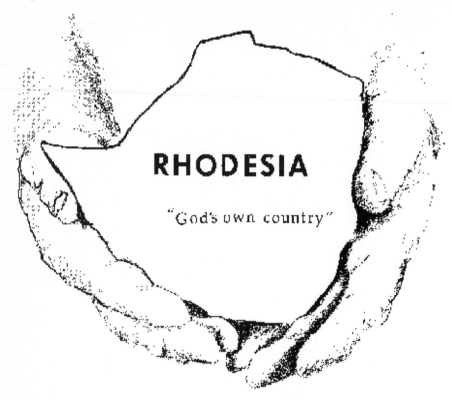

Figure 1

participating in this Mass, as one at odds with the dehumanization of modern society. 'We' are still "soldering on" against 'them' is the recurrent theme. In a poem called 'Never a (sic) Ex-Rhodie!' the author explains his grammatical error in a footnote 'The use of a instead of an is a subtle, rebellious insult to the English language and race':

> Rhodesia might be dead and buried,
> But still I am a Rhodie not a Ex-Rhodie.
> And when I pass on I will still be a Rhodie.
> Rhodesia lives within me, even though she does not exist on any map.
> (H.Ref. 6)

It could be that many ex-Rhodesians, like many other dispersed peoples, have difficulties identifying with their new homelands. Being a 'Rhodie' may be a way of dealing with the sense of alienation and smallness. The web enables the sharing of memories; the celebrating of differences and a way to scorn the sensibilities of a mass that threatens to consume this distinctiveness.

Conclusion

'Computer-mediated communication begets a vast array of virtual communities', observes Manuel Castells (1996: 22). The digital natures of these communications, which exactly reproduce content, allow expression in contexts entirely different to those of the 'original' (whatever that now means). The 'derealization' of space and self implied resembles, and perhaps epitomizes, the description of the post-modern subject as having 'lost its traditional form of closed interiority encapsulated in a boundary' (Kirby, 1996: 51). As Kirby's discussion of Jameson's conception of post-modernity emphasizes, the challenge to 'boundaries', both spatial and sociological, is a complex process: 'Boundaries of all kinds are on the one hand highly emphasised and deemed necessary, but on the other problematized and metaphorized' (1996: 51). There is, therefore, a contradiction in the community-forming characteristic of informational societies. Castells continues: 'Yet the distinctive social and political trend of the 1990s is the construction of social action and politics around primary identities'. Such politics of identity may be based on notions of historical or geographic rootedness and often expresses a 'newly built-in anxious search for meaning and spirituality' (1996: 22).

The net that we cast, and in which we are caught, is spun of the complex fabric of late twentieth century social life. The search for connectedness arises from the dispersal, fragmentation and alienation of late industrial societies. The technology of the Internet provides a means for imagining new commonalties of existence, including those related to nationalist projects. The potentiality of the Internet for enabling the production of meaningful communities rests on the need of dispersed peoples for political, ideological and spiritual identity. Such need is certainly shaped by communicative acts but may not be entirely reliant on them.

In this brief resumé of the considerable and rapidly growing 'virtual Rhodesia', plasticity and invention in the uses of the Internet are evident, rather than abstraction and disembodying. These pages contain a rich imagery of photographs, anthems, waving flags, recipes, reminiscences, novels, noticeboards, virtual embassies and more. The 'primary identity' they evoke is based in creative play with historical and geographical realities. The meanings attributed to being a 'Rhodesian' or even 'never a ex-Rhodie' requires an inventive plasticity, a stretching of Geography on the Internet rather then its rejection. Relations of space and time are considerably distorted in these accounts. However, this is a refraction, an extension and elaboration of the past and locale, not its abolition.

The meaning and significance of communities on the Internet requires a mapping process. A process that begins with the recognition of the continuing importance of geographical realities in social life, and the recognition that these geographical realities were always virtual.

References

Adorno, T., (1994), *The Stars Down to Earth and Other Essays on the Irrational in Culture*, Routledge, London.

Anderson, B., (1983), *Imagined Communities: Reflections on the Origin and Spread of Nationalism*, Verso, London.

Anderson, B., (1986), The Cultural Roots of Nationalism, in Donald, J. and Hall, S. (eds), *Politics and Ideology*, Open University Press, Milton Keynes.

Beach, D.N., (1979), 'Chimurenga': The Shona Rising of 1896–97', *Journal of African History*, vol. 20 no. 3, 395–420.

Castells, M., (1996), *The Information Age: Economy, Society and Culture Volume 1: The Rise of the Network Society*, Blackwell, Oxford.

Crook, C. and Webster, D.S., (1997), 'Designing for informal undergraduate computer mediated communication', in Martin, J. and Beetham, H., *CTI Active Learning*, No. 7 December 1997, 'Teaching in the Twenty-First Century'.

Elliott, P., (1986), 'Intellectuals, the 'information society' and the disappearance of the public sphere', in Collins, R. and Curran, J. (eds), *Media Culture and Society: A Critical Reader*, Sage, London.

Frederikse, J., (1982), *None But Ourselves: Masses Vs. The Media in the Making of Zimbabwe*, Raven, Johannesburg.

Hobbes, T., (1651/1968), *Leviathan*, Penguin, Harmondsworth.

Holderness, M., (1998), 'Who are the world's information poor?', in Loader, D., *Cyberspace Divide: Equality, Agency, Policy in the Information Society*, Routledge, London.

Holmes, D., (1997), 'Virtual Identity: Communities of Broadcast, Communities of Interactivity', in Holmes, D. (ed.), *Virtual Politics: Identity and Community in Cyberspace*, Sage, London.

H.Ref. 1: Rhodesian Association of Western Australia, *Bundu Times* December 1995/January 1996. http://www.rhodesia.com/oz wa/b12 all.html#rww.

H.Ref. 2: *Welcome to the new web site of the Rhodesian Government in exile!* http://www.geocities.com/CapitolHill/Lobby/9465/index.html

H.Ref. 3: *Rhodesians At War*. http://members.iinet.net.au/~henshaw/.

H.Ref. 4: Rhodesian Association of Western Australia, *Bundu Times* December 1995/January 1996: Our Kind of People, RHODESIANS IN THE 90s http://www.rhodesia.com/oz wa/gregory.html

H.Ref. 5: 'The *Rhodie' Ontario Association*. http://www.accessv.com/~docd/page3.html.

H.Ref. 6: *Never a Ex-Rhodie!* http://www.rhodesia.com/docs/poems/glover/never.htm

Jameson, F., (1984), 'Postmodernism, or the cultural logic of late capitalism', *New Left Review*, 146: 79.

Kirby, Kathleen M., (1996), 'Re: Mapping Subjectivity. Cartographic Vision and the Limits of Politics, in N. Duncan (ed.), *Body Space: Destabilizing Geographies of Gender and Sexuality*, London, Routledge

Lan, D., (1985), *Guns and Rain: Guerillas and Spirit Mediums in Zimbabwe*, James Currey, London.

Mills, C. Wright (1959), *The Sociological Imagination*, Oxford University Press, New York.

Poster, M., (1997), 'Cyberdemocracy: The Internet and the Public Sphere', in Holmes, D. (ed.), *Virtual Politics: Identity and Community in Cyberspace*, Sage, London.

Ranger, T., (1979), *Revolt in Southern Rhodesia 1896–7*, Heineman, London.

Ranger, T., (1985), *Peasant Consciousness and Guerrilla War in Zimbabwe*, James Currey, London.

Wilson, M., (1997), 'Community in the Abstract: A Political and Ethical Dilemma', in Holmes, D. (ed.), *Virtual Politics: Identity and Community in Cyberspace*, Sage, London.

Windrich, E., (1975), *The Rhodesian Problem: A Documentary Record 1923–73*, Routledge and Kegan Paul, London.

Yuval-Davis, N., (1997), *Gender and Nation*, Sage, London.

Part 3: Mass and Persons

Introduction to Part 3

Too often a key concept rocks us between the 'many' and the 'one', between individuals and society, between members and group, between persons and their community. Mass is no exception. Social theory slips and slides between talking about an inchoate mass of sheer numbers and theorizing a hegemony of the same.

In looking at materials, the chapters in this third and final section find a tension which helps keep analysis *between* the individual and the social. Asking what people are *doing* with their materials, they set out from a view of the relations between persons and mass that has so far been muted: the *instrumental* account in which persons 'grow' and manipulate mass for effect. It is clear, however, in what follows that these manipulations affect 'subjects' as much as 'objects'.

Persons are masses too. We participate in social life through the masses of tissue that constitute our bodies and the wide range of material extensions available to us. Being 'mass' not only gives us the power to exercise others, mass *works* us. At the same time mass makes us vulnerable, because not every body is consumable. Persons can be consumed only if they are 'prepared' properly.

The four chapters in this section take this matter of consumability as their point of departure. The authors are all aware that it is wrong to treat people as things. If one is showing persons the respect they properly deserve – as *human* persons – one should refrain from eating them alive, from speaking for them without listening properly and from staring at them as if they were goods on display.

Joanna Latimer's theme is regeneration and her chapter puts into question modern notions of improvement. After noticing how 'values' are no longer left to guide, but are themselves becoming *pressed* into service, she surveys the social scientific literature on consumption. She finds attention tilted toward the consumption of 'things' and away from the consumption of persons. Taking as its motif the wasting disease of 'consumption' (tuberculosis), her analysis goes on initially to redress this imbalance by addressing the means by which persons 'body forth' their relations. In so doing, she makes the crucial point that it is by rendering ourselves 'consumable' by others that we gain cultural membership.

Here the killing of an Etoro baby because it is plump and well, is contrasted with employees who make themselves unconsumable in today's 'culture of enhancement' by complaining of change and harking back to tradition. Her central concern, however, is with a peculiar consonance of critical discourse and late-capitalist ideology. From the left comes the view that we are de-centred and flexible; from the right comes the order that we become de-centred and flexible. Outlining a materialist view of passion and creativity, Latimer challenges this consonance and highlights how the contemporary *call* to quality incites people into making themselves consumable.

Nick Lee compares a novelist's account of a prison visit with a photographer's front cover of *Vogue* magazine in order to explore relations between essence and appearance and articulacy and visibility. He argues that some forms of identity politics discourage the consumption of persons by appearances and encourage a deeper 'reading' of persons. We should not judge books by their covers, or persons by the semblance of their mass.

The ambivalence over essentialism that can be found in late twentieth century critical discourse arises from this competition between deep reading and shallow stereotyping. For many years commentators have taken the view that the possibility of *dignity* rests on the abandonment of the visual register and the promotion of a more literate consumption of persons, which takes time, conversation and reflection. Meanwhile, as more literate commentators wrangle over the merits and demerits of this 'strategic essentialism', glamour is being performed and created through the denial of essence and through the spirit that is offered by visual registers.

Taking up themes of cannibalism and vampirism, **Cristina Pallí Monguilod** sharpens the topic of dangerous representations in a reflection on her own consumption practices in two ethnographic studies, one of Roma (the 'gypsy' community) and one of bio-tech scientists. Ethnography involves spending time with persons so as to take something away. The ethnographer then eats this something-that-belongs-to-others publicly, and undergoes a transformation in the eyes of her or his peers. If there is something disturbing about her imagery here, how profound the disturbance becomes when she points out that social scientists eat people in order to be *fair*.

Marginalized groups, like the Roma, apparently need representation, and the cannibalism of social science acts as a form of hospitality. At least two alternatives to this view were developed in the late twentieth century. If we view social science as a kind of fiction, for example, we can retreat from the ethical implications of representation. On the other hand, we might seek to cleanse our representational/ consumption practices by insisting on a radical particular-ism, trying our best to turn away from the path of generalization. The chapter reminds us that such examples of straight thinking are unlikely to reduce the ethical ambiguities of practice.

A number of the book's earlier themes are recapitulated in **Robert Grafton Small**'s endpiece, which cuts and pastes its collage of anecdotal examples, minor marginalia and found objects into an auto-consumption of mass. For example, a pair of see-through knickers reminds the reader that a demand for *transparency* is growing alongside the consumption of mass. An irony not lost on his Glaswegian informants, one of whom remarks: 'If I dress as I like, why am I holding myself accountable and to whom?'

Drawing on the landscapes of twentieth century biography and ethnography, Europe is imagined as a vast land mass of 'borders' whose geometries are equally insubstantial, fragmentary and shiftless – an abyss of absence where we no longer are and its writers never have been. Moving impressionistically, back and forth between different moods of consumption, the reader trips and slips across the border-lines, through the void of Libeskind's Berlin, the Piet-a-terre of Mondrian, the blues of R.S. Thomas and Kitaj's diastrophic 'cult of the fragment'. This is a journey of arrivals that satisfyingly critiques the vaulting ambition of projects like that of understanding a consumption of mass.

All-consuming passions: materials and subjectivity in the age of enhancement

Joanna Latimer

Power, passion
What-are-we goin' to do?
Union,
Union,
Union City Blue.
   (Blondie, 1979)

Introduction

This chapter explores the problem of *consumability*, not of nature, but of persons. Social beings do not just consume goods and bads in the performance of identity. To be social, persons figure and refigure themselves – and each other – as 'cultural materials', as available for consumption. But not anything goes. What makes up consumability is culturally specific, and, as will be seen, ambiguous. In what follows I show how this consumability of persons helps accomplish a culture of enhancement.

Post-enterprise societies are characterised by what Strathern (1995) ironically refers to as a 'culture of enhancement'. In enterprise societies, everyday life can be understood as interpellated by an economics-based model of social action: the call for greater productivity simply meant more. In contrast to traditional practices based on *regeneration*, a culture of enhancement reflects how contemporary social life has become enmeshed within practices of *reformation*. Yet enhancement is not quite the 'progress' of modernization. Unlike Beck's (2000: 18–19) reflexive modernization, which he defines as being driven by the 'dynamic power of technological and economic innovation', enhancement is a cultural process in which the values of society are themselves becoming harnessed.[1] Increasingly, purposiveness is connected to augmenting meaning and adding value (of selves, property, work and community.) The turn is from making more in terms of quantity, to a morality deriving from making more in terms of *quality*.

The demand created by a culture of enhancement goes to the heart of the social: mimesis, repetition and reproduction. These alone cannot capture how the social goes along. For the sake of the future, it is no longer enough to circulate what has gone before. For example, Strathern (1991: 39), drawing on Haraway, discusses how the cyborg helps us to understand that the 'politics of a postscientific world must talk not of a rebirth, producing something equal to the producer, but of regeneration, that is extension'. Consumability is thus connected to a promise of improvement, but not in ways that take persons beyond the pale.

This emergent project constitutes a reversal of the iron cage: by putting values back in it deploys what merely bureaucratic rationalities have drained out. For Weber, to have a 'calling' is precisely not to be a bureaucrat; it is 'to have passion as well as an ability to calculate consequences' (Walker, 1993: 148). So that the very characteristics of persons with a calling, which Weber considered so essential to the making up of the social and political, are incited and deployed within the culture of enhancement. In a framing of things which puts Dean Swift's motto 'Not more, different!' into quick reversal, improvement must stay within boundaries envisaged and governed by a *process* of enhancement. By deploying regeneration (at the very moment of denying it) the new processes of enhancement are much harder to resist.

The rest of the paper focuses upon this tricky space, the space between stability and change. To explore this space I move between the motifs of 'consuming passions' and 'consumability'. This movement in focus allows aspects of the consumability of persons and its relationship to the culture of enhancement to come into view. Indeed, by examining the problematic of passion, power and creativity, the analysis suggests that only some subjectivities and objectivities will do. The aim is to show how consumability depends upon the *jointing* of performances of particular kinds of subjectivities and 'objectivities' (cf. Latimer, 1999; Latimer and Lee, 1999.)[2]

The chapter begins by re-calling the (usually invisible) co-constituting nature of emotion, subjectivity and materiality (cf Adam, 1998). I then go on to review some of the ways in which theories of consumption reproduce notions of the subject/object, social/material divide. Drawing on the work of Munro and Strathern, the analysis suggests that, as they consume, social beings are in 'extension': that is people materialize socio-cultural relations to perform themselves *as* social. However, consumability is not settled one way. It is not that subjects, or anything else, become 'fluid'. Rather, consumability elicits 'motility' (Munro, 1996b, 260–262; 1999). In a culture of enhancement the motility is between, one moment, regeneration (showing that you know what has gone before) and the next, valorizing 'the new', in the form of creative change.

Passion

Passion confounds the usual divisions, between reason and emotion, (non-human) nature and (human) culture, spirit and body, emotion and mind, heaven and earth, self and others.

159

Lovers and madmen have such seething brains,
Such shaping fantasies, that apprehend
More than cool reason ever comprehends.
The lunatic, the lover and the poet,
Are of Imagination all compact:
One sees more devils than vast hell can hold,
That is the madmen, the lover, all as frantic
Sees Helen's beauty in a brow of Egypt:
The poet's in a fine frenzy rolling,
Doth glance from heaven to earth, from earth to heaven,
And as imagination bodies forth
The form of things unknown, the poet's pen
Turns them to shapes and gives to airy nothing
A local habitation and a name.

(A Midsummers Night's Dream, emphasis added)

Passion is associated with creativity, a chiasmic crossing of mind and body. Lovers, madmen and poets share something in common: imagination. Although they are all consumed by a passion their effects are very different. Critically, imagination, apprehends what 'cool reason cannot comprehend' and brings into being what has *not* gone before. So passionate people – lovers, madmen and poets – are alike in that their passion kindles their imagination, but they differ in that it is the poet who brings forth something into being which is in a consumable form for others. It is the poet who alone travels between heaven and earth, and 'bodies forth' the form of things unknown, giving 'to airy nothing a local habitation and a name'. And it is this consumability that makes something creative, rather than merely personal, recreational or procreative. As Shakespeare says, it is *the poet's pen* which makes the difference.

Still, not anything goes. Poems too materialize relations: they circulate *who* has gone before, even where they transgress or deviate from traditional forms to innovate and enhance. So, at the same time as the poet performs his or her distinction, she or he must make her poems in a consumable form by others. Consumabilty rests then in part on *how* the poem materializes, and this in turn rests upon the poet's discipline: as the poet works the language, the language and the writing, as materials of extension, exercise and work the poet (cf. Foucault, 1979; Strathern, 1991).

Consumption

Much of the literature on consumption has little to say on either passion or creativity. It is mainly concerned with the issue of lifestyle and taste, in terms of how both are socially constructed. Although persons certainly reproduce 'distinction' (Bourdieu, 1984) in terms of class and status, studies increasingly explore lifestyle practices in terms of leisure activities, such as sports, music, shopping, style, and fashion.

The focus is on recreation – what is being re-created is self, and with this more 'alternative' identities. Here, materiality emerges not for itself, but as significant in terms of the *expressive* and *symbolic* aspects of social life. In the circulation of goods and bads, persons participate, to perform themselves, however momentarily, as a part of some fashionable (and therefore temporary) domain of culture. But the implication is that what is being consumed is the 'freedom' to choose who you are: the turn to consumption seems to celebrate the liberation from the oppression of convention and tradition. Working a particular complicity between consumption practices and the body, it is *as if* almost anything goes.

But there is surely something contrived here about such performances of identity? On the one hand, the body is being reconstituted by the auto-erotic, egocentric rituals of adornment, pampering, mass-aging, piercing, and exercising, as the new altar of worship in the worshipping mass of individualism and choice. On the other, there is little attention to the visceral, or for that matter embodied *relations*. All too quickly the body loses its materiality and immanence, and re-emerges as a site of representation in the endless play of signs. This is circulation without regeneration. It is not that we are what we desire. *Desire* gets left out of the picture, desire is reduced to taste, or to a sign. Nor is it that 'I consume because of what I am'. Rather, it is a matter of 'I consume therefore I am'.

Alongside these ideas that consumption helps make up self-identities are understandings that consumption practices also make up social spaces. Museums, shopping malls and Stonehenge are regarded as *spaces of consumption*.

Examining the shopping mall as a site of consumption, Langman (1992) for example, asserts that self-hood and subjectivity are appropriated by the commodification process and trapped in the 'neon cage' of mall-based seeing and being seen. For Langman (1992: 66), shopping for subjectivity is compelling to selves who are 'enfeebled', seeking 'more and more mall-based empowerment and recognition'. Feelings, of gratification at being seen, are mass produced through the hegemony of the mall.

The implication is that a commodification of lifestyle is possible because of a human need for identity, experienced and confirmed by *recognition* from Others. In Langman's view, the shoppers are exploitable *because* they are located in the necessity of appearing, in a revealing of self-identity, as a function of their post-modern condition: rootlessness and role-lessness. Shopping for visibility substitutes for the iron cage of bureaucratic rationalities to trap subjects and delimit their freedom.

Overall, these subjects appear to be more acted upon than acting: they interact, but as little more than cultural dopes. And *what* acts upon them is not the stuff that they consume, but a set of disembodied abstractions. Treating consumption as *displays* of self-identity misses something. While studies like

161

Langman's help us to see the negative effects of globalisation in action, the lack of detail misses how consumption is also (re)productive of *social relations*, that is how it is also socially (de)constructing.

Consumption as cultural praxis

Consuming goods and bads are practices: they involve interactions, between materials and people and across time and space. The ways in which people and things interact have profound implications for social relations. The kinds of social relations (re)produced will be very specific to how activities of consumption are conducted. The spaces of consumption then are not just made up by the conspirators of fashion, stalking the world, to trick the consumer with a semiotic seduction into the hegemony of the mall. As people consume, they also (re)make the world.

The world then that consumption practices make up, depends upon *how* they are conducted. For example, Hetherington (1992), in his examination of Stonehenge as a site of consumption, attends to how at the moment of consumption there is also a moment of production, the production and reproduction of the significance of the goods to be consumed.

Nor are these spaces just made up of practices of consumption. Rather, they are made up of, and by, practices of division (see also Munro, 1997). This work of distinction has considerable political effect. For example, Hetherington makes explicit how the world that consumption practices (re)make depends upon the making up of the significance of the object which is being consumed: its meaning emerges in the practices which consume it. Hetherington shows how the object of consumption (Stonehenge), rather than being a part of a happy-go-lucky, 'ludic, post-modern game', can be considered as heterotopic, figured and refigured through people's symbolic and discursive practices as they perform their belonging to one kind of group rather than another. So that what is being consumed (Stonehenge) takes on multiple forms, each having serious political associations. These include 'festival', expressive of the freedom to create a lifestyle, as well as 'heritage', as the desire for continuity and control through enclosure. Thus Hetherington implicitly points to how there is a relation between the significance attributed to the object of consumption and the subjects doing the consuming: goods do not simply travel, they are not versions of Latour's (1987) immutable mobiles, rather goods are made up by the practices which consume them. Consumption practices thus emerge as creative acts, conditioned by and helping to accomplish particular and normative notions of social order.

As such, practices of division also entail matters of inclusion, exclusion and disposal (Munro, 1992; Latimer, 1997; Strathern, 1996.) People, or the parts they perform, also form materials for consumption. We are used to thinking about this in terms of the theatre when actors explicitly embody or represent socio-cultural relations. But we also consume people, through their cultural performance (cf Munro, 1999). Thus, a focus on the consumption and circulation of cultural goods highlights the contemporary anxiety over visibility: visibility is the new substance of human existence. This is best understood in terms of Strathern's idea of extension.

Extension

Drawing on ethnographic material relating to her work in Melanesia, Strathern (1991, 1995) develops the possibility for the performance of social being as extension. The materials of extension 'body forth', or in-corporate, relations of significance to the culture concerned (see Strathern, 1995, drawing on Fortes). For example, Strathern (1991) suggests that through the traditional way of composing a head dress, worn in a ritual dance, the bearer performs his participation and, thereby, his relatedness: the head dress is made up of tokens given to him by others and signifies his participation in relations. And, it is only through such participation that he exists as a social being.

Strathern is stressing the importance of performance *as* participation: it is by magnifying relations, bodied forth in materials or evoked through particular practices, that identity is composed and, critically, displayed. In this particular case the person who is to wear the head dress does not make it up: his identity is incorporated in a head dress which is made up by, and of, others. Indeed in making up his own display of identity, some of the efficacy attached to him would be lost. Made up by the head-dress of others he bodies forth his relatedness, and thereby his efficacy.

Thus through processes of prosthetic extension, participants' practices help make their relations, or those of others, visible as objects *of a certain value*. To *classify* themselves, and each other, participants perform their relations through attaching and detaching themselves from cultural materials, such as clothes and particular styles of food (cf Munro, 1995). Critically, that these materials are considered actually as parts of persons, is made explicit in a Melanesian context: it is *parts* of persons, bodied forth in materials, which are circulated in the making up of significance. As Strathern puts it (1991: 118): '... it is persons who extend persons'. I should add here that processes of extension are also characterized by moments of severance. Indeed, because people and things are all of the same material, it is only through the creative act of severance (Strathern, 1991: 118), that one person is visible as an extended part of another. Through this the 'partial connections' between persons come into view, locating differences in identity.

Critically, then, the efficacy of persons depends upon their consumability. To render self consumable, subjects deploy materials of extension which are suitable to the culture that they occupy. Being consumable is to a certain extent dependent upon persons performing 'parts' which are circulatable, in other domains and in the domains of others. The question is now: how to *dispose* of those relations in ways that magnify self.

Consumability

The question of disposal is a vexed one. Extending an idea of Munro's (1992, 1995), Strathern (1999) presses how efficacy rests upon persons materializing their social relations in *consumable* form. Speaking of Etoro men, Strathern states that they were very conscious of keeping the capacity for producing significance, their creativity, alive, but that the capacity to produce significance had to be consumed by others to be realized. Elaborating this idea, Strathern goes on to speak of a strong sense of the social as being 'where people deliberately put themselves into positions of extracting – draining away – meanings from one another'. (p. 47) Indeed a person's *creativity* (the flow of the life force) is only sustained by the fact that there were other persons willing to *consume* it.

Where persons embody blockages, or short circuits, to the flow there are problems: they are not in a consumable form so that their creativity is not sustained because others cannot extract meaning from them. There is then a need to 'dispose' (Munro, 1992) of the meaning they embody. So that disposal becomes as much a cultural demand as consumption. For example, Strathern cannot dispose of the image of a new born Etoro baby being suffocated by having its nose pressed to the earth. The person doing the pressing is the baby's mother. Strathern suggests that while she might find it only tragic if circumstances (such as poverty, illegitimacy, disability) led to the mercy killing of a puny child, getting rid of one in good health seems wanton. She cannot get rid of the image because of the reason – 'its meaning':

> ... the fat baby born to the Etoro mother is not healthy, or at least not for others. Such children are witch-children, identified by a special name ... they were evidently witch-children precisely because they were fat. (p. 45)

The massivity of the child is problematic because it is an image of an excess of creativity which is not in a consumable form by others. Persons and their bodies, are images of giving and receiving, and the massivity of the body takes on its significance as an image of this flow. The baby's fatness is an image of a blockage to the flow of the life force, and this is why it is a witch: witches cannot, like other men and women, bestow life force in others, rather they feed on others and so accumulate substance.

The amassing of substance on the body signifies that the baby is not in circulation. The outside body is at once 'an aesthetic medium for the effect that persons had on one another and the enactment of that effect'. (p. 51) The one who registered the effect, received the message, was the *consumer* of the body. A fat body was an image of where this relation had gone wrong. The fat baby is an image of excess, of the accumulation of too much substance, it must be a witch, and witches cannot dispose of their life force: the life force in the baby is not available for consumption by others, thus it must be disposed of by other means.

The baby's death is consuming for Strathern, she cannot dispose of it, partly perhaps because she thinks of the baby as an individual: the baby is significant and therefore consumable, as the embodiment of a 'person' in a discrete and independent form. In contrast, for the Etoro, the baby embodies a blockage to the flow of social relations.

For the Etoro, the consumability of persons is thus deeply connected to circulation, to the circulation of the life force as the substance that bodies forth social relations. But a persons *creativity* (the flow of the life force) is sustained only by the fact that other persons are willing to *consume* it. Consumability depends upon persons bodying forth, either in extension or by their own bodies, social relations of value. They do this by circulating what is recognizable: materials of worth to the culture they occupy. The significance of these materials, like the baby's body, are prefigured.

Enhancement

Consumability appears at first to be very different in Euro-American contexts. Within contemporary social theorising, culture is characterized by detraditionalization and the crisis of identity. For example, according to Giddens (1991), identities have to be reflexively managed within post-traditional cultures. Relations are not prefigured in ways which provide a map for conduct. The effect, we are told, is fluidity. Fluid identities are supposedly managed through the consumption of goods, not as displays of relations, but of distinction. My earlier discussion on the literature concerned with the consumption and circulation of cultural goods highlights this as a contemporary anxiety over visibility: visibility is the substance of human existence. But we could understand this effect differently.

Euro-Americans draw upon materials of worth to the culture they occupy to reveal and make explicit their distinction. Others consume these distinctions in the making up of their identities. In late modernity, it is not just goods that have to be produced, managed, circulated and consumed, but subjectivities. Sometimes, within democratic, enterprising societies consumability should not be (visibly at least) connected to being 'in' relations. Rather, it seems that consumability is increasingly dependent upon not performing embeddedness, but *individuality*. To *classify* themselves, and each other, participants perform their identities through attaching and detaching themselves from cultural materials, such as cars. However, as discussed above, this is to draw attention to their distinctiveness, their individuality, not their connectedness. Indeed, distinction performed through connectedness might smack of elitism and nepotism – it is important that you *own* your car.

Materials of extension, in contrast, are increasingly mass produced and increasingly available to the point of surfeit: these materials are so *non-human* that they cannot be thought of in terms of circulating persons, not even their parts. This is important: you can own cars, while owning persons would be deeply problematic.

So that within Euro-American contexts, it definitely does not appear to be *parts* of persons, bodied forth in materials, which are circulated, and consumed by others, in the making up of significance. This would be to detract from significance, the significance of the individual as a discrete, self-invented subject. Re-membering goods is to radically reinvent Euro-American culture. But to leave analysis there would be to miss a further key point.

The mass of subjects are also massaged: appearance of fluid identities have also become the fix of very specific, very contemporary modes of organizing. Flexible, responsive and mobile masses are being elicited by modern industries and institutions, sure. To put up a fight and insist on precedent or tradition, is to complain, and to complain is to risk rejection. But a culture of enhancement fixes the elicitation in very particular ways. Clearly not anything goes – to avoid the Etoro baby's fate, persons need to body forth relations of value in consumable form. But in a culture of enhancement, significance is connected to accountability (Munro, 1996a; Strathern, 2000). And for Strathern:

> ... *the financial and the moral meet* in one turn of the century rendering of accountability..Only certain social practices take a form which will convince, ones which will persuade those to whom accountability is to be rendered..Only certain operations will count (page 1–2, emphasis added).

Consumability then is connected to a jointing, of the financial and the moral. While, as Strathern states, '*only certain social practices* take a form which will convince', and '... *Only certain operations will count*', I want to suggest that the registers across which quality is assessed are multiple, and frequently contradictory, and not necessarily explicit. There are therefore possibilities for disparity, incongruity, and ambiguity. Indeed, it is not just that significance is never settled, nor is it just that significance must be continuously accomplished, although both these are characteristics of post-enterprise societies. Rather, it is that what may seem appropriate at one moment, may need to be reversed the next.

Within this framing of things, there is a need for persons to body forth innovation and change, but not in ways which are so extreme or excessive that they destabilize. Indeed, innovation and change are emerging as aspects of cultural performance which reproduce stability, *because* they characterize contemporary social life. The call then is for creative and productive subjects. But traditionally, creative subjects are consumed, passionately, by what they do. This can make them excessive, a loose cannon, asocial. A good example is Luzhin, Nabokov's chess playing hero in *The Defense*. Nabokov creates a figure consumed by a fatal passion, for chess. His passion is a way of life, which while it helps him transcend the social life that has so damaged him, it also makes him virtually *asocial*. Passion represents then both a crucial and a tricky space, because it mixes worlds that should be held apart, that of the mind, productivity, the life force and the emotions.

All-consuming passion

As discussed earlier the relationship between creativity and passion is well rehearsed in Euro-American writing. Indeed, passion is often the cultural material for the performance of creativity.[3] But passion and creativity are also connected to the depletion of substance. For example, the Romantic figures of the early nineteenth century are often figured in the act of creation as consumed *by* passion, love or tuberculosis. The assumption is that their all-consuming passion makes them neglect their material and social status, leaving them poor and susceptible to diseases such as TB. Indeed, TB itself was referred to metaphorically as 'the consumption', and sufferers, like Chopin, were referred to as consumptives.

As Romantic subjects are consumed by passion, their expenditure results in their bodies being dissipated, exhausted, depleted, or burnt up. As the body burns up or spits blood, there is a simultaneous divinity. Man is at his most sublime, but also at his most self destructive, in his acts of creation. Thus, creativity, stemming from a passion which depletes substance, puts subjects in an ambivalent relation to industrialized societies which emphasize productivity.

Byatt (1990) keeps in play these potential spaces of passion and productivity to reinvigorate their contemporary importance. Her heroine, Cristabel, is a late nineteenth century feminist attempting to live an independent and creative life as a poet. She had chosen a way, 'a life of the mind' (p. 187.) Her passion is for literature and for a devout, disciplined and ordered life which feeds the spirit and kindles the imagination. Yet this passionate life becomes threatened by another kind of passion:

> ... flame licked, flame enfolded, flame looped veins – burned up and utterly consumed ... I cannot let you burn me up. I cannot. I should go up – not in the orderly peace of my beloved hearth here – with its miniature caverns of delight, its hot temporary jewel-gardens with their palisadoes and promontories – no – I shall go up – like straw on a dry day – a rushing wind – a tremor on the air – a smell of burning – a blown smoke – and a deal of white fine powder that holds its spillikin shape only an infinitesimal moment and then is random (p. 194–195)

At her hearth, as desire runs through her blood, Cristabel is in extension, an assemblage of the human and the non-human: associated on the one hand with stability and on the other with the caverns of delight which kindle imagination.

Cristabel evokes an image of the consummation of her and her lover's passion as consuming her. Her lover is the most famous Victorian naturalist-poet of his day. He is also married. She sees a consummation of this kind of passion as an act of destruction, not creation, and contrasts the possibilities with her current life, a life ordered to enrich the imagination. The possibility of consummation is not regenerative: she feels that if she allows his passion, its consummation, she will be burned up and utterly consumed. For Cristabel, being consumed by her and her lover's passion will bring forth her *inchoateness:* she will be returned to a formless mass. All her work to define herself as a distinctive and creative being will be lost. And of course she is playing on the dilemma here: as her lover is himself married their union can never be made respectable, and her reputation as well as her art will be destroyed.

The irony is that her lover loves her for her creativity, materialized in her poetry and her beautiful life, yet she sees in submission to that love a loss of her creativity *and* her social status. She materializes that loss in the dematerialization of her self. And, as dematerialized, she will no longer be consumable. Thus there is a transformation of subjectivity in relation to the effects not of what is being consumed, but in what is doing the consuming. A passionate life, tempered by the discipline of writing, and dedicated to the creation of poems is not all-consuming – it is *regenerative.*

To be consumed by her passion for poetry holds Cristabel in consumable form. In contrast, under particular conditions, being consumed by a 'romantic' passion can also be figured as degenerative, and is likely to render the figure of self inchoate. This remember is the post-Romantic era, the Protestant ethic is flourishing. Cristabel's life and poems body forth a particular *conceptual* relationship: the relationship she bodies forth is between discipline, the elevation of the spirit and creativity. Her life helps to enhance herself and, where that life's project is materialized in her poems, the world. Indeed, the image of her life to date is one of creativity and enrichment, evoked by her reference to the jewel-gardens and caverns of delight of her beloved hearth. In an age of invention and enterprise, Cristabel's creativity is not out of line. But at the same time as she makes something new (her independent life, her poems), Cristabel also regenerates social relations: her celibate life bodies forth her conformance and displays her embeddedness in certain relations of value. Indeed she is suggesting that without that life she could not be creative. Rather, her creativity depends upon it. Her individuality is thus in a consumable form. She and her poetry both circulate the domains of others and circulate in the domains of others. So that while she is different from most women, she is not so different that her way of life threatens stability. In contrast, being consumed by romantic passion embeds her in the wrong kinds of relations and is potentially degenerative: the consummation of her sexual passion threatens to put her beyond the pale because it bodies forth relations which are devalued by the culture she occupies.

Disposal

Cristabel does lets herself be taken by her lover. Desire, despite prevarication, proves too much:

He felt her face, hard and wet on his shoulder, and imagined the living skull, the living bone, fed with threads and fine tubes of blue blood and inaccessible thoughts, running in her hidden cavities.

'You are safe with me'.

'I am not safe, with you. But I have no desire to be elsewhere'.

In the morning, washing, he found traces of blood on his thighs. (p. 284)

This passage reinvents Cristabel. She is no longer, as in the passage above, in consumable form. It is not that she has become inchoate. On the contrary, in his thoughts Cristabel is refigured – she is redefined as all body, dependent, turned in on herself, her ideas and her mind hidden and inaccessible. Her blood, her life force, does flow out, but it is not in a consumable form by others, it merely flows around a now broken, but individual, circuit.

Unfortunately, the consummation of their passion resolves itself in pregnancy and the loss of Cristabel, even from the poetic scene. Cristabel hides her self, and her pregnant body. The massivity of that body bodies forth the wrong kinds of relations. But she defers disposal. By fleeing Britain, having her baby in secret and arranging for her married sister to adopt the baby from birth, Cristabel avoids the baby inheriting the stigma of degenerate relations. Cristabel's passion refigures itself in her sacrifice to the child's future: she is known to her daughter, who despises poetry, only as her aunt.

This story of Cristabel helps elaborate how what constitutes a consumable form in cultures concerned with reformation and regeneration, like the late Victorian era, cannot just rest upon the performance of what has gone before; what has gone before must be *improved*. What is called for is that the essence of selves – spirit, integrity, passion, imagination – get utilized in producing the future, as *better* than what has gone before. There is therefore room for self, but a *harnessed* self.

Consumability is thus connected to a promise of improvement, but not in ways that take persons beyond the pale. For Cristabel, the pale was fairly clearly demarcated by the morality of her time: as for the Etoro, the consumability of form is prefigured. But in contemporary fragmented societies, while the elicitation is for persons who are to some extent creative, the 'new' must stay within the boundaries governed by *a process of enhancement*. So that while at one moment they may need to perform their individuality, the next persons also need to perform their *conformance*, and their embeddedness in relations of value to the culture they occupy.

Discussion

In Byatt's book there are also two post-modern anti-heroes, two literary academics, possessed by Cristabel and her lover, following their footsteps to detect their story. These two parallel protagonists are in a continuous state of reflection, and recognize their difference: as they make up and deconstruct the text of their romantic counterparts, they detect their own post-modern condition, of being only ever text. Their lives spell out the impossibility of heroism, the obliteration of self and individuality, the loss of passion and love, and of course, exaltation. All these they discern as the effects of a socially fabricated world, so that they have become as dry as dust, longing only for a pure white bed of solitude. And of course, they know nothing can be engendered there; the white solitude of the single bed before them represents sterility.

If being consumed by passion is an impossible condition in post-modernity we are once again presented with disenchantment, and the dry, white and sterile space of a social constructivism misread. Certainly, where passion is rendered 'only personal' (Scott-Fitzgerald, 1967) then it may be uninteresting to social theorizing. Giddens (1991) certainly argues that passion has been privatised, and consequently trivialized by contemporary popular culture (page: 162–3). Passion as 'those moments at which an individual felt in contact with cosmic forces, with a realm beyond day-to-day experience' (p. 162) has regained its currency, according to Giddens (drawing on Alberoni) only in the context of falling in love. For Giddens (p. 206) while sexuality, retains a 'moral charge and a generalizable significance', falling in love is 'intense, exalting and specifically extraordinary'.

But passion can also be understood as more than just a display of the life force: critically, as we have seen in the example of Cristabel, the specificities of passion body forth particular forms of human relatedness. The idea of passion is certainly troubling, it is also interesting. Understood as a personal space passion is dangerous: it can burn you up. And passion, juxtaposed as *against* reason, and rethought as involuntary, implies a space beyond choice, the God of late modernity (Bauman, 1998). So that passion reminds us that we are not just rational, calculating individuals, reflexively engaged in identity management as we choose which goods best perform our distinction. Passion is also the stuff of enhancement: passion bodies forth the form of things unknown. But to be enhancing, passion must not take the subject beyond the pale, rather passion must be for a calling, a life, of the spirit and the imagination, materialized in the perfection of a craft, and tempered by the calculation of consequences.

Conclusion

This chapter has explored the problem of the consumability of persons. I have emphasized that consumability is accomplished in ways which continuously reconnect persons to the culture they occupy. Specifically, persons draw upon materials of worth to the culture they occupy to reveal and make explicit their distinction. Others consume these distinctions in the making up of their identities.

I have also emphasized that within post-enterprise societies, such as the UK, we are becoming embedded in the demand for enhancement. Here, in all walks of life, regeneration no longer works as before, and the complexity is in knowing how to go along to be consumable. Consumability is connected to more than *reproduction*, or the rematerialization of what has gone before. Within a culture of enhancement the consumability of persons seems to be being reconnected to creativity and the elicitation of subjects who put their *selves* on the line. Indeed, within this unlikely space, what is being consumed is indeed parts of persons. There is not just an amassing or even a circulation of goods, but the consumption of 'parts' of selves. This situation is very different from that implied by an emphasis on the fluid, rootless and role-less individuals figured by the consumption literature.

I am suggesting that the emergent project of a culture of enhancement puts values back in, to deploy what merely bureaucratic rationalities have drained out. This consitutes a reversal of the iron cage. That is, the demand is precisely for Weber's passionate subjects who, unlike Cristabel, have an ability to calculate consequences. So that the very characteristics of persons with a calling are incited and deployed within the culture of enhancement.

Consumability seems to be being reconnected to the flow of the life force, a flow which must improve, not just reproduce, what has gone before. Within this framing of things consumability is connected to a promise of enhancement, but not in ways which take persons beyond the pale. That is, creative persons themselves must be in consumable form: their creations must body forth relations of value to the culture they occupy. And this is the problematic: how to regulate creativity.

Figured as excessive, passion has been associated not just with transcendence but with a simultaneous depletion (Bataille, 1989). Within this view, what gets circulated is a cultural display of the life force; but one which consumes substance. The risk to organization is that creativity, associated with passion, expenditure and excess, may be too depleting.

A culture of enhancement excites peoples' need to be in a consumable form; in this then there is a self-limiting effect on the kind of creative subjectivities which will do. A person's *creativity* (the flow of the life force) is only sustained by the fact that there are other persons willing to consume it. For others to be willing to consume it, creative subjects have to be seen to be *improving* the materials of extension through which they perform their creativity, but in ways which are of value to the culture concerned. So that their creativity moves between performing their distinctive individuality by improving on what has gone before, and performing their sociality by doing this in ways which regenerate, not reinvent, the conceptual relations bodied forth by these materials.

To be 'consumable' creative subjects need then to be regulated, regulated by attention to their consumability by others: indeed the products of creative passions only get constituted as creative *in* their consumption by others. This is the twist. It is not so much that there is an elicitation of subjects to become 'fluid', reflexively managing identity to fit with the multiple social spaces of post-modernity. Rather, consumability elicits 'motility'. In a culture of enhancement the motility is between regeneration, as rematerializing what has gone before, and 'the new', extension in the form of creative change. The consumability of persons rests then in part on *how* subjects materialize their life force, and this increasingly rests upon their discipline: as subjects work the materials of their passion, such as language and writing, these, as materials of extension, exercise and work them, regulating and harnessing their selves.

As discussed above, processes of enhancement, such as audits and quality programmes, connect significance to accountability, and accountability joints the moral and the financial. But the registers across which quality is assessed are multiple, and frequently contradictory, and not necessarily explicit. So that what may seem to be being privileged at one moment – for example ethics rather than efficiency – may need to be reversed the next. Nothing is prefigured one way, but neither does anything go: it's left to you to work out how to stay consumable. All this, as discussed, requires a *motility* to give social organization its suppleness and stability. The difficulty is the future: it is not clear what kinds of subjects are desirable at any one time. Hence the need for ambiguity.

Notes

1 Embedded within the culture of enhancement are what I have called elsewhere (Latimer, 2000b) 'technologies of assessment'. These as processes of enhancement, include evaluation technologies such as the Research Assessment Exercise and Teaching Quality Audit. To register as success stories, performance is assessed, simultaneously, across multiple registers.

2 These motifs of consuming passions and the consumability of persons trouble the division between the human and the non-human in relation to how the social is regenerated. Critically, to perform consumability social beings deploy, invent and consume cultural goods, including self and other.

3 Stephen Berkov, the *enfant terrible* of British theatre, drew on this relationship in a radio interview with Anthony Clare: in the interview he performed his transgressive creativity by stating that when he is engaged in theatre productions his passion eats his body up (with gastric ulcers).

References

Adam, B., (1998), *Timescapes of Modernity. The environment and invisible hazards.* London: Routledge.

Bataille, G., (1989), *The Tears of Eros.* Hong Kong: City Lights Books.

Bauman, Z., (1998), *Work, Consumerism and the New Poor.* Buckingham: Open University Press.

Blondie, (1979), *Union City Blue.* Written by Harrison and Harry, Chrysalis Music Limited: Chrysalis Music Records.

Bourdieu, P., (1984), *Distinction. A Social Critique of the Judgement of Taste.* London: Routledge.

Byatt, A.S., (1990), *Possession. A Romance.* London: Vintage.

Foucault, M., (1979), My body, this paper, this fire. *Oxford Literary Review,* 4 (1): 9–28.

Giddens, A., (1991), *Modernity and Self-Identity.* Cambridge: Polity Press.

Hetherington, K., (1992), Stonehenge and its Festival: Spaces of Consumption. In R. Shields (ed.) *Lifestyle Shopping: The Subject of Consumption:* pp. 93–98. London: Routledge.

Langman, L., (1992), Neon Cages: Shopping for Subjectivity. In R. Shields (ed.) *Lifestyle Shopping. The Subject of Consumption:* pp. 40–82. London: Routledge.

Latimer, J., (1997), Giving Patients a Future: the constituting of classes in an acute medical unit. *Sociology of Health and Illness*, 19 (2): 160–185.

Latimer, J., (1999), The Dark at the Bottom of the Stair: Participation and performance of older people in hospital. *Medical Anthropology Quarterly*, 13 (2): 186–213.

Latimer, J., (2000a), *The Conduct of Care: Understanding Nursing Practice.* Oxford: Blackwell Science.

Latimer, J., (2000b), Personhood and Time: technologies of assessment, ambiguous identities and people with a future. British Sociological Association Annual Conference, *'Making Time – Marking Time'*, York.

Latimer, J. and Lee, N., (1999), Looks are deceiving? *Sociality/Materiality: The Status of the Object in Social Science.* Brunel University, September 1999.

Latour, B., (1987), *Science in Action.* Milton Keynes: Open University Press.

Munro, R., (1992), Disposal of the Body: Upending Postmodernism, Proceedings of 10th Anniversary, SCOS conference, *Organization and Theatre* (Lancaster University).

Munro, R., (1995), Disposal of the Meal. In D. Marshall (ed.) *Food Choice and the Food Consumer:* pp. 313–325. Glasgow: Blackie.

Munro, R., (1996a), Alignments and identity-work: the study of accounts and accountability. In R. Munro and J. Mouritsen (eds) *Accountability: Power, Ethos and the Technologies of managing:* pp. 1–19. London: Thomson International Business Press.

Munro, R., (1996b), The Consumption View of Self: Extension, Exchange and Identity. In S. Edgell, K. Hetherington and A. Warde (eds) *Consumption Matters.* Sociological Review Monograph: pp. 248–273, Oxford: Blackwell.

Munro, R., (1997), Ideas of Difference: Stability, Social Spaces and the Labour of Division. In K. Hetherington and R. Munro, *Ideas of Difference:Social Spaces and the Labour of Division:* pp. 1–22. Sociological Review Monograph, Oxford: Blackwell.

Munro, R., (1999), The Cultural Performance of Control, *Organization Studies*, 20 (4):, 619–639.

Munro, R., (2000), Punctualising Identity: Motility, Time and the Demanding Relationship. British Sociological Association Annual Conference, *'Making Time – Marking Time'*, York.

Scott-Fitzgerald, F., (1967), *The Great Gatsby.* Harmondsworth: Peguin Books.

Strathern, M., (1991), *Partial Connections.* Maryland, USA: Rowman and Littlefield Publishers Inc.

Strathern, M., (1995), *The Relation. Issues in Complexity and Scale.* Cambridge: Prickly Pear Press.

Strathern, M., (1999), The Aesthetics of Substance. In M. Strathern, *Property, Substance & Effect.* Anthropological Essays on Persons & Things. London: The Athlone Press.

Strathern, M., (2000), Introduction: New accountabilities. In Strathern M. (ed.) *Audit Cultures* London: Routledge.

Walker, R., (1993), Violence, modernity, silence: from Max Weber to international relations. In D. Campbell and M. Dillon, *The Political Subject of Violence.* Manchester: Manchester University Press.

Becoming mass: glamour, authority and human presence

Nick Lee

Introduction

As social participants, we often feel an intense need to supplement our visible, physical mass with some other invisible presence, be it our 'character', 'personality' or 'spirit'. 'Being persons' requires more of us than being human bodies in animation. In the normal run of things one must bring the invisible out of hiding (Bull, 1999). Special forms of animation are often needed to constitute the presence of a person. For the vast majority of people, this extra shaping of animation very often takes the form of speech. Thus, bodies frequently issue the demand to be heard as well as seen.

Performances of personhood, then, extend through media of language and audibility as well as through light and visibility. But matters are a little more involved than this. As I will go on to suggest, language and light are sometimes drawn into conflict, a conflict between visible appearances and whatever they may conceal.

This chapter focuses on the bodies that form people's most highly localized visible manifestations. It is not my purpose to draw attention to the fact of personal embodiment as if flesh were a rock on whose mass our thoughts about human presence could find firm foundation. Our bodies do not tell us how to be persons. I write instead in the light of the mundane observation that within social interaction, physically embodied presence alone is not *usually* enough to constitute a full 'person'. The points I am going to make and the questions I will raise throughout the chapter all branch off from the question of how visible human mass is supplemented in the production of persons. The material presented here, however, works toward the identification of a source of dignified human presence that I refer to as 'glamour'. This 'glamour' relies for its effects on the denial of and refusal of the normal need to supplement one's material presence. This glamorous, dignified presence trades off fundamentally ambiguous relations between humanness and mass and places itself beyond the powers of articulate authority and accountability.

Spirits and politics

We often perform the presence of the invisible parts of ourselves against a background awareness that if we do *not* present the invisible, then other social participants may make their own attributions concerning us. To our dismay, others may satisfy themselves that they know all they need to know about us on the basis of our appearance alone. Thus, practices of the supplementation of the visible, practices in which we bring our personhood to presence, are thoroughly political. Modernity's complex, shifting patterns of the marginalization and re-recognition of 'non-standard' human variants (women, 'blacks' and more recently children (Lee, 2001)) has, in the past, been informed by the efforts of the non-standard to capture the quality of 'hiddenness', to know that, for them personally and as individuals, there is more to them than meets the eye (Bull, 1999). This underlies late 20th century concerns with 'voice' and the politicization of 'experience' and of 'recognition'. When this 'hiddenness' is captured and revealed in language, then language takes on a very specific power, the power to *contradict* the visible.

Persons whose bodies are marked as 'non-standard' have developed many different responses to the facts of their marginalisation. Some of these responses have been institutionalized; a child, for example, may require an adult to stand between him/her and social judgements based on his/her visible youth, using the adult as a supplementing 'shield' to gain access to otherwise forbidden places of entertainment such as cinemas and theatres. Some of them buck existing institutions; African-american civil rights demonstrators' calm insistence on their dignity and rights of access to segregated institutions and transport services, their insistence that they did not need supplementation or extension beyond their own self-possession to accede to fully human status and dignity. One strategy, however has been particularly prominent in struggles against the injustices of gender discrimination; to perform oneself in such a way as to establish that one's bodily manifestation provides *no* information about one's person, that one's visible presence *does not* matter to oneself and *should not* matter to others. In the following section we exemplify this strategy through a discussion of an article by the novelist Joyce Carol Oates.

Authority: a woman of substance

'One cannot take through the eye without at the same time giving'. Georg Simmel (Frisby and Featherstone, 1997: 112)

'... the sociological charm of being, by virtue of adornment, a representative of one's group with whose whole significance one is 'adorned''. Georg Simmel (Frisby and Featherstone, 1997: 210)

The novelist Joyce Carol Oates took a guided tour through a New Jersey prison in 1984 in her capacity as Professor of Humanities of Princeton University. She was accompanied by a number of other academics and some lawyers. This was an occasion for persons who were, by profession, articulate and well-informed, further to inform themselves by eye-witnessing the objects of their professional concern. In a newspaper article (Oates, 1998), Oates reports that she was shamed and humiliated during the tour. We will turn to the shaming and humiliating events shortly. For the moment let us record that these events so poisoned Oates' articulacy that she felt unable to discuss them for several years.

The tour allowed Oates and her companions to observe the conditions under which prisoners lived. It also allowed them to see the prisoners. We might describe the informed and concerned scrutiny of the tourists as part of a 'scopic regime' (Metz, 1983), specifically the scopic regime of research into social problems, which examines selected individual lives to shed light on society.

To call this scopic regime pornographic (Kappeler, 1986) would be harsh. However, just as some genres of pornography aim to make flesh sexy by mirroring gendered relations of inequality, so, in the scopic regime of the tour, the prisoners were interesting as emblems of social problems. Through the tour party's gaze, large-scale social problems, such as inequality, became ready for view. Though the prisoners were scarcely 'adorned' by being representative of a group phenomenon, Simmel's 'sociological charm' is a useful term for the effects of this scopic regime. To witness the prisoners was to witness poverty, disorder, or, perhaps 'capitalism', telescoped and condensed into a form consumable with the eye – open to being seen, not just discussed. The tour allowed for an inspection of the 'micro' for traces of the 'macro'.[1]

From Oates' account it seems that the tour guide, a prison officer, may have seen the tour as an opportunity to staunch bleeding hearts by showing the party what prisoners were *really* like. He was trying to block the scopic regime of informed concern. Following the tour, rather than see the prisoners as emblems of macro-scale problems beyond their individual control, perhaps the prisoners' physical presence would loom so large in the tourists' imaginations as to disrupt informed concern. A case of the micro being awesome enough a spectacle to make recourse to the telescopy of research, and its forgiving politics, seem fanciful.

So the tour presented Oates and her companions with the *appearance* of prisoners. Seen as a piece of ideological theatre, stage-managed by the tour guide, the tour's dramatic content came from the uncertainty of the connection between appearance and essence.[2] What would the tourists *really* see when they finally saw the prisoners before them? Large scale social problems, or small scale venality? Politics or morals? Social structure or individual choice? The scopic regime of social concern would be satisfied if the prisoners' appearance revealed the essence of American society – inequality and the brutalization of the socially excluded. The tour guide would be satisfied if the tourists came to know the prisoners, and them alone, for what they were, seeing their brutal essence through their appearance. If the prisoners were vile enough, perhaps then the visitors would be educated.

The visible and the articulable

Before conducting the tourists inside the prison, the tour guide laid out some ground rules. On no account were tourists to interact with prisoners. Specifically, on no account were tourists to make *eye contact* with prisoners. Oates describes the smell of the prison, the sweaty heat and the eye-aching fluorescent light. She then describes the architecture of the prison and its approximation to the panopticism (Foucault, 1977) that makes prisoners relatively more visible than any other occupants of the building – the arrangement that allows for seeing without being seen.

> The 30 man block was structured with cells arranged around an open space, like a common room, containing tables and chairs; the fourth wall of this rectangular space was an elevated guard station in which a window, wire enforced as usual, was inset. No privacy for these men except at the very rear of their cells, and these cells measuring six feet by eight. The effect was like that of a zoo enclosure or an aquarium. (Oates, 1998)

Looking down on this enclosure, Oates did what she was not supposed to do. She '... met the startled gazes of two young inmates ...'. (Oates, 1998). They stared back with consternation, resentment and fury. Confused and embarrassed, she smiled. Within seconds, '... excited calls and cries spread through the cell block ...'. (Oates, 1998) and prisoners gathered, staring at her, pulling faces and mouthing words she could not hear through the reinforced window. One can only imagine what they were saying. Oates could hazard a guess, and she was fearful. It didn't matter now that she was Professor of Humanities. By making eye-contact she had broken the scopic regime of concern in the moment that she broke the panoptic spell of invisibility. She had lost her position. The result;

> It was as if I stood naked before strangers, utterly exposed and in such exposure annihilated ... A woman: cunt. What these eager men would do to me, if they could get hold of me'. (Oates, 1998)

Objects of concern became subjects. It mattered now that they had minds of their own. Where previously their presence had been minimized, their appearance telling of elsewhere, they were now intensely present for themselves. A concerned subject became objectified in turn. Oates was humiliated because she was reduced to a body and, in that reduction, became '... contemptible, because anonymous, mass-produced'. (Oates, 1998). She was now the objective of a scopic regime such that she was no longer herself but 'woman' in general. By becoming nothing but a body she was de-individualized – made a representative of her group. Her reduction to a body can be described as a 'becoming-mass', becoming effectively speechless and maximally visible. Her ordeal lasted a few minutes. She wanted to make it clear that she wasn't just a body.

She wanted to tell the prisoners;

But this isn't me! I am so much more than what you see'. (Oates, 1998)

Her appearance, her sudden coming to light in the eyes of the prisoners as a mass of female flesh, belied her essence – her Professorship, her professional identity. By her own report she was ashamed because she had foolishly broken the spell of invisibility. She was humiliated in the prisoners' eyes and thus in her own. This experience led her to write;

We enter the world as purely physical beings; and leave it in the same way. In between we labour pridefully to establish identities, selves distinct from our bodies. Not what we are but who we are. This is the crux of our humanity'. (Oates, 1998)

The specifically gendered nature of her prison experience seems to be key for Oates, but, in the quotation above, she also gives us a view of the human condition that is universal in its implications. Though it is expressed as a universal, this view still bears the trace of one particular feminist viewpoint. For Oates, identities are separate from and distinct from bodies. A human life of dignity is made by enforcing that separation. As long as you are more than what can be seen, more than your body, you may have dignity. The separation collapsed during her prison visit and, with its collapse, her dignity evaporated. Oates casts the visible and the articulable as two axes in a cruciform arrangement. Humanity suffers at the juncture.

Just as some feminisms require a distinction between material 'sex' and social 'gender' to make the pursuit of female dignity thinkable,[3] so Oates bases the possibility of dignity in general on the maintenance of a division between the material and the immaterial, the visible and the articulable (Deleuze, 1988). In Oates' view, and she is painfully honest about this, her 'essence' – who she really is – is made up of and sustained with words. In the prison, she was trapped in the visible, defenceless, since her only defence is what she can articulate – her title, her novels, her academic writing. The articulable is where she keeps her pride.

The title 'Professor' is like an adornment in Simmel's sense (Frisby and Featherstone, 1997). Like jewelry made of precious metals, it is symbolic because it brings a whole system of valuation and respect to presence. Oates' pride is rendered portable by the adornment 'Professor' because that adornment brings a system of valuation to presence. Especially valuable, as she points out, for a woman, a person who's body, when it is just a body, renders a patriarchal system of valuation portable.

Concerning Oates, it is clear that the sources of her identity and dignity are principally articulatory. Much the same could be said of anyone who lives through words. If we live always 'in extension' (Strathern, 1991; Munro, 1996) and find our identity in the extensions that are available to us, then language is a major form of extension, and some of us are more dependent upon it than others.

There are many circumstances, however, in which language is less than readily available. There are many ways of life in which words are *just words*. For us all there are circumstances in which words are not heard, or in which the transport of articulatory values, such as the transport a title may achieve, is blocked. Even academics and novelists have to walk down the street. In the circumstances of the prison tour, Oates' path to human dignity was largely closed off. Articulation was impossible, and in all likelihood, futile. The more our essence, or our substantial presence, rests on the invisible, the articulable and the immaterial, and the more store we set by effacing our embodiment, the harder things will go with us in such circumstances.

Civil inattention and star status

So what happens when the strategy of separating visible matter from articulable meanings becomes a failing strategy? What happens when the articulable is not available as a medium of presence, pride and significance? Are there visual ways of performing one's essence? Further, are there visual ways of performing one's essence that can transport a degree of dignity commensurate with the title 'professor'?

When we cannot perform our essence through words, we have to perform our essence through appearance. This suggestion is hardly novel. For Goffman (1963) the economy of visibility practised in 'civil inattention' comprises a social contract of normalcy. Civil inattention is the visible analogue of the articulation 'I'm okay; you're okay'. We come to know ourselves as essentially normal when we recognize each other's presence and recognize it as *unremarkable*. Thus we peaceable 'pass' each other as mutual equivalents so long as our glances *are* mutual and muted.

If Bauman's (1995) analyses of city life are correct however, civil inattention is not the only strategy available to city dwellers to manage the 'opportunity and threat' (Bauman, 1995: 137) that the constant presence of strangers presents us with. At least one alternative to civil inattention is available – to perform oneself as *remarkable*. This strategy exploits the mutual recognition pattern of civil inattention. The performer is seen, indeed intends to be the cynosure of all eyes, but betrays no sign of seeing. If civil inattention is a contract, the *remarkable* person defaults and makes their viewers default. This maximizes the potential to walk the street as the star of one's own movie. It also maximizes the threat that others present. The performer must be on guard against mutuality and the reciprocity of gaze.

Whenever we see, we are also seen. We must make a stand and present ourselves as persons of substance. But when we make ourselves known for what we are, we are exposed and at risk. We show people what we are made of. We can be seen and our essence judged. But we *can* make ourselves present and yet face down the risk of exposure. In other words, the panoptic spell can be rendered portable. Further, the passage between the need to expose oneself and the risk of exposing oneself ensures that some of the highest degrees of animacy and presence, some of the strongest concentrations of essence that we can achieve are delivered by performances of self as *inanimate*, performances which involve a certain blanking of the hidden, the immaterial and the essential. We are safest to consume others and to be consumed by others when we are becoming-mass. When articulation is unavailable, we are at our most substantial, and at our most intensely present when we pass ourselves off, albeit momentarily, as matter and nothing more. A purely massy presence then, is the visible analogue of the articulatory strategy of 'speaking objectively'. Just as a maximum of articulatory presence can be achieved by rhetorically effacing oneself as the origin of one's words (say by avoiding the personal pronoun), so a maximum of visible presence can be achieved by pretending that one has no spirit.

These relations of spirit, matter and dignity, composed as they are by humans in their worldly creativity, are exceedingly complex. Sometimes a becoming-mass may serve as the footing for a later bid for articulate authority. Bauman (this volume) reflects on one example of this from the film 'Elizabeth'. A stylistically blanked face effaces Elizabeth's private personhood, giving her words the status of non-negotiable public declarations. The question remains of how we as film viewers are capable of getting this point.

Fashion: the ambiguity of mannequins

> From the beginning one of Foucault's fundamental theses is the following: there is a difference in nature between ... the visible and the articulable ... Between the two alliances are formed and broken, and there is occasional overlapping on particular strata and thresholds'. Deleuze (1988: 61–63)

Deleuze (1988) examines Foucault's (1972) analytic distinction between the discursive and the non-discursive. In this distinction he detects a more general concern in Foucault's work (Foucault, 1975; 1979), a concern with the shifting alignments of the 'articulable' and the 'visible'. For Deleuze's Foucault, these are two distinct kinds of 'there is' (Deleuze, 1988: 61) – language and light.

We can understand the articulable and the visible as analytically distinct modes of 'extension' (Strathern, 1991) composed respectively of statement and of spectacle. As Deleuze argues, the visible and the articulable are not reducible to one another, and no single law or pattern determines how they are related. Their relation is a non-relation. Hence the empirical cast of Foucault's philosophy and its distinctiveness from 'contemporary analytic philosophy' (Deleuze, 1988: 50).

Foucault's recognition in principle of the autonomy of the visible puts him quite at odds with the notion that statements become true on the condition that powerful people *say* that they are true. Foucault, then, presents us with rather more than 'speech acts' (Austin, 1962; Searle, 1996), and an understanding of his work as 'relativist' is cursory at best. Authority and power are not felicity conditions external to statements. Rather, 'games of truth' (Deleuze, 1988: 63) involve a 'dream' (Deleuze, 1988: 61) of isomorphism between the two modes of extension, an epistemological fantasy in which what we see and what we say seem identical, and in which saying and seeing confirm each other in an unbroken loop of reference. The production of truth is the attempt to realize this dream, and as Deleuze (1988) notes, in the birth of the clinic and of the prison, this involved the subordination or 'overcoding' (Deleuze and Guattari, 1988) of the visible by the articulable. In this sense 'truth' stems from the temporary alignment of what is to be seen with what is to be said.

But what would a 'game of non-truth' look like? How could we recognize a set of procedures in which truth was irrelevant? Perhaps such a game would typically be encountered as dream-like, as an evanescent, lesser reality? Perhaps we would find 'authority' undercut by such a game, words confounded by images in a quadrille of ambiguity, rather than secured by the neat accompaniment of well-crafted illustrations?

Figure 1 is the front cover of the October 1949 edition of American *Vogue*. The photograph was taken by Norman Parkinson. The foreground is occupied by a blurred mirror-reversed letter, indicating the photograph was taken from inside what looks to be a plate-glass window. The background is a street scene containing people and cars, blurred and in motion. The model, displaying the clothes, exhibits every sign of being in motion and of going about her business unobserved. Perhaps her attention has momentarily been caught by a display in our window. While she continues walking she turns her torso to the left and drops her left shoulder slightly to look behind her. It looks like she is not going to hold that posture or that position for very long. The attitude of her left hand still indicates a forward motion.

Fashion has not always been an industry. Ewing (1985) credits a certain Charles Frederick Worth with making the first steps towards industrialization. By 1864, Worth employed a thousand workers, producing garments for private customers and patterns for dressmakers and manufacturers to copy in France, England and America. For our purposes, Worth's most significant innovation, however, was the 'mannequin'. Before Worth, Ewing writes, garments were customarily displayed to private customers, shop-buyers and dressmaker copyists on inanimate 'dummies'.

Were it economically viable to tailor a suit of clothes for each prospective customer, and were it convenient for each prospective customer to do so, no doubt, customers could have served as their own models. As it was, Worth took

Figure 1

to exhibiting styles on the body of a *human* mannequin. This term, ofte
an inaminate dummy, captures the ambiguous role of these early fashi..
quite neatly. When modelling clothes, the mannequin had to be present and
absent at the same time. She was required to lend the support of her body to the
clothes on display, and depending on cut, fabric and type of clothing, she was
also required to lend animacy to the clothes, to display how they would look in
real life. However, as a temporary surrogate for the client, dressed only to give
an impression of how another might look in those clothes, the mannequin was
also obliged to efface herself. The likelihood is that the former seamstresses or
shop-girls doing the modelling already had plenty of experience of pretending
'not to be there' when in the presence of wealthier women. As was the case in
other service roles, the models' visible presence and movement was absolutely
necessary, but any articulate presence was not. Further, one can imagine how
vital it was to a sensitive sale opportunity that the mannequin not disturb the
consumer's assessing gaze by returning it. Being a mannequin then, was a
peculiar performance requiring a woman's simultaneous presence and absence to
make the clothes consumable. Mannequins had to be animate mass and mass
alone, and their animacy had to be worked on so as to prevent the intrusion of
mannequin's character into the moments of display. The work of the fashion
house in producing the clothes was supplemented by the work of the mannequin
in managing her presence. The fashion industry and the display of fashion were
shot through with artifice which was intended to manage any ambiguity over
who the clothes were for.[4]

Glamour

Lloyd (1986) comments on figure 1 as follows:

Parkinson gives his cover ... a new journalistic look by catching his model,
on the move, through a shop window'. (Lloyd, 1986: 60)

So far, in my consideration of figure 1, I have followed Lloyd's brief reading
of it. I have accepted that the model was 'on the move' and, following the
model's attitude and posture, have endorsed the view that she had been caught
by the camera while in motion. However, a further reading can be made, a
reading that is not in direct conflict with Lloyd's, but takes some of the
implications of her description a little further. I suggest that rather than being
'journalistic' and simply recording a live subject, Parkinson is capturing a
journalistic 'look', through artifice.[5] He is also making witty play of the
ambiguities surrounding the nature of the mannequins presence. The chief
ambiguities are over whether she is present simply as mass or as animated mass
and whether she is present simply as object of gaze or as gazing subject.
  First let us consider the question of animacy and inanimacy that is posed by
the term 'mannequin'. For all the signs that she is in motion, the model's

183

posture and attitude look awkward. She seems so stiff that she could almost be a showroom dummy. For Parkinson to be journalistic and to show a woman in movement, it was necessary to have a real woman stand stock still in such a posture as would imitate a moving woman. To bring animation to presence on the cover of *Vogue* required a brief performance of inanimacy. In the light of these suppositions what are we to make of the shop window that stands between the camera and the model? It is a useful prop in bringing the 'woman going about her business' to presence. It suggests that she was snapped unawares in her natural habitat, the natural habitat of the post-war American 'woman about town', passing through a major shopping district on her way, perhaps, to a lunch appointment. We can fill in a whole life for this woman, a life of articulacy and independent action. A monied life, despite the caption above her that reads 'more taste than money'. At the same time, however, the shop window draws our attention to her inanimacy. It could be that we are looking into, rather than out of, a shop window. Looking at a clothing display. And of course we are looking at a clothing display. This did not escape Parkinson's attention even as he produced the 'new journalistic look' for the *Vogue* front cover. This goes some way to accounting for the *glamour* of the photograph. The model looks so good, she is so smart, her clothes so fresh and unruffled, that she could almost be a showroom dummy, untroubled by such considerations as weather, limited time for the preparation of her appearance and the countless inconveniences of life that degrade real people's appearance and put them in the way of negative assessment by others.

Let us now turn to the question of the direction of gaze. Parkinson is presenting us with a woman who is at once going about her business, emanating gaze (looking at something to our right, perhaps in our window) and who is also on display, the object of gaze. Through the device of the shop window, Parkinson reminds us that the woman is being looked at. The street she walks along is her shop window. As a photographic model the woman is merely displaying the clothes, but if she were as 'real' as the journalistic features of the photograph imply, she would also be displaying her 'self'.

The word 'glamour' means attractiveness. 'Glamorous' also means enchanting, bewitching. The glamorous are able to cast a spell over others. In one, now largely forgotten, usage, glamour was a spell of invisibility (Priest, 1984). Bearing this in mind, we can suggest that Parkinson is giving the readers of *Vogue* a lesson. How is one to be the focus of others' gaze and simultaneously protect oneself from any negative assessment?

This is a vital question if one's appearance is the shop window of one's soul. What would allow one to attract the gaze of others and simultaneously to ignore the gaze of others, is if one was assured of the high quality of one's display and, thus, that the regard one was receiving was positive. To put oneself on display, to expose one's essence, requires protective glamour – the ability to act as if one was invisible, whilst attracting the gaze of others. Parkinson's glamour lesson turns the 'becoming mass' of the mannequin from a performance undertaken momentarily, and for pay, by low status women such as seamstresses and shop girls, into a freely-given cultural performance, a positive asset for Parkinson's monied female contemporaries.

Conflicts of the visible and articulable

Today, the 'mannequin' has become the 'supermodel', fêted for her ability to display clothes. Supermodels are some of the richest women in the world. They are now in a position to endorse clothes by agreeing to model them, and to endorse a wide range of other consumables – cars, restaurants, books, social events – by appearing with them, or at their launches. When they lend their presence, they bestow grace. They are certainly valued for their beauty, for their qualities as masses of flesh, bone and skin. But they are also valued for their mastery of glamour maximizing the amount they are looked at while minimizing any awareness that they are looked at. They are valued for their ability to become-mass. On the catwalk they move as if unaware of the audience's attention, physical beings innocent of the critical and promotional chatter that surrounds their performance. As the catwalk fashion show has become a ritual of major cultural and economic significance, the becoming-mass of the mannequin has become a highly valued cultural performance.

The profile of becoming-mass as a cultural performance has not been decreased by supermodels' accession into the category of the super-rich. Their characters as individuals have not yet become so awesome and intrusive as to spoil the catwalk performance. Even though biographies are now written exploring models' characters, motivations and inner lives, stereotypes of models as stupid, empty-headed clothes-horses still refer to the becoming-mass performance that they live by. Articulacy seeks to avenge itself on visible glamour, knowing that its means of producing its own authoritative dignity are as nothing to the unaccountable and glamorous.

The spaces where such conflicts occur are numerous. In the UK, marketing organizations produce free exercise books for schoolchildren adorned with images of products and personality-light pop-stars. Clothing manufacturers worry about their limited penetration of male markets and television shows challenge sober masculinity and encourage men to enjoy dressing up. Feminists feud over the values of image and word, allowing and proscribing clothing and make-up styles (Chancer, 1998). Questions are raised over whether 'Government' is an attractive brand. In each of these locations people are offered choices between our two different paths to human dignity.

Conclusion

The present argument may be reminiscent of Hebdige's (1988) comments on the postmodern mood of 'style over substance': 'Reality is as thin as the paper it is printed on. There is nothing underneath or behind the image and hence there is no hidden truth to be revealed'. (Hebdige, 1988: 159). It should be recognized, however, that becoming-mass is rather different from the performance of self as depthless surface without essence. It is different because it is productive. It is not productive of truth but of certain non-negotiable presence. Becoming-mass is a performance that alludes to the qualities of the performer; glamour, intensity of presence and human dignity. While the postmodern mood of depthless transience and the meaningless carnival is an option, we should not imagine that its performers have brought the play of appearance and essence, visibility and articulacy to an end.

It is still not so very long since the evanescence of appearances, fashion and glamour dissuaded dowdy social scientists from their concerted study. There was at once nothing worth saying about them *and* a problem making words stick to such a changing surface. Those who made the attempt risked infection by the topic's triviality (Weinstein and Weinstein, 1991), and their work seemed to suffer a lack of systematicity (Featherstone, 1991) – a danger signal for any attempt at disciplinary authority. There was a discomfort with regard to the visual on the part of those who made themselves through words. A problem, then, that those who live by articulacy have with the visible. This discomfort can still be detected as social commentators grapple with the 'end of the book' (Derrida, 1976: 6), finding an analytic mid-point between the gleefully disgusted celebration of the surface, and lamentation at our contemporary 'loss of depth' in the supervenience of the image, all too infrequently (but see Stallabrass, 1996).

But the time has, perhaps, arrived for social scientists to develop sufficient 'engaged detachment' (Rojek and Turner, 2000) with regard to visibility and articulacy to begin to understand the shifting grounds of human dignity and presence in highly-mediated and highly individualized societies in terms of their relationship.

Glamour is the heart of fashion's game of non-truth, a game which stands outside the authoritative articulacy which has controlled the marking of bodies and the distribution of human dignity throughout modernity. It is as positive and as deceitful a force as authority's vanishing trick of objectivity.

Notes

1 It should be clear that the sociological imagination rests on this scopic regime to the extent that it transforms persons into case studies, examples or data points.
2 As Taussig (1993) argues, appearance and essence are often understood as, at least clearly separable, and sometimes as each other's opposites. I suggest, with Taussig, that the appearance/essence division is a cultural artefact and that it is malleable. Thus we know that appearances can be deceptive, but we also habitually take them as a guide to persons' qualities.
3 This familiar theoretical strategy is answered by Irigaray (1991), amongst others, who would see in a sex/gender, material/immaterial division a repudiation of the flesh that mimics, rather than challenges, patriarchy.

4 On this matter of ownership, it is interesting to note that right up until the beginning of the 20th century '... early model girls are reported as having invariably worn tight-fitting, high-necked, long-sleeved black garments under the fashions they displayed'. (Ewing, 1985: 13). It is unclear whether this was primarily to satisfy requirements of decency, or whether this black barrier kept the garments free of the real or imagined traces of the mannequin so that her priority as wearer of the garment could be safely forgotten by the customer.

5 This is not to deny that 'realistic' photo-journalism involves artifice. Quite the opposite. The realistic image requires that the artifice and mediation involved in its production efface themselves and conceal themselves from view.

Image

A: Norman Parkinson, Oct 1949, American Vogue in Lloyd, V., (1986), *The Art of Vogue: Photographic Covers.* London: Octopus Books

References

Austin, J.L., (1962), *How to do Things with Words.* Oxford: Clarendon Press

Bauman, Z., (1995), *Life in Fragments: Essays in Postmodern Morality.* Oxford: Blackwell

Bull, M., (1999), *Seeing Things Hidden: Vision, Apocalypse and Totality.* London: Verso

Chancer, L.S., (1998), *Reconcilable Differences: Confronting Beauty, Pornography and the Future of Feminism.* Berkeley: University of California Press

Deleuze, G., (1988), *Foucault.* Minneapolis: University of Minnesota Press

Deleuze, G. and Guattari, F., (1988), *A Thousand Plateaus: Capitalism and Schizophrenia.* London: Athlone.

Derrida, J., (1976), *Of Grammatology.* Baltimore: The John Hopkins University Press.

Derrida, J., (1994), *Spectres of Marx: The State of the Debt, the Work of Mourning, and the New International.* London: Routledge.

Ewing, E., (1997), *History of Twentieth Century Fashion.* London: Batsford.

Falk, P., (1997), 'The Scopic Regimes of Shopping', in Falk, P. and Campbell, C. *The Shopping Experience.* London: Sage:177–85.

Featherstone, M., (1991), 'George Simmel: An Introduction', *Theory, Culture and Society* 8 (3): 1–16.

Foucault, M., (1972), (Trans. A.M. Sheridan Smith) *The Archaeology of Knowledge.* New York: Harper Colophon.

Foucault, M., (1975), (Trans. A.M. Sheridan Smith) *The Birth of the Clinic: An Archeology of Medical Perception.* New York: Vintage/Random House.

Foucault, M., (1979), (Trans. Alan Sheridan) *Discipline and Punish: The Birth of the Prison.* New York: Vintage/Random House.

Frisby, D. and Featherstone, M., (eds)(1997), *Simmel on Culture.* London: Sage.

Goffman, E., (1963), *Behaviour in Public Places: Notes on the Social Organisation of Gatherings.* London: The Free Press of Glencoe.

Hebdige, D., (1988), *Hiding in the Light: On Images and Things.* London: Routledge.

Irigaray, L., (1991), *The Irigaray Reader.* London: Blackwell.

Kappeller, S., (1986), *The Pornography of Representation.* Minneapolis: University of Minnesota Press.

Lee, N.M., (1998), 'Childhood and self-representation: the view from technology', *Anthropology in Action.* 5, 3, 13–21.

Lee, N.M., (2000), 'Faith in the Body?: Childhood, Subjecthood and Sociological Enquiry', in Prout, A. (ed.) *The Body, Childhood and Society.* London: Macmillan.

Lee, N.M., (2001), *Childhood and Society: Growing Up in an Age of Uncertainty.* Buckingham: Open University Press.

Lloyd, V. (ed.), (1986), *The Art of Vogue: Photographic Covers.* London: Octopus Books.

Metz, C., (1983), *Psychoanalysis and Cinema: The Imaginary Signifier.* London: Macmillan.

Munro, R., (1996), 'A Consumption View of Self: Extension, Exchange and Identity', in Edgell, S., Hetherington, K., and Warde, A. (eds) *Consumption Matters: The Production and Experience of Consumption.* Oxford: Blackwell.

Oates, J.C., (1998), *Jail Bait.* The Guardian, Oct 10th 1998.

Priest, C., (1984), *The Glamour.* London: Jonathan Cape.

Rojek, C.and Turner, B., (2000), 'Decorative Sociology: Towards a Critique of the Cultural Turn', *The Sociological Review*, 48 (4): 629–648.

Searle, J.R., (1996), *The Construction of Social Reality.* London: Penguin.

Stallabrass, J., (1996), *Gargantua: Manufactured Mass Culture.* London: Verso.

Strathern, M., (1991), *Partial Connections.* Maryland: Rowman and Little.

Taussig, M., (1993), *Mimesis and Alterity: A Particular History of the Senses.* London: Routledge.

Weinstein, D. and Weinstein, M.A., (1991), 'Georg Simmel: Sociological Flâneur Bricoleur', *Theory, Culture and Society* 8 (3):151–68.

Ordering others and othering orders: the consumption and disposal of otherness

Cristina Pallí Monguilod

The consumption view of others

This is the story of my addiction: I can't stop consuming others. I observe and persecute them, trying to pick up, make sense and digest the tiniest of their actions, conversations or products. I talk and write and write and talk about them, representing them. And here I go once more. But probably we all know what this is about, since many of us live off consuming and representing others (and no, this is not simply to speak figuratively): oppressed computers and desired women, abused children and stressed bodies, devastated 'favelas' and colonized brains, Argo-Nuers and deep-significant cocks, dominant scientists and modest oncomice. The most gluttonous of acts: never-ending others to consume and represent. And since single others were not enough, I went for the most filling meal of all: communities. A community of gypsies in Badalona (Barcelona, Spain), and a community of scientists in a biology laboratory (UAB, Spain) (Pallí, 2000).

Don't look at me in that way, with those horrified eyes. Yes, I know what you call those who eat human flesh, those who drink human blood. But before you rubbish me, before you name me too fast (tell me, am I a Cannibal? a Vampire? Both?) listen to my story. Because it may be yours too. (Are you sure you have never tasted such delicacies?). This is going to be a story of selves, others and quasi-others. Of teeth and blood, of wars and hunting, of love and haunting. Of dirty work. Which means, that it is also going to be an ambivalent story. Ambiguous enough to make you doubt its monstrosity. After all, we can't easily tell who is a vampire, can we? Maybe you will forgive me if I promise to tell this story only once, 'I won't do that again'. But then, can you trust a monster's word?

Representing others

Gold, spices, ebony and ivory have been consumed by Western people on our conspicuous 'travels' around the world; bodies too. Outside and inside our borders, we have been consuming, above all, Otherness. So much so, that Baudrillard (1993) warns us to take care of whatever Otherness we still have left before we run out of it. It came as a surprise, though, we really thought we were simply representing others. We were just holding an immense mirror in front of the world, in front of other people, in front of other cultures, in order to send their images back home. Nothing could be more innocent, more spiritual, less material. Optics and panoptics. And if you hear noises of machines, maps, engineering, it's just our engineering of images, just a few things: telescopes, periscopes, microscopes, lenses: 'don't you worry, we are simply watching, we are not going to hurt you', we were saying, while laughing at the ingenuous Indian who thought that pictures could steal their souls. However, they were right after all. We have produced, consumed and disposed of their souls ... and bodies. We have been producing others for our consumption and disposal (Clifford and Marcus, 1986; Law, 1994; Munro, 1995; Said, 1978; Sampson, 1993; Wilkinson and Kitzinger, 1996).

Dialoguing did not turn out to be less problematic. If the other is too far away, we need mediation (But is this really a contact, humanists ask? Is it really you who speak at the other side of the line?). And what if the Other speaks a language we don't understand? The End – unless we translate. But then, they say, this is no less mediation. Not even in our own language can we escape mediation. Hermeneutics has it that our prejudices are mediating every conversation; and there is never complete understanding (Gadamer, 1975). But relax, there is no call for despair because you can't even have direct contact with your self or your experiences. Language speaks us, remember? Damn these omnipresent mediations! No way out. No direct access to the other. There are only mediations, only translations.

We really tried to get it right. If the other's voice could not be heard, we could represent the other, speak for the other. But the spokesperson was usually challenged: 'What right do you have to speak on our behalf? Why are you consuming us?'. Thus, the more we were trying to represent and celebrate the other, the more other they become – every attempt of representation being a further constitution of others. On looking for the perfect spokesperson, in an identity relation with the group (from like to like), what happened was that similarities and commonalties were fading away. What appeared as a group with common identities, melted into further divisions on closer look. Until when the divisions and differences? Are communities melting away? Despair, loneliness.

We have had to learn, painfully learn, that there is no way to 'speak for' without 'speaking about' (Callon, 1996; Latour, 1987; Lee, 1994). No way to represent (Vertretung) without re-presenting (Darstellung) (Spivak, 1987). There are no others, but othering (Wilkinson and Kitzinger, 1996). Stories which order and disorder others (Law, 1994). And what follows is not less a story – or is it stories? There is no unmediated dialogue – does this mean no connection is possible? There is no communion – does this mean no community is possible? There is no pure sameness to represent identities – are we doomed to inhabit individual islands?

On being affectionate to monsters

Let us try and sort these issues out. I have not been working alone, but with[1] the monster. For even monsters have come to fatten the list of represented others (what? did you think that impure, monstrous flesh could be spared from the mass(ive) consumption, the mass-acre?). This may seem surprising. Why are we interested in monsters? Are they not scary? But then, maybe we could start by asking why are monsters scary? A first answer is that we are afraid of them because they are unknown. But this answer poses some problems, first logical (why should we be afraid of what we do not know?), and foremost, ethico-political, for it justifies the political view that it is 'natural' to be scared of foreigners – and therefore defensive, even aggressive (see Stolcke's critique of the Homus Xenophobicus, 1995). On the contrary, it is precisely what we know of them that scares us (oh, the look of the mad – yes, it could have been otherwise, it could have been me ...). It is precisely what rests beyond/along/between our greedy networks of power-knowledge where the Other escapes us. The Other is Lem's (1961) ocean-planet Solaris: unknown, impenetrable, ununderstandable, meaningless, unassimilable, Baudrillard's radical foreignness (1993) -which does not mean unreachable, unconnected. Rather, the Other is what makes us stop, what sets a finitist ethics (Lee and Stenner, 1997), to our gluttony. The indigestible. Our limit.

Nevertheless, let's be wary. If we are caught in the poetics of the Other, we will miss quite a lot. For it is quite ingenuous (ingenuous?) to say that the other is inedible. Now we know a lot (which does not mean enough) of the perversity, persistence and corrosiveness of the gastric juices of our power-knowledge stomachs. Others are edible. Ask Baudrillard's (1978) anthropologists, who discovered, to their horror, that the population of Tasaday was diminishing. The 'critical mass' was reaching its lowest level. 'Where's all that mass gone?'. Ask our mothers. Ask The Edible Woman (Atwood, 1969). Ask the Alakaluf, who ended up calling themselves 'alakaluf', 'give, give', their consumption inscribed in their names (Baudrillard, 1993). Ask immigrants. You can probably add your own examples.

And here it is when we encounter our monster. The capture of radical foreignness into the net of differences – ending in the absurdity of 'the right to difference' (Baudrillard, 1993; Stolcke, 1995). The creature who/which is made other. And when I say 'made other', I mean it. The monster is not excluded due to being a monster, rather, the border between normality and monstrosity depends on the existence of the monster. Mary Douglas (1966) dixit. To keep those borders clean is the dirty work monsters are made to endure (Lee and Stenner, 1997). A symbolic mark, the 'marked group' (eg, Apfelbaum, 1989). But not only. It is a proper mark on the flesh. It is an heterogeneously material (Law, 1994) as well as symbolical construction.

The monster has thus a disadvantage: it demonstrates borders; it is marked, it is excluded, it is demonized. It is not represented – which does not mean it is unrepresentable. Sometimes it is made invisible – like when the recruitment of immigrant women in the U.K. after II World War permitted the identity of indigenous women as primarily wives and mothers (Webster, 1998); at others, too conspicuous – as is the case nowadays with the various persecution of immigrants in the European Union (Stolcke, 1995). However, the monster has an advantage too: it demonstrates transgression. Not only is it contradictory and heterogeneous, but even worse, it is ambiguous: is it similar or different to us? Is it simply a monster or does it have human features? Maybe, like a memory of its exclusion, we can still read its previous humanity. For the monster has one foot in each world, master of ambiguity and in-betweenness: '*le monstrueux, qui participe des deux mondes*' (Montadont, 1987, p. 170). Can it possibly be one of us?

Maybe this is why it exerts this powerful attraction on us. Well, some monsters more than others, though. There are some monsters so clearly inhuman, that nobody can regret their exclusion – they deserve it, we say: Who wants a Cannibal in one's life? In other cases, it is not so clear, poor Frankenstein. And sometimes, we even surprise ourselves feeling attraction for others. We all know vampires are dangerous, but isn't Dracula irresistible? But we'd better watch out, for, however strong the attraction, the monster is not defenceless. As Haraway says, the monster cannot pretend not to know, to have forgotten, it cannot feign innocence. You'd better not 'romanticize' the monster, if you don't want to be a guest at their table, or preying in its mind ... For the monster is subversive, and without realizing, you end up asking weird questions to yourself: '*le monstre ce n'est pas l'autre, c'est nous*' (Montadon, 1987, p. 72).

If monsters break the Aristotelian doctrine that 'like produces like' (Huet, 1993), what can the monster show us?

Of cannibals and other teratogenies ...

Allow me to tell you a short story of cannibals, as Lestrigant (1997) tells it. When Columbus stepped on new land, not only did he discover a New World, but also the Cannibal. Real otherness, so resistant to our understanding that we were all too eager to find one explanation. For some, stripped of its ritual aspect, cannibalism was reduced to a mere matter of nutrition.[2] The poor Cannibal lived in an environment of such limited resources that, had they not eaten human flesh, they would not have survived. But if it is for nutrition, how can we accept that such practices were possible among humans, how could the polluting threat of such a bestial and demonic act be held at bay? It was excluded by literal distance. Cannibalism was confined to Robinson's island, to Flaubert's and Sade's deep primitivism, to Medusa's raft. The other as a scapegoat, carrying all our impurity, the black(ened) alter ego. A process of degradation of the Other, with the help of science and colonialism.

Others – Montaigne among them – produced the symbolic dimension necessary to keep them in the kingdom of humans. It was not nutrition, but revenge: an act full of meaning, still human. Not only is the Cannibal understandable, but it is also noble, brave and defiantly talkative: it gives out more than it takes in. Moreover, it symbolizes our own misery: after all, isn't it better to eat the dead (as most of them do) than to live off the living (alienation and exclusion) as we do? Cannibals as a mirror to see our own sins. *Le monstre c'est nous*, we are all Tupinambas. At the discovery of this '*le bon cannibal*', the missionaries' appetites suddenly woke up. Jesuits, Capuchins ... all in search of souls to fatten up the Holy Body. Missionaries giving themselves to be consumed in order to consume. The assimilation appeared to be mutual, the eaten eater. A symbolic fusion with the Other. (Well, not only symbolic: the consumption of some (missionaries) bodies was rather literal. Even though this was quite a bargain: a few missionaries as exchange for the massacre of many cannibals' souls and bodies ...).

But now, how to stop the ghost of cannibalism? It was said that human flesh was inedible; the problem being that those affirmations were followed by culinary suggestions ('Spaniards are not very good to eat because the flesh is too tough, unless it is marinated and softened for two or three days before eating' (ibid, p. 127) and gourmet's distinctions ('The Spaniards are cruel as they are indigestible; but the French please both the palates and the ears of these barbarians, who thereby demonstrate their undeniable good sense, tact *and good taste*' (ibid, p. 129 – a French man wrote. This is consumption for belonging!!). Thus, alas! given this succulence, it was difficult to repress the irrepressible question: what can human flesh possibly taste like? (Mmm, look what I've got for you, do you want it?). For this is the problem of the symbolic hypothesis, it forgets the flesh: Cannibals don't eat meat, but symbols, 'the noise of teeth and lips is shifted towards the domain of language' (ibid, p. 12).

Cannibalistic appetites ... or vampirical seductions?

And we, as social researchers, why do we do it? Why do we represent others? Why do I consume gypsies and scientists? All right, here are some answers. One: it is a matter of nutrition: food is food, a job is a job, and we all have to survive. By representing others, after all, our curricula are growing, our faculties too. Women's Studies and MAC on science. Centres of Technology (oops, this is the end of my belonging!) and grants to spend months following scientists around. And what about the display, identity and belonging we obtain from this consumption? (Which do you reckon is more profitable in terms of symbolic capital: the gypsies or the scientists? Which works more for my distinction? (Bourdieu, 1979)). My career is feeding on my gypsies, on my scientists. Have a look at this paper: nutritious others.

But, like Montaigne's Cannibals, we have more sublime reasons. We consume others because we feel it is fair, it needs to be done, it is politically necessary. The representation of the other is linked to an emancipatory project. We detect poor innocent others to rescue; or dirty others: we are all too willing to go to the margins, to eat this (maybe succulent, but polluted) flesh. And while eating these others, we offer ourselves to be eaten (our position, our voices, our power of representation in order to achieve their emancipation). A communion by consumption.[3] We strive to say the same: to talk on their behalf, or to make sure that when they talk we say the same. We need to speak in an only voice. Only one voice.

And here lies the problem with emancipatory project – in the 'only'. If they are to be seen as legitimate such projects require an other who we speak for, an other which is 'already there'. A fixed and united category which is not put into question. For it is easier to eat 'the gypsies' or 'the scientists' in one bite than to hunt and eat each and one of them. It is easier to mobilize and consume others if they are categorized in one pack. This effect, which has not gone unnoticed (eg, Wilkinson and Kitzinger, 1996) brings the reification of the other. And a dichotomic and bellicose definition of the world: 'Gypsies' and 'Payos', 'scientists' and 'lay people', 'women' and 'men', 'blacks' and 'whites', 'immigrants' and 'natives', etc: a fat list of others to consume.

Without this other, it is difficult to sustain the need for a spokesperson. Thus, and perversely, the more reified the other, the more legitimized the self. The more fixed, secure and stable the identity of the other is made, the more secured the identity of the spokesperson becomes: the other can become more a flag to be waved to mark one's position than an active, mobile participant. Who would I be without my 'others'? What would happen to my identity as social researcher if we question the existence of 'gypsies' or 'scientists'? We live out of our others.

However ... only one voice for emancipation's sake? All well and good if what you are representing are excluded gypsies. Or, for that matter, disciplined and obedient proteins. But, what if I am representing scientists? Now not only is the other well kept behind a category, but also, the category becomes bloody. For this is a curious situation in which the concern about speaking in one voice gives way to an active search to say different things, or even to prove those represented wrong: 'they – the scientists – still believe they are representing a reality out there!' Now we seem not to fight for the emancipation of an other from some societal demon (eg, against the alienation of Gypsies), but for the emancipation of society from some evil other (eg, against Science's power effects). Here we find one of those situations in which the ambiguous and mobile union of 'speaking for', and 'speaking about', allows us strategic sleights of hand (Lee, 1994). For more than a community of consumption, this seems a hunting. This is no communion, this is the war.[4] For it must be symbolic, but I can also hear the sound of teeth ...

Is it just chance that 'my scientists' called me 'Psycho-killer'?

Nevertheless, things are not so clear in this orgy. For the ethnographic relationship destabilizes the distribution of selves and others. What happens with the differentiation between self and other, between 'we' and 'they' when you are actively working to be in? The work to belong awakens appetites: you start desiring being one of them. The devil melts into a desired vampire. I

194

wonder whether they know, ('my' gypsies, 'my' scientists), how much I wanted to be in, and how relieved when I was out. (Attracted and repelled by the security of their identities, by the beauty of their worlds, by the fascination of their practices). Longing for belonging. Can you please bite my neck?

This is not a call to stop political projects. Because, yes, I do want to take sides as well (Star, 1991). But does this lead us to an eternal war between two sides? Can we take sides together? Can we take sides through commitment? Is there any alternative between communion of the same and war of differences? Between in and out? To whom are we telling that things could be different? (Spivak, 1990). Maybe there are ways; ways that enable us to agree and disagree, construct and deconstruct through commitments. I am with Spivak: 'it is especially important to choose as an object of critique something which we love, or which we cannot not desire, cannot not wish to inhabit, however much we wish also to change it' (Spivak, 1996, p. 7). Connecting, myself connecting (Brown and Capdevila, 1997). Who is there, at the other side of the line? Wait for me ...

They called me 'Psycho-killer'. I call myself Psycho-killer. I *am* Psycho-killer. And what's worse: I like it.

Encounters in a pre/post-modern world

Allow me to present the point with some reflections from both sides of my fieldwork: with Gypsies and with scientists. In the case of the Gypsy community – where, allegedly, it seemed very clear that we were dealing with two different, clear-cut communities, where it was possible to decide who belongs to which – things proved not to be so clear. When I joined a team of my University to work with a Gypsy community, I was neither Gypsy, nor did I especially want to be. The Gypsies of the community were very proud of being Gypsy, and would have been quite horrified at the thought of being 'Payo'. But they claim to be Spanish: of course, they have been living in Spain for about five centuries. No contradiction at all. But still, they are not Payos, and they claim a different culture. Indeed, our worldviews were very different, different interpretations arising everywhere. Was that the impenetrable (sic) barrier of cultural differences?

After some forging of relationship, the immense difference started to be put into question. Instead of a sheer incomprehension, a process of continuous negotiation seemed to be bearing some kind of understanding. The possibilities of relationship and contact seemed to be opening up, spaces where communication was possible. Well, more than possible. For among 'us', a new way of making sense of their culture was appearing. And with it, an awareness that other ways of relating to the world and life were not only possible, but could also be more desirable: we found ourselves following some of their habits, advice and models, looking at situations in our everyday life in a complete different way (Crespo, Pallí and Lalueza, in press).

But still, we were not Gypsy.

However, on gaining more and more knowledge of the community, the very security or stability of what it means to be 'Gypsy' started to disappear. For they explained to us that even though you were born 'Gypsy', this didn't assure you 'Gypsyness' at all: you were only considered a 'Gypsy' if you complied with the Gypsy law and, what is tantamount to the same, followed the authority of the elder (Crespo, 1998). And this is no joke, for this means that you and all your acts in every dimension are open to the gaze and control of the whole community, every day of your life. To be a 'Gypsy', you have to work for it your whole life; until your very last day you could be excluded. And, of course, they had anecdotes of non-gypsy people who had lived among them, sharing their practices and observing the Gypsy law, thus 'being more gypsy than ourselves'.

But still, I am not Gypsy.

However, what this example shows is that if I am not Gypsy, it is not because there is an insurmountable distance between two cultures. Neither because there is an alleged Catalan essence (sic) that prevents me from acquiring 'Gypsyness', nor a Gypsy essence impossible to make sense of. It is because I haven't worked hard enough, I have engaged neither in 'Gypsy acts' nor with a form of life. To be Gypsy, there is no passport: you have to earn it.

The situation was different in the ethnography in a biology laboratory. We, social psychologists who present ourselves more as anthropologists – nevertheless seen as clinic psychologists. They: biologists and biochemists. For the situation now is one of 'researchers studying researchers'. This, as many have realized, provokes some problems (Latour, 1988a; Woolgar, 1988), for it challenges directly the supposed distance which ethnographers are supposed to be endowed with. Among us, was the relationship one of self-to-self ('scientists studying scientists') or one of other to self (non-scientists 'studying' scientists)? In other words, the question arose of whether we belonged or not to the scientific community.

With the initial negotiations, some degree of similarity was recognized (after all, wasn't I a young researcher, a PhD student like them?). And I wanted to be in, I was working to be in. (Had I gone native – our taboo or our secret desire?). But then, at some point the situation changed. More than half way through the study, (for reasons too long to explain), a debate arose about whether we were or not scientists. In order to find the answer, they asked some questions ('Is it true that you [social sciences] don't publish and that you don't have journals? Isn't your work too subjective to accumulate knowledge?'). Internal debates – always in our absence, of which we had news through leaking – went on for some days. So much so, that in the end they were complaining that they did not know any more what science was!

Interestingly, debates turned back into a crude categorization 'we-they', 'natural scientists-social scientists' ... and eventually, the last category was disposed of: the consensus was that, surely, we were not scientific enough to be scientists. Result 1: we were out of science. The end of (one of) our belonging(s). Result 2: I am lost, moved by the ethnographic position/relation: not knowing whether I was scientist or not; whether I was a 'proper' PhD student or not; recognizing myself completely neither as a 'scientific biologist', nor as 'non-scientific social psychologist'; not knowing where I belonged, where I wanted to belong (definitely, this paper will cost me my belonging – one of my many).

Limits, the very idea

What is happening with belongings then? Are you one of us or one of them? A Gypsy or a Payo? A scientists or a lay person? Different or similar? Self or Other? Pure or Monster? National or Foreign? Do you belong or are you excluded? In both stories on Gypsies and on Scientists, what counts as a 'we' or as a 'they' was disturbed. On leaving behind historical narratives of selves and others (Michaels, 1996), and observing particular situations/interactions, belongings do not appear as taken for granted and unproblematic affiliations which sustain the relation, but the other way round: it is in relation where belongings and exclusions are (re)produced, negotiated, attributed, negated and so forth. (You need membership work, to show that you belong – whether this means to comply with the Gypsy Law of the elders, to publish and be known in particular spheres, to prove you know the code, or any other way in which loyalties and moralities are put to the test and need to be shown). Thus, whether or not you belong to the Gypsy or a scientific community, that is, whether or not you are a Gypsy or a scientist, is always in the making.

As Garfinkel (1967) taught us, it is this very membership work, the work required to sustain belongings and exclusions, that is constructing those very identities and communities which define us and to which we strive to belong. (The same communities that grant our identities, come into existence precisely because of our work to belong). Thus the Gypsy community is constituted out of attempts to be Gypsy; science is constituted out of attempts to be scientists. The boundaries between collectives which differentiate identities, (those same boundaries that are supposed to make communication difficult), reveal themselves as being always in the making. In this sense, we are always on the boundary: always doing boundary work, through which the very boundaries, mobile and flexible, are continuously (re)constituted.

And it is in the way boundaries are drawn that selves and others, similarities and differences are constituted. In the previous story, had they accepted us as scientists, this would have had dramatic repercussions, for if we were 'scientists', their concept of 'science' and their own identities as 'scientists' would have been challenged. Our exclusion was somewhat necessary if their identities were to be secured – a categorization for disposal (Latimer, 1997). In this way, the construction of us as 'other' to science worked for their stability: the borders of disciplines and identities were re-done and maintained. In a similar move, a clear surveillance on (and for a long time, avoidance of) the relationship between Gypsies and Payos, works for a preservation of the boundary, of a clear-cut categorisation that keeps the two groups separated. Boundary work to create selves, others and quasi-others. In other words, through othering, ordering was achieved/performed.

Thus, selves and others are not what grants relationship, but the other way round: they are constituted through the relationship (Mead, 1934). They are effects of ordering (Law, 1994). There are acts of differentiation and identification, not differences and identities (Latour, 1988b, p. 169). Labour of division: production, consumption and disposal of differences for belonging and exclusion (Hetherington and Munro, 1997). Inclusions and exclusions can be performed (and even, held open and undecided for a while) so as to perform order, mobilize others, exclude alternative orders. Ordering others and othering orders, this is the mass consumption of otherness, the consumption of massive others.

Beloved others ...

If belonging is always in the making, always depending on ordering, we will have to conclude, with Munro (1997a, 1999), that membership is partial and incomplete. Like the Gypsies, until the very last day of our lives, we are exposed to exclusion. Like in the laboratory, identities are worked and reworked to negotiate belongings. We must work for belonging; membership is an on-going achievement; we always risk exclusion: a self can become an other. Therefore, by showing the impossibility of belonging completely and for ever, we open ourselves to the experience of being marginal, monstrous – even if only for a while. We can live the precariousness and instability of selves, identities, belongings, houses, communities, and so forth.

Confronted with the categorization self/other, the stranger is always the other; but on considering the heterogeneity between self and other, the degrees of belonging, the eternal work of membership, we start tasting our own foreignness, we become more and more strangers to ourselves. We are always on Borderlands (Anzaldúa, 1987), always on the margins. Thus, the encounter with the monster can challenge our belonging: We are never at home, we are not the master of the house anymore.

This does not mean that there are no categories, homes, belongings, identities or selves. Not at all, for not everything is so fluid and emergent in our world: there are Textuality *and* Tectonics (Curt, 1994; Lee, 1996). But one thing is to accept their existence, and the other is to accept them as 'already-there'. Rather, the interesting thing, then, is to see how stability is made possible, what holds entities in place[5] (Latour, 1987). For the security of these entities is frequently based on the work of others. Others who are then pushed and excluded into the margins, becoming invisible (Star, 1991) – whether these are women sustaining the work of men, black women managing the house of white women (Webster, 1998), technicians supporting scientists' work (Shapin, 1989), or slaves supporting the identities of free people (Morrison, 1987), just to give a few examples. This is the exclusion of everything dark into the lands of the monster what makes appear our home secure and stable. The more secured the other, the more secured the self.[6] So, when you see a category working, look for all the work that is needed to keep it there.

The recognition that our identities/communities are frequently sustained in exclusion, makes us all monsters: we are all feeding on others. Selves and houses and communities are made with others. Invisible others whose presence always haunts us: our (Beloved) ghosts. We all are made of them, we live thanks to and among them. We all depend on ghosts' hospitality. This is why, rather than 'tolerating the other' (you have the right to be different; how generous I feel), we'd better admit that we vitally depend on the other. I need the other's hospitality to keep on moving, to endeavour in being. (It would seem, then, that not everything can be swallowed up (Law, 1997); or brought to your own language. Time to admit the agency of the other (Bhabha, 1994).

Opening up spaces: bridges and horizons

At this point, the ambiguity and ambivalence of the monster comes in handy. On the one hand, the figure of the monster calls our attention towards the continuous making and remaking of selves and others, and therefore, de-essentializes these notions, showing them as effects of relationships, rather than previous entities to it. On the other hand, however, precisely because selves and others are mutually constituted in relation, it is in these very relations that new possibilities come into being: the figure of the monster opens up a space in which limits can be subverted. Thus, the boundary play allows for both, moments of subjection and power (Munro, 1997a) and moments of resistance and change. As Star (1991) puts it, there is plenty of space and possibilities in the 'as-yet' labelled, in the 'in-between' positions (Anzaldúa, 1987; Bhabha, 1994), in the perversion of borders (Haraway, 1991, 1997), at the hyphen (Fine, 1994).

The acceptance that categories and communities are in the making does not render them less useful. Not all categories and clear belongings are always bad or ways of disposing of others, and some can be useful to articulate political fictions (Burman, 1996) or hopes (Bhavnani, 1999). Rather, the other way round: to show this on-going construction opens possibilities of construction, of commitments, of association (Pallí, submitted). For the experience of monstrosity that we all have makes us question kinship. 'Who are my kin in this odd world of promising monsters, vampires, surrogates, living tools, and aliens?' asks Haraway (1997, p. 52). How can one say 'count me in'? If it is true that 'cannibalism is a radical form of hospitality' (Baudrillard, 1993, p. 144), could you then, please, eat me? Hope and appetites, affects increasing our possibilities of acting. Performances of encounters in the centre, in the margins and in-between. Wait for me, I am coming. Connecting, myself connecting ...

Contacts with otherness, then, have the power to allow novelty into different collectives. At the zone where encounters happen, a Gypsy can challenge politicians with a highly politicized speech; a Gypsy woman can silently (and not even that silently) subvert the authority of male voice. Some Payo women are made to confront the power of emotions in ethnographic relationships. Some biologists can start thinking what is going on in science, when nobody knows what It is. A social psychologist trained at biting the jugular of scientists falls in love with them all, starting to feel the instability and insecurity of belonging once one is moved. Encounters with the Other, in which we are moved by something other than ourselves[7] (Pallí, 2000).

It is then when differences and similarities, limits and borders can be questioned. At this zone, then – precisely at the zone in which we encounter our limit, that which we are not, that which stops us – we find what can bring us forward beyond ourselves. In other words, if the other is our limit, it is not a limit that enclose us into borders; the other does not confine us, our limits are not our prison. Rather, it is the very possibility of relationship, of interaction. What saves us from 'the hell of the same' (Baudrillard, 1993). A refrain, a repetition which is never the same (Brown and Capdevila, 1997) The other is the potential you (Shotter, 1989), the 'you' that stretches our horizon: Gadamer (1975), who taught us a while ago that there is never perfect communication, who showed how we find limits in the other which open us up, said, too, that those very limits were what projects us in the world. If there is no way of going outside our limits, it is a matter of building bridges, building connections with the other. 'A boundary is not that at which something stops but, (...) the boundary is that from which something begins its presencing' (Heidegger, 1975, p. 155). Connecting, myself connecting. No way out of mediations and translations? Then, let's mediate and translate and connect worlds and languages. Encounters that turn the allegedly problematic barrier of difference into a source of possibilities. For better or for worse, it is up to us.

Refrains

This is the story of my addiction. I can't stop consuming others. Does this make me monstrous? Or do I still belong? But belong where? Longing too much to go bio-native as to be a good ethnographer, and psycho-ethnographer enough so as not to believe that going gypsy-native is so easy. Too strong a Catalan accent to be at home, too much English in my thoughts to be a foreigner. So, will you accept my account? For we all know that only some accounts will count; and, of these, some accounts will count more than others (Munro, 2001). For my account is ambiguous enough. Stepping some limits, but not crossing others completely. In spite of selves, affects and monsters, this story performs also the membership-work of belonging for 'those who know the code' (Douglas and Isherwood, 1978, p. 5). So, nothing is closed yet. Is this paper too much of a Cannibal or does it have a hue of vampirical pollution?

Maybe if I promise that I won't tell this story again ... for it is said that monstrous stories can only be told once. But then, can you trust a quasi-monster's word?

And what about you? Do you thing you are more pure? Look at our eyes and consume the abyss. Come on, join us. We know you wonder what human blood must taste like. Eat me and join us – if you find the Spaniard flesh too tough, you can always marinate it two or three days .... But if you decide (decide?) to avoid pollution, before you send me to do the dirty job, think twice. While ones order others, others disorder orders. Remember, no story can tell it all. Which does not only mean that there is still territory uncolonized (Lee and Brown, 1994), but also, that your house is never yours completely. The ghosts never leave the haunted house. Ghosts ex machina. Who said the world was disenchanted? *We all depend on ghosts' hospitality* ....

Listen to my story, for it might be yours too.

This is the story of my addiction: I can't stop consuming others.

And you ... ? Can you?

Notes

1 In some disciplines, the consumption of the preposition 'with' displays a self concerned with dialogue, dialectical relationships .... However, in some manual crafts, to work with gives quite a different sense, involving manipulation, creation .... It is the ambivalent interplay of both senses that I would like to keep here.

2 This move is not infrequent in monsters either. It has even been suggested that vampires were in fact nomads from Asia who would drink the blood of their cattle, for need of vitamin B!!

3 Political project? Partly. Partly guilt for having been born Western, perhaps? (Baudrillard, 1978). Maybe we are trying to win our place in heaven – or our place of heaven on earth. This is our mission. And we do not mind being consumed too: 'eat me', we ask, 'eat my flesh'. Communion by consumption: we are all welcome at the table (Williams, 1973), for redemption and salvation.

4 Is this revenge? (If we are not a science, we'll see who is). Do we want to use them as a mirror to show our own faults (they search for power, but who doesn't?). Do we want them to do all the dirty jobs? (as if we could, an ant (sic) biting an old, hard-skinned elephant. I still hear them laughing). But we always have the option of accusing them of being dominant, destroyers, male-omnipotent; not like us, feminine social sciences, dolphins and other weak natures (Mulkay, 1991).

5 Like passports and customs. Or the 'Schengen border', permeable to goods, but not to African monsters.

6 Only because one has many others working to stabilize one's identity that one knows who one is. And the more the self knows, the less the other can find itself.' Garner called and announced them men – but only on Sweet Home, and by his leave. Was he naming what he saw or creating what he did not? (...) It troubled him that, concerning his own manhood, he could not satisfy himself on that point. Oh, he did manly things, but was that Garner's gift or his own will? (...) Did a whiteman saying it make it so?' (Morrison, *Beloved*, p. 220).

7 Suddenly, our own and master language does not run so fluently as before, and we find ourselves saying something like 'me understiendes o no me understiendes?'. It is now that we can start to understand how the translation might turn 'German into Indian' (in Benjamin, 1975) – or Catalaspanish into English, for that matter ...

References

Anzaldúa, G., (1987), *Borderlands/La Frontera. The New Mestiza*. San Francisco: Aunt Lute.

Apfelbaum, E., (1989), Relaciones de dominación y movimientos de liberación. Un análisis del poder entre los grupos. In J.F. Morales and C. Huici (eds), *Lecturas de Psicología Social* (pp. 261–95). Madrid: Uned.

Atwood, M., (1969), *The Edible Woman*. Toronto: McClelland & Stewart-Bantam Limited.

Baudrillard (1978), *Cultura y Simulacro*. Barcelona: Kairos.

Baudrillard (1993), *The Transparency of Evil: Essays on Extreme Phenomena*. (J. Benedict, Trans.). London: Verso.

Benjamin, W., (1975), *Illuminations* (H. Sohn, Trans). New York: Shocken Books, 1968.

Bhabha, H., (1994), *The location of culture*. London: Routledge.

Bhavnani, K., (1999), Paper presented in the Action-Research Conference. Manchester, U.K., July, 13–16.

Bourdieu, P., (1979), *La Distinción. Criterios y bases sociales del gusto*. Barcelona:Taurus.

Brown, S.D. and Capdevila, R., (1997), Perpetuum Mobile: Substance, force and the sociology of translation. In J. Law & J. Hassard (eds), *ANT and after* (pp. 26–50). Oxford: Blackwells.

Burman, E., (1996), The Spec(tac)ular Economy of Difference. In S. Wilkinson & C. Kitzinger (eds), *Representing the Other. A 'Feminism & Psychology' Reader* (pp. 138–40). London: Sage.

Callon, M., (1986), Some elements of a sociology of translation: Domestication of the scallops and fishermen of St. Brieuc bay. In J. Law (ed.), *Power, action and belief: A new sociology of knowledge?* (pp. 196–233). London: Routledge & Kegan Paul.

Clifford, J. and Marcus, G.E. (1986), *Writing Culture*. Berkeley: University of California Press.

Condor, S., (1997), And so say all of us? Some thoughts on 'Experiential Democratization' as an aim for Critical Social Psychologists. In T. Ibáñez & L. Íñiguez (eds), *Critical Social Psychology* (pp. 111–146). London: Sage.

Crespo, I., (1998), *La adolescencia en el contexto cultural gitano*. Research project, Universitat Autònoma de Barcelona.

Crespo, I., Pallí, C. and Lalueza, J.L. (in press). Minority/majority relationships: An educational alternative for the empowerment of a Gypsy community in Barcelona. *Community, Work & Family*.

Curt, B.C., (1994), *Textuality and tectonics: Troubling social and psychological science*. Buckingham Open University Press.

Douglas, M., (1966), *Purity and Danger: an analysis of the concepts of pollution and taboo*. London: Routledge.

Douglas, M. and Isherwood, B., (1980), *The World of Goods: towards an anthropology of consumption*. Harmondsworth: Penguin.

Fine, M., (1994), Working the Hyphens. Reinventing Self and Other in Qualitative Research. In N. Denzin and Y.S. Lincoln (eds), *Handbook of Qualitative Research* (pp. 70–82). London: Sage.

Gadamer, H.G., (1975), *Verdad y Método I*. Salamanca: Sígueme, 1996.

Garfinkel, H., (1967), Studies in Ethnomethodology. Englewood Cliffs, New Jersey: Prentice-Hall.

Haraway, D., (1991), *Simians, Cyborgs, and Women. The Reinvention of Nature*. London: Free Associations Books.

Haraway, D., (1997), *Modest Witness@Second Millennium. FemaleMan© Meets OncoMouse_^{TM}*. London: Routledge.

Heidegger, M., (1975), *Poetry, Language, Thought*. London: Harper & Row.

Huet, M.H., (1993), *Monstrous Imagination*. Cambridge, USA: Harvard University Press.

Latimer, J., (1997), Giving patients a future: the constituting of classes in an acute medical unit. *Sociology of Health & Illness, 19*, 2, 160–85.

Latour, B., (1987), *Science in Action*. Cambridge, Mass: Harvard University Press.

Latour, B., (1988a), The Politics of Explanation. An alternative. In S. Woolgar (ed.), *Knowledge and Reflexivity. New frontiers in the Sociology of Knowledge* (pp. 155–176). London: Sage.

Latour, B., (1988b), *The Pasteurization of France followed by irreductions* (A. Sheridan and J. Law, Trans.). Cambridge, MA: Harvard University Press.

Law, J., (1994), *Organizing modernity*. Oxford: Blackwell.

Law, J., (1997), Traduction/Trahison: Notes On ANT. published by the Centre for Social Theory and Technology, Keele University at http://www.keele.ac.uk/depts/stt/jl/pubs-JL2.htm

Lee, N., (1994), Child Protection Investigations: Discourse Analysis and the Management of Incommensurability. *Journal of Community & Applied Social Psychology*, 4, 275–286.

Lee, N.M., (1996), Two Speeds: How are real stabilities possible? In R. Chia (ed.), *In the Realm of Organisation: Essays for Robert Cooper*. London: Routledge.

Lee, N. and Brown, S., (1994), Otherness and the Actor Network: The undiscovered continent. *American Behavioral Scientist*, 37 (6): 772–790.

Lee, N. and Stenner, P., (1997), Who pays? Can we pay them back? In J. Law and J. Hassard (eds), *ANT and After* (pp. 90–112). Oxford: Blackwell.

Lem, S., (1991), *Solaris*. Kent: Faber & Faber. (Original published 1961).

Lestringant, F., (1997), *Cannibals. The discovery and representation of the Cannibal from Columbus to Jules Verne*. Trans. Morris, R. Oxford: Blackwell.

Lorde, A., (1980), *The Audre Lorde Compendium. Essays, Speeches and Journals. (The Cancer Journals, Sister Outsider and A Burst of Light)*. London: Harper Collins Publishers.

Mead, G.H., (1934), *Mind, self and society*. Chicago: Chicago University Press.

Michaels, M., (1996), *Constructing Identities*. London: Sage.

Montadont, A., (1987), La beaute monstrueuse de la sirene. In The Monstrous. *Durham French Colloquies*, 1, 59–72.

Morrison, T., (1987), *Beloved*. London: Vintage, 1997.

Mulkay, G., (1991), *Sociology of science. A sociological Pilgrimage*. Buckingham: Open University Press.

Munro, R., (1995), The disposal of the meal. In D.W. Marshall (ed.), *Food choice and the consumer*. (pp. 313–325). London: Blackie Academic & Professional.

Munro, R., (1997a), Power, Conduct and Accountability: re-distributing discretion and the new technologies of managing. *Proceedings of the 5th Interdisciplinary Perspectives on Accounting:* 4.1.–4.2.10, Manchester: University of Manchester.

Munro, R., (1997b), Ideas of difference: stability, social spaces and the labour of division. In K. Hetherington & R. Munro (eds), *Ideas of Difference*. Oxford: Blackwell.

Munro, R., (1999), The cultural performance of control. *Organisation Studies*, 29 (4): 619–40.

Munro, R. (2001) Calling for Accounts: numbers, monsters and membership work. *The Sociological Review*, 49.

Pallí, C., (2000), *Jugant als límits: Selves, others and monsters en el viaje etnográfico*. Research project, Universitat Autònoma de Barcelona.

Pallí, C. (submitted). Communities in Context: Undefinitions, Multiplicity and Cultural difference.*American Journal of Community Psychology*, special issue.

Said, E., (1978), *Orientalism*. New York: Pantheon.

Sampson, E.E., (1993), *Celebrating the Other. A dialogic account of human nature*. London: Harvester Wheatsheaf.

Shotter, J., (1989), The social construction of 'you'. In K. Gergen & J. Shotter (eds), *Texts of Identity*. London: Sage.

Spivak, G., (1987), *In Other Worlds: Essays in Cultural Politics*. London: Methuen.

Spivak, G.C., (1990), *The Post-colonial Critic. Interviews, Strategies, Dialogues*. London: Routledge.

Spivak, G.C., (1996), *The Spivak Reader*. London: Routledge.

Star, S.L., (1991), Power, technology and the phenomenology of conventions: on being allergic to onions. In J. Law (ed.), *A sociology of monsters: Essays on power, technology and domination* (pp. 26–56). London: Routledge.

Stolcke, V., (1995), Talking culture. New boundaries, New Rhetorics of Exclusion in Europe. *Current Anthropology*, 36 (1): 1–24.

Webster, W., (1998), *Imagining Home. Gender, 'Race' and National Identity, 1945–1964*. London: University College London Press.

Wilkinson, S., (1997), Prioritizing the Political: Feminist Psychology. In T. Ibáñez and L. Íñiguez (eds), *Critical Social Psychology* (pp. 178–94). London: Sage.

Wilkinson, S. and Kitzinger, C., (1996), (eds), *Representing the Other. A 'Feminism & Psychology' Reader*. London: Sage.

Williams, R., (1973), *The country and the city*. London: Chatto & Windus.

Woolgar, S., (1988), Reflexivity is the Ethnographer of the Text. In S. Woolgar (ed.), *Knowledge and Reflexivity. New frontiers in the Sociology of Knowledge* (pp. 14–34). London: Sage.

Border Blues: between Maastricht and Dada disorder

Robert Grafton Small

Mass for Hard Times
Because we cannot be clever and honest
and are inventors of things more intricate
than the snowflake – Lord have mercy. (R.S. Thomas, 1992: 11)

When Picasso died I read in a magazine that he had made four thousand masterpieces in his lifetime and I thought, 'Gee, I could do that in a day.' So I started. And then I found out, 'Gee, it takes more than a day to do four thousand pictures.' You see, the way I do them, with my technique, I really thought I could do four thousand in a day. And they'd all be masterpieces because they'd all be the same painting. And I started and I got up to about five hundred and then I stopped. But it took more than a day, I think it took a month. So at five hundred a month, it would have taken me about eight months to do four thousand masterpieces – to be a 'space artist' and fill up spaces that I don't believe should be filled up anyway. It was disillusioning for me, to realize it would take me that long. (Warhol, 1975: 148)

Mass, if central to the topography of present-day European society, is equally insubstantial, fragmentary and shiftless, an abyss of absence where we have not yet been or no longer are. Polyphonic politics apart, this might all sound a little Greek to those less obdurate monoglots who trouble and strive with an otherness more than mere double Dutch. It is. Rather, it may be, assuming the first mention of Europe as a geographical entity was Theocritus' attempt (Parks, 1998: 13) to distinguish the Peloponnese, to demonstrate that a small peninsula had not been engulfed by the amorphous bulk of an ever-invasive Asia.

Playing on the same divide, Singh (1998: 7–8) insists that while Pythagoras gathered many mathematical tools and techniques from both the Babylonian and the Egyptian civilizations of his time, their accounting systems and their elaborate buildings, it seems the peoples of these well-established social orders treated each computation as a recipe which could be followed blindly to solve a practical problem, say, the reconstruction of field boundaries lost in the annual flooding of the Nile. Why these calculations worked was irrelevant, only that they should. The Greek's, indeed the Greeks', subsequent development of geometry, literally the measurement of the earth, as a set of principles, a realm of thought independent of its physical or communal origins, is implicit in our own understandings of space and time, our everyday ability to handle notions of distance and land mass, to impute borders and negotiate cultural boundaries, even our capacity for inferring social structures from the realised masses of architecture.

Corbusier raises suitably monumental parallels (1978: 50–52) between the ordering of industrial life, and entire cities as we might recognize them, and the buildings of the Acropolis, massed together in accordance with their plans – each structure as the architectural expression of a particular geometry – and designed to be seen from a distance as one solid block. However, for all that our understandings of mass and surface are informed by this underlying aesthetic with its various encodings of rhythm and propriety, the ability to impose a given order on our physical surroundings merely by looking at them is very much a societal rather than a mathematical construct and open to endless individual reinterpretation (Virilio, 1991: 110–111).

A hint of the distance between outlook and organization, between landscape and belonging, can be glossed from Paul Carter's (1996) impressive overview of European perspectives and their impact upon a civilized world. He begins, though, with a detailed discussion (1996: 121–123) of Giorgione, a painter from turn of the sixteenth century Venice, whose curvilinear sense of space was, at the time, just one among many offering fluid, rather than fixed points of view to a Lagoon society, physically and figuratively at home with the parabolas of navigation and the sea's ceaseless shifting. Typically, then, Giorgione's landscapes and buildings refuse to narrow towards their more distant edges. Where we might expect convergence on a common vanishing point, they splay out, and even though viewed obliquely, turn to face us.

If this seems difficult to picture nowadays, even disorientating, particularly to anyone unfamiliar with Cubism, it is because we, like the navigators of Columbus' generation, have generally adopted as somehow natural and true, the Florentine perspective (Carter, 1996: 136), a flatteringly one-sided format that makes our viewpoint the vanishing point of any prospect while, in effect, abstracting us from our own perceptions. Similarly, the underlying geometry, via Alberti, from Roman constructions of scale and proportion, grid and plan, may have enabled European explorers to reach the Americas (Carter, 1996: 123–124) but we are as blind as the sea-goers were to those other ways of seeing, sited in each local habitus rather than imported and imposed by outsiders.

Still we feel a sting from the Aztec seer (Carter, 1996: 136–139) who combined the coming of Cortés with an inherited illustration and circular notions of time to tell of a Mexico invaded and possessed by a mass of monocular men, every one a Cyclops. Significantly, this grim yet glorious visual pun, a sight gag on the conquistadores' helmeted heads and singular vision, has far outlasted its creation and its creative use, though only as an arcanum, the detritus of empire, its critical ambivalence largely lost on those who brought the new barbarism to the New World.

The dismissiveness of the colonizing gaze is so acute, and replicated so readily by the abstract geometries which inform it, that in Australia where the Aborigines were once entirely migratory, rooted in movement and routed along folding, not planar, surfaces, the nominal outback was seen and enacted by incomers as a cultural waste land as well as a desert. This serial supposition, this mapping of maps, is in itself a shell, a contemporary creation, though the apparent absence at its heart has come to encode a signal slippage between writing under erasure and the erasure under writing of those clans and communities who made, and reaffirmed, themselves and their place in a protean world through sequences of song and sand painting, drift-line and dance (Carter, 1996: 345–346).

Ethnographic fragments apart, some Aboriginal Australians have made subtle and revealing attempts to explain their situation (Carter, 1996: 42–46), developing mimicry to the point of taking on European styles of landscape painting, then returning the cultural imposition by relaying established, indigenous stories of a restless earth to the settlers – the stock-still, the utterly other – in the only medium they might understand. More recently, bolder native artists (Carter, 1996: 350–356) have transferred the dots and dashes of their own sacred material to murals and canvases, a radical shift in perspective on many levels yet one which protects the producers' notions of the available landscape as part of an unfolding performance, not static but ceaselessly mobile. Traditional sand paintings were, and are, meant to be viewed from above – a map to us, an installation, and more – though the marks and the significance of each composition will vary with every telling of the tribe's terrain, each artful account another step in their rippling pilgrimage 'ab origine ad interim'. This 'talk of the walk' completed, the contents of a contingent continent move on, while the finished – exhausted – designs are left to blow away.

In these terms, permanent patterns, without song or shift, are 'white man's toys' (Carter, 1996: 345) and not at all serious, especially when, hanging on a wall, they are literally at odds with the world. Ironically, recalling the Aztec's Cyclops, these visible proofs of cultural astigmatism are highly prized and fetch good prices at auction, meaning relatively cheap if you consider their illustrious, and remarkable, predecessor. Long before Tom Paulin (1998: xiv) made the link between Navajo sand painting and journalism, Andy Warhol had already taken the further step from mass-produced small ads in the popular press to polymer paint on canvas, from commonplace consumer items to cultural icons, even the quarter-revolution from underfoot to up against the wall. So much for the vertical expression of a horizontal desire. ...

His 'Dance Diagram-Tango' was completed in 1962 (Shanes, 1993: 24) and depicts precisely what you'd not have looked for then in a gallery: two interwoven tracks of numbered footprints – left and right – with directional arrows showing the proper, if not the ritual, movements of the dance on display. Clearly, Warhol is trafficking in the same cultural improprieties, the same glide across boundaries of outlook and expectation, as in the more recent

Australian works but turning our gaze in the opposite direction, from our domestic demotic to the heights of contemporary fine art. Andy may equally well be seen as challenging notions of cultural hierarchy and the primacy of a particular perspective, where the Aboriginal artefacts are derivative or kitsch, for Warhol has moved only within, and against, the confines of his own artistic embeddedness. You can take your time – 4/4, in this case – working through the mass of plays on popular dance as both mass movement – perhaps the Tango's spread from Argentina – and the movement of mass – his and hers, theirs, what have you. Note, also, the body of music which is vital under any circumstances, and absent, yet which we can evoke from the steps and the silence, given an appropriate upbringing.

However, even Warhol's groundbreaking variation assumes the otherness of broken ground. He, too, adopts an architectural aesthetic, an orchestrated arrangement of smooth surfaces and radiused rather than radical curves, where the violence implicit in rendering rainforest hardwood as the sprung and polished floor of a dance hall is barely a beat in the rhythm of our everyday lives. Then again, as Christopher Hill (1996: 91–92) reminds us, this terrible combination of a single overarching vision and a willingness to shape, to force, the flesh and the fabric of the world accordingly (Hill, 1996: 95–97), was evident as long ago as the late sixteenth century, in the establishment of England as a society structured around centralized government and liberty within the law for property-owning individuals (Hill, 1996: 162) but only oppression and exclusion for the poor and the dispossessed.

Hill also demonstrates in convincing detail (1996: 19–43, 90–91) how the resultant assault on highly localized traditions of communal landowning, and the importance of both vernacular understandings and oral history to the interpretation of law and the maintenance of parochial order, was so severe that numbers of successful yet self-sufficient small communities dissolved, or decayed into day-labouring and vagabondage, sometimes even emigration – often to North America (Hill, 1996: 163–164). Here, as settlers, the same people helped to foster many previously insubstantial or fragmentary notions of republicanism and freedom without privilege (Hill, 1996: 169–176, 188–189), while treating the indigenous population to an array of the founding abuses. Irony, irony ....

Limned in these liminal states, the instruments of power presage colonial expansion in their – literal – field trials on domestic but outlying systems of tenure, hierarchy and perception. Equally, as the written law (Hill, 1996: 20–21) comes to signify absent structures of authority that are not amenable to local needs, or concerned to be so, the powerless and the impoverished are relieved of their most intimate feelings of self and belonging – displaced from their home ground without going anywhere. Here, too, in principle, is an end to customary weights such as the stone, petrine in name and nature yet inconstant, meaning more or less according to what's being scaled and where. A way out also for traditional tallies and counting systems, and for measures culled from our own bodies, like the hand and the span.

These strategies of estrangement are with us still, in more extreme yet for all their presence, less obvious forms: ours. Daily, the bulk of Western society struggles to accommodate itself within a topography of flesh (Klein, 1997: 34–37), mapped out in mass-produced clothes and measured in industrially standard sizes. The contours and declines, the rhythms and folds, of our own shapes and appetites are foreign country to us now, an embodiment of alimentary alienation (Klein, 1997: 93), whether we eat or not. A parallel play of place and paradox emerges from the broader, more familiar strictures and structures of the built environment when wandering – down these one-way streets a man must go who is not himself one way – after Walter Benjamin (1997: 236): 'How are we to imagine an existence oriented solely toward Boulevard Bonne-Nouvelle, in rooms by Le Corbusier and Oud?' Consider, then, the following.

One evening, an intimate and I were in adjoining seats at Cinema 2 of the Glasgow Film Theatre, waiting to see a movie called 'Marvin's Room' – how many projections can you find, even now, and where are our margins maintained? – when a conversation broke out in the darkness behind us.

'Want wan?' The rustling cellophane suggested a packet of crisps being opened in situ.

'What flavour?'

'No flavour.'

'Aye, fine ....'

'I like tomato flavour'.

'D'ye get tomato flavour?'

'Aye. I'll tell ye where ye can buy them – at the Post Office. Walker's Tomato Flavoured Crisps.'

The two concerned were men in their sixties but a couple out together, a meeting of friends or perhaps a chance pairing? It's hard to tell. The lights were down and there are certain well-observed constraints, or limits of good taste, against eavesdropping too openly, especially when it might involve something as obvious as turning round or some other significant shift in your seat, in brief, the body language of intrusion. Not to mention making hurried notes in the flickering afterglow of the trailers, before the main feature has begun – what manner of aside is this?

By the same token, how are we to picture the 'first transnational university in Europe' (Ayre, 1998), which unites an institution in Limburg with another in Maastricht yet acknowledges the border it straddles between Belgium and the Netherlands? As one of the Limburgers remarked, a don, I gather, from the southernmost Dutch province, not a fellow from the Flemish fiefdom, 'It is interesting to find out in daily life, people living so near can belong so much to a different culture.' Disbelief suspended, and these difficulties apart, the notionally concerned parties all appear to view their joint venture as both interesting and important, a foretaste of the future perhaps, a cornerstone of the united Europe to come.

For all its apparent modesty, this small step is a signal response to other more ambitious attempts at such a feat. A trace of one particular instance, itself within living memory, was evident when the Institute of Contemporary Arts agreed to a display of annotated photographs (I.C.A. Concourse, August, 1977) by John Fieldhouse and Rupert Gardner, postgraduates from the R.C.A. The exhibition was entitled 'Blockhausen' and sought to demonstrate dominant characteristics of the '1,000 Year Reich' but for some reason, the show was cancelled at brutally short notice. Without witnesses, then, or the chance to attend, those unused posters that announced the forthcoming event became, in effect, a new venue for the very feature they trailed, a metonym for what the exhibitors might have had in mind.

Assuming we can envisage, much less admit, being at a non-event, this was intended, the creators claim, as an analysis of the largest and most enduring aspect of Reich architecture, the one artefact designed to last any time at all – The Atlantic Wall. As the structure is monolithically militaristic and its construction only possible through terrible sacrifice and a feudal use of labour akin, maybe, to the raising of the Pyramids, the nature of those powerful few whose ideology is encoded in the Wall is explicit. Millennial aspirations apart, however, the Wall is now a husk of hideous ambition, a mark of its makers' instability, rendered obsolete, like the Maginot Line it engulfed, by the parabolas of rocketry pioneered within Nazi Germany and from without by Oppenheimer's otherworldly A-Bomb, the end of both blitzkreig (Akizuki, 1981: 137) and the thousand bomber raid.[1]

Revalued to the point where we scarcely bother our heads over thoughts that were once capital offences, the Wall still encompasses Corbusier's (1978: 31) definition of architecture as 'the masterly, correct and magnificent play of masses brought together in light'. This in concrete form is the will to power, the Modernist project as an enforced interpretation of the drama inherent in the Parthenon, say, or the emergent engineering of American grain elevators (Corbusier, 1978: 33). Here are the cubes, cones and spheres, the cylinders and pyramids, our eyes are made to see, images which because they are distinct within us, tangible and unambiguous, are necessarily and indisputably the most beautiful of all shapes (Corbusier, 1978: 31). In Glasgow, but:

'After all that fuss about nae knickers, you bought see-through? Two pairs ....'
'Aye, they're nice. See? Well I like them and they're snug.'

Clearly the play of masses brought together in light, and as for magnificence, an entire book – a whole volume, so to speak – has been built around high regard for haunches and the beauty of bahookies (Hennig, 1975), yet unambiguous or made to be seen, let alone tangible? And how are we to take transparency? Not light, but darkness visible? Risible. There is also that one word interrogative. Does it echo the logic revealed in Corbusier's primary forms, addressing the seat of his argument, perhaps, or are we to infer a competing rationale, based on snugness and the sovereignty of self-determination, 'nice' being such an elastic term it will stretch to cover most things. Do we include the boundaries of self and society? If I dress as I like, why am I holding myself accountable, and to whom?

Where, now, are the foundations of morality à la mode, our understandings of propriety, gender and common decency, when a woman's underwear can be debated – displayed in discussion if not splayed out – in public? Slips of the tongue aside, the paired panties, those transparently mystifying tokens of industrialised eroticism, give rise to other seminal issues, like questions of where, or wear, the good might lie in consumer goods, and how it is consumed. Fundamentally, Corbusier declares (1978: 268), we are facing a problem of adaptation, in which the realities of our life are both formed and destroyed by a persistent disagreement between the modern state of mind and a stifling accumulation of age-long detritus.

His resolution, his counter to the coming revolution, is a new world order, regular, logical and clear, where things that are useful and usable are produced in a straightforward way (Corbusier, 1978: 268). Appropriately, making the case and snapping it shut, all this is captured in the single enduring image which concludes 'Vers Une Architecture' (Corbusier, 1978: 269), the photograph of a briar pipe. Not Corb's corncob, you'll notice, for this is no pipe dream, but obviously a form dictated by its function and equally a route to reducing our tangled past, our common roots, to ashes. True, the self-deprecating humour of a pipe-and-slippers parry to an impending upending, a mass-produced revolution against industrial order, is hardly consistent with Corbusier's prior account though perhaps fittingly for an architect, his whole life seems to have been an attempt to bridge the gap between human choice and natural or mechanical evolution, to reconcile his own inner and outer landscapes (Jencks, 1982: 142–148). Autocritique apart, however, it wouldn't require the self-regard of hindsight to read a book ending in a burner as a profane rebus, foreshadowing the final solution (Jencks, 1975: 67,72,77) when one society in particular was 'filled with a violent desire for something which it may obtain or may not' (Corbusier 1978 : 268).

Are we drawn instead, or do we draw, towards an idea of unfamiliar and eccentric gravity; Magritte's 'Ceci n'est past une pipe', one of the twentieth century's most imitated artworks, as a Dark Star over Corb's 'Ville Radieuse'? How are we to make our way among everyday goods and signs when a single surreal icon – a Belgian kakemono – shows industrially sponsored functionalism and all the related postulates of Modernist philosophy to be cultural constructs in themselves, every bit as slippery and inconstant as the interplay between picture and representation in this seething version of the Cretan Paradox. What does it mean to write 'This is not a pipe' across a bluntly literal painting of a pipe? Don't walk away, René ....

To compound the question, by addressing it, there is not only 'Ceci n'est pas une pipe', Michel Foucault's fecund discourse on Magritte's fascination with 'mystère', the ineffable alienness beneath the surface familiarity of the world, but in one translation at least (Foucault, tr. Harkness, 1983: 60), a curious misreading which implies any attempt to solve the riddle will itself appear full of holes as a result. We are told that in 'The Shock of the New', Robert Hughes speculates on René's canvas conundrum as a painted riposte, brushed on to brush away Corbusier's banal use of the briar's image. Not so. An acknowledged adept in the aesthetics of Modern Art, Hughes unhesitatingly asserts himself and his analysis (1981: 244), though on the basis of Magritte's 1928–9 variation rather than the 1926 portrayal preferred by Foucault (1983: 15).

From a fracas over footnotes, these seemingly minor marginalia will bear expansion on two fronts, beginning with 'la trahison des images', the picture reckoned to rebut Corbusier and more importantly, one of a forty year series of oils – another in the 'pipe' line – by which Magritte fuelled his drive to establish 'the mystery evoked *in fact* by the visible and the invisible' (Foucault, 1983: 57). While each of these paradoxical paintings is unique in fine art terms, with its own title and provenance, their thematic unity, their individual and collective 'aura' (Benjamin, 1992: 214), is subject to decay through those processes of reproduction and exchange that result in, say, 'the betrayal of images' as a postcard, reducing our reading of the surreal to quiet daze in cliché.

Artwork apart, the further inference from Harkness' hiccup offers hints of Magritte's hidden hinterland by taking at face value archetypally Modernist skills and commodities like communal literacy and cheap printing. A capital, if not an upper, case in point (Paulin, 1998: 309–310) concerns a distinguished American critic who became so fascinated by the strange, suggestive phrase 'soiled fish of the sea' in Herman Melville's novel 'White Jacket', that he based a deal of interpretation upon a demonstrable misprint. Omitted from the author's original, as well as the American and English first editions, this literary literal was created inadvertently – cast against type – by a miscast typesetter for an additional printing.

To an expert reader, though, the fault was far from self-evident, either as a small part of a particular word or sentence or in the broader context of the host novel, offering us at least the possibility of the critic's misapprehension as a plumbing of hitherto unhazarded depths and uncharted backwaters in the manner and material of Melville's marine writing. Does it help, then, to be given the authorized version (Paulin, 1998: 309): 'I wondered whether I was yet dead or still dying. But of a sudden some fashionless form brushed my side – some inert, coiled fish of the sea; the thrill of being alive again tingled in my nerves, and the strong shunning of death shocked me through.'

Meanwhile, in a ward at Beatson Cancer Hospital, a husband is visiting his wife on her deathbed.

'Margaret, whit ur they two tubes fur?'

'C'mere,' she whispers as her life washes away. 'They've put a fuckin' twin adapter in.'

A wheezy chuckle softens her last words. Rinse. Final Spin. End of Programme.

Rage, rage against making light of the dying ....

And yet, as Georges Bataille (1991: 34) is at pains to remind us, the heirs and the haute monde, the helots and the hedonists of consumer society, death, in its fatal and inexorable form, is undoubtedly the most costly of all conceivable luxuries. 'It constantly leaves the necessary room for the coming of the newborn and we are wrong to curse *the one without whom we would not exist.*' And yet.

'Is that you having chips the day, again?'

'Aye, the ugly bastard in front o' me got the last pie ....'

In Livingston, a living monument to the breath-taking – ho, ho – nature of Scots industrial catering, and from beneath the chip pan's permafried pall, bearing in mind the nation's appetite for heart attacks, all too solid evidence – the proof is in the eating – that the 'acts of life have neither beginning nor end' for 'everything happens in a very *idiotic* fashion' (Tzara, 1992: 11). This de facto display of up-to-date demotic Dadaism is doubly disheartening because the original avant-garde version was on the verge of Bataille's ultimate indulgence, a symbolic sacrifice of self and space, when 'Vers Une Architecture' was first published – in 1923.

By then, though, the Dadaists had already determined that the apparent order of an emergent 'machine aesthetic' (Jencks, 1975: 32,34–35,162–169) (Corbusier, 1978: 15–24) could be undone from within through the creative use of atypical texts and irregular typefaces (Tzara, 1992: 15–17) – graffiti, maybe, or Burroughs' 'cut-ups' to us. These polemists, poets and performance artists also supposed everyday life in any industrial society must include at least an element of practical semiotics, an assertion they were able to demonstrate experimentally!

'Dada' itself was coined – Zurich, 1914, Saussure, Emmentaler, my dear Watson – to have no discernible meaning, to be impenetrable (Tzara, 1992: 4), only becoming a precise commonplace word when its popular repetition had given it a specific set of associations, first with the Dadaists' own attitudes and behaviour, then later – here the plan fades – with a broader communal acceptance of the same organic defects and contradictions (Tzara, 1972: 111). All this before the Weimar lecture in 1922, when Tristan (Tzara, 1992: 109) insisted on the absolute impossibility of monolithic categories like 'Beauty' and 'Truth' – the cornerstones of Corb's conceit (1978: 31); individual variations in culture, background and psychology would guarantee that every use of a term, every human perception, must be unique and context-dependent. And when there is only context, what does the enclosed void signify? Where, if at all, might it begin or end? Dadaist overtones or no, the problem is genuine enough and mushrooms – sautéed, no doubt – out of 'Eat Fat' by Richard Klein (1997: 66–67), a big dilation with a little name and the corporation responsible for a mass-produced polemic on behalf of overeaters everywhere, encouraging them, and us, consumers at large, to adjust our perceptions, not our mass or our appetites. To this end, Klein lards his text with exhortations to eat, garnished throughout with more than ample examples of 'Fat Beauty' (Klein, 1997: 111–146) spilling in folds from the art galleries of the Western world.

With one exception, that is. Klein (1997: xx) cites 'Turkish Bath' by Ingres in his list of illustrations and sure enough, on the appointed page, there is a sufficient, indeed, a plumply welcoming opening between eulogies to Boucher's particularly erotic way with the painting of female fat (Klein, 1997: 141) and the simple legend 'Turkish Bath' by Ingres. Otherwise, though, there is nothing, an unsettling event in any text, or context, but to belie these billowing belles, for a paean to adiposity to lack substance? How are we expected to swallow that? Is it cultural snobbery on Klein's part; we should all know Ingres, for Chrissakes. A step beyond Benjamin, perhaps: a once-ripe image worn so thin by reproduction, its 'aura' has eroded to nothing. Or is this some interactive affair: we are meant to look elsewhere for the image shrouded in mystery rather than steam.

Nor is the vacant page – if such it is – a self-evident misprint; the crux of 'The Bellman's Speech' in Lewis Carroll's (1980: 16–17) 'Hunting of the Snark' is an ocean-chart that is both a perfect and absolute blank and avowedly the best available precisely because it ignores all conventional signs. You may decide for yourselves about this text which has at its core a discussion of voids at the core of texts. Not that a void has to be heartless to be devoid of meaning (Virilio, 1991: 107). Recently, for a special promotion of the 'Ka', Ford had two on display in Glasgow's Princes Square. One, by the upward escalator, was in showroom condition and very much as you'd expect to buy it, while the other, at the foot of the escalator from the first floor, had been fitted out as a fish tank, complete with parti-coloured koi, and labelled 'Karp'.

'Och, no way!' said the black leather besom behind me to her man.

'Sumdy cannae spell "Krap"'.

Out of a space in the heart of Glasgow to a hurt in the space of Berlin; commonly the Jewish Museum and known to Daniel Libeskind, its architect, as 'Between the Lines' (Libeskind, 1997: 34) because, physically and philosophically, the project follows two lines of thought, about organization and relationship. One line is straight but broken into many fragments, the other tortuous yet unending, and their interplay develops through a distinct – limited – dialogue. They also fall apart, become disengaged and are seen as separated, exposing 'strangely intersecting galleries and apparently inexplicable concrete voids' (Merrick, 1998) which characterize the building as equally the presence of absence and the absence of presence.

Libeskind's dice with dualities draws on an invisible matrix of connections and relationships between Germans and Jews which he imposes upon the structure of the museum, and the reading of that structure, as the museum itself is imposed upon the physical traces of Berlin. Similarly, the holes in the construction's fabric are a token of the measureless gaps and lesions there will be, must be, in our understandings of the site and its significance. These critical evocations are underpinned by an unexpectedly four-square foundation for a project by a deconstructive architect (Ryan, 1998: 22–24). Libeskind (1997: 34) began with a selection of those people, 'particularly certain writers, composers, artists and poets', who formed the connection between Jewish tradition and German culture. He then plotted an irrational matrix, linking the addresses where these chosen ones had lived or worked, into a system of 'intertwining triangles that would yield some reference to the emblem of a compressed and distorted star: the yellow star which was so frequently worn on this very site' (Libeskind, 1997: 34,55).

So does Daniel summon ghosts to labour as Pharoah once enslaved the Children of Israel? The prospect is far from frivolous for Libeskind's (1997: 34) second source was Arnold Schönberg, in particular 'Moses and Aaron', the opera he could not complete. For some reason, the logic of the work, which hinged upon the relationship between 'the revealed, unimaginable truth and the spoken, mass-produced people's truth' (Libeskind, 1997: 34) led to an insoluble impasse and Schönberg was never able to orchestrate his own libretto. In the end, Moses doesn't sing at all, he just speaks – 'Oh word, thou word' – an unaccompanied declaration, in complete contrast to normal opera where the score is vital to a voice's context, carriage and even confusion.

Consider, then, that this, the third act of 'Moses and Aaron', was written during the composer's exile (Merrick, 1998) and echoes still within Diasporist – displaced, usually Jewish – art as part of Kitaj's (1989: 59) 'cult of the fragment', itself a byroad to Walter Benjamin's (1992,1997) discourses on detritus and industrial life. In short, Schönberg's spoken libretto depends on Moses' 'tessitura', the voice's ordinary range of pitch, to lay down the word, a glittering fragment of Mosaic Law, defining the moral underlay of Jews' everyday existence as tesserae do the mosaic floors beneath our feet. Think here, too, of the promised land, described by the prophet and denied by death, or some closer Cymric Canaan, detailed by the Reverend Thomas (1987: 12) and defiled by life:

'Coming in late,
Rising early
To flog the carcase
of the brute earth;'

In an elegant counterpoint, given that Goethe calls architecture frozen music, the Jewish Museum – a building in 'no known style' (Merrick, 1998) – is Daniel using his first commission (Libeskind, 1997: 113–114) to make an unaccompanied declaration in his own voice, for his entire previous output had been cities of words – though hardly Tony Tanner – sketches, macquettes and computer simulations. Deconstruction notwithstanding, Libeskind is also upsetting professional boundaries by being a writer who builds rather than a builder who writes, like Corbusier. This emphasis on text continues through the third aspect of Libeskind's (1997: 34,37) work, an interest in the identities of people deported from Berlin during the fatal years of the Holocaust. The missing – the missed? – are listed in two very large volumes – Gedenkbuch – which contain nothing but the names, dates of birth and deportation and the presumed places of execution where these citizens were murdered. Again, the invisible matrix is extended, to Riga, Lodz and all the other concentration camps where Berliners have died.

The final elevation of Libeskind's Jewish Museum (1997: 34) is formed by Walter Benjamin's 'One-Way Street' (1997: 45–104) and incorporated into a continuous sequence of sixty sections along the zigzag, each of which represents one of the 'Stations of the Star' described in an absent author's prescience, a personal apocalypse of Berlin. By the by, while Libeskind admits (1997: 34) his fictional structure is built upon the ruins of Benjamin's capital, the mesh of their invisible matrix easily stretches to include the Dublin laid down in James Joyce's 'Ulysses' (Paulin, 1998: 21–24). Remember Bloom, his émigré Hungarian father – stateless, unspoken for, and his own wanderings – wonderings – between fantasies of the Jews after their escape from Egypt and his everyday life in an Ireland bounded by bondage to the British. But that way madness lies. Maybe. ... In this bottomless Ilium, this textual Troy, we can all be Heinrich Schliemann for a day.

With its special emphasis on housing the Jewish Museum, Libeskind's project is an attempt to give a voice to a common fate – the inevitable integration of Jewish history and Berlin's, of each and incineration, massacre and Modernism (Libeskind, 1997: 34), 'despite the contradictions of the ordered and disordered, the chosen and not chosen, the vocal and silent, the living and dead'. So the new building is conceived as an emblem in which the invisible, the Void, makes itself apparent as such (Libeskind, 1997: 34,46,47,54), through structural features that have been gathered in the expanse of the city and exposed in an architecture where the unnamed – the collective other – remains in the names which go unspoken. This Void is something that every participant in the museum will experience as his or her own absent presence (Libeskind, 1997: 34). Likewise, the matrix, the extraordinary web of intersections (Merrick, 1998) Libeskind has used to determine almost all of the available geometry within the structure, hints at those untold Jews who were exiled or executed. Yet when Derrida (Libeskind, 1997: 110) says the Void was the most expensive piece of the puzzle to complete, he is acknowledging, surely, that whatever the cost of volumes which invert our ideas of order and propriety by admitting our sight but not ourselves, the dear departed are the greater part of the price, however we make the trade.

Officially, Libeskind's project is an extension of the facilities already established in a baroque Berlin mansion (Libeskind, 1997: 34,121), though their only union is underground, preserving the contradictory surface autonomy while binding them both to a common root in the capital's physical and cultural fabric (Libeskind, 1997: 34). Put simply, we are witnessing a classic play of plan and perspective, a drama of mass and morality that employs a zigzag – even a flash of the SS 'lightning bolt' insignia, note – with a structural rib, which is the Void of the Jewish Museum, running across it. That's why this building is a new type of organisation (Libeskind, 1997: 34). It's arranged around a core of what is not, the richness of Berlin's Jewish heritage reduced to archival and archaeological material, become a Void which is visible but inviolable, vacant but unavailable, unavoidable. For all that it is not there, this Void is a troublesome thing.

More so when there is a bookish precedent to Libeskind's lacuna, his intercellular space. In 'The Voidoid', a novella first published a generation ago, Richard Hell (1996: 20) allows us access to a single room in the teeming concrete hives, the urban bunkers, of America's Modernist melting pot:

'The skeleton is named Skull and the vampire is named Lips. They live together in New York City, where they have a rock band, the Liberteens. (Daniel, Daniel. ...)

The two of them had gradually reached their present identities on the other side of life at about the same rate as they had acquired facial hair.'

(Daniel, Daniel, bearding the lion in his den. ...)

In this perverse caesura, this space where the unnatural breathe and natural breathing pauses, we meet only the embodiments of Death – a sign of our common fate – and the Undead that feed on living flesh, the memories that will not fade? So, privileging sight with a mass-produced yet private viewing, we consume a text by reading it and become a medium for those things which live again through us. For myself, etched with curiosity and ever a creature of habit, I have to wonder: does the Voidoid shop at Gap?

To R.S. Thomas (1993: 287), though, 'The Gap' is the locus of human life, between perfection and the world as we make it. His Void is also a paradox (Thomas, 1993: 361), a sure sign of the hidden God:

It is this great absence
that is like a presence, that compels
me to address it without hope
of a reply. It is a room I enter
from which someone has just
gone.'

Despite their obvious differences in outlook, Derrida (Libeskind, 1997: 111) makes a notably similar assessment of the sealed cells – the 'theological spaces' – in Daniel's Jewish Museum. The reverend gentleman (Davies, 1998: xiv) is also adjudged 'always to have had a consciousness of some 'otherness', even in himself', in other words, 'to be good on *mystery'*. Even so, the implicit comparison to Magritte (Foucault, 1983) reveals a telling contradiction in Thomas' linguistic landscapes when his autobiographies (1998) are openly compared with the painter's secret mining (Foucault, 1983: 37), those excavations of words that make the 'old pyramid of perspective' 'no more than a molehill about to cave in'. Any apparent industrial analogy is misleading, however, for R.S.T. is utterly pastoral (1998: 71,76,80–81) and cuts his cloth to suit, preferring rural parishes and the areas of Wales which remain within a culture of native Welsh speakers rather than (Thomas, 1993: 287) 'spurious metals' and 'the cold acts of the machine'.

Like Joyce (Paulin, 1998: 25–26) and Libeskind (1997), Thomas (1998: 67) writes of places he knows do not exist, and times that will never return (Thomas, 1998: 58,74,99), the discrepancy being his resolute refusal to consider either the people (Thomas, 1998: 11,52,64) or the issues (Wintle, 1997: 13) of the everyday world he does inhabit. This is curious because the emptiness that prompts his 'hiraeth' – the long hurt of having a past like the Welsh (Wintle, 1997: 14–15), their hunger for an older, less aggressive order (Thomas, 1998: 98) – is shared by compatriots who also have the inner lives R.S. has assumed they lack (Thomas, 1998: 62,85). Equally, for all the priest's willingness to learn Welsh (Thomas, 1998: 10–12,50,54) as a means of addressing his concerns, the same medium magnifies the differences, the very nonconformity, he will not acknowledge. As a second south Walian (Wintle, 1997: 12–13) explains of himself, unlike the poet he didn't grow up to write in 'high culture Welsh, BBC Welsh. Very precise, classical, but lacking in sinew'. Notably, too, there's 'a lot of Gwynedd' in the Reverend's vocabulary, a vital detail when the folds and creases of the native landscape are so closely mirrored in the commonplace language of most competent Welsh speakers that each may locate another precisely, by town and valley, even community and street, simply through minute variations in idiom and accent.

Had Thomas talked to his moorland parishioners more (Thomas, 1998: 11–13), he might also have unearthed the significance of 'cynefin', the 'almost mystical interdependence' (Hopkins, 1998) between a farmer and his land that could lead him to give names and identities to particular fields or landmarks. Clearly here there is no avoiding an intense commonality with Carter's (1996: 128) contradiction, his paradox of Western vision: 'to gaze fixedly at something is to lose sight of everything about us; conversely the useless activity of 'staring into space', allowing the world back in, may be to see everything at once'. In Carter's eyes, we prefer – we privilege – the former, the hunter's outlook, though the second may constitute another form of knowledge, allowing us, perhaps, to hear as well. Remember Schönberg's impasse and wonder, was he caught, open-eyed in amazement, between these two perspectives?

True, the Reverend R.S. is a proven pacifist (Thomas, 1998: 44,95; Wintle, 1997: 138–139, 155, 189), yet wherever his parish, he walks Wales alone (Thomas, 1998: 41,53–54; Wintle, 1997: 87), not quite the watcher of flocks you might expect (Wintle, 1997: 14) but an inveterate ornithologist (Thomas, 1998: 35, 55, 57, 58, 60, 61, 66–67, 70, 78, 80, 99–100)[2], Orion in symbolic form. Cast – ill-starred? – in Cardiff and raised in Holyhead, never Caergybi, this neb Nimrod remains English enough and sufficiently Anglican – or is it the Reithian Modernism of his BBC Welsh – to populate his colonizing perspective with archetypes like Iago Prydderch (Thomas, 1998: 54), spelled 'Prytherch' so the incomers will pronounce it properly. We've already seen a visual equivalent in Warhol's 'Dance Diagram-Tango', for while these are patently the steps to tread, they're not the measure of anyone we know, and Andy's artistry is far from that informal gauge we each take in our stride.

Back at the Moor, Iago would lie better with us if Thomas hadn't also attributed a 'Shropshire accent' to both the miners of Chirk (Thomas, 1998: 42–43), a border-country town in Clwyd, or Denbighshire as it once was, and the Welsh of Manafon (Thomas, 1998: 54), meaning Powys now and mid-Montgomeryshire then. Following the tracks of his train journeys home through Ludlow and the Marches (Thomas, 1998: 10), this hint of a collective other is more a product of R.S.T.'s cultural cartography than any lasting confusion over the flux of margins or the march of fluxion.

Beyond our by-line delight at the play of a poet so well versed in footwork, there is another, Tom Paulin (1998: 60), with a plaint for the oral English of Ireland, which lives 'freely and spontaneously' in a 'rich carelessness' of provincial and spoken forms yet rarely appears in print, a discourse without lexicon or literature – literally homeless – to the bafflement of its many would-be users. This 'strange creature of the open air' (Paulin, 1998: 60) becomes easier to appreciate in more immediate terms if we take holy orders, in a secular sense (Thomas, 1998: 144), and go 'to the parts of Wales where the language has disappeared and where the place-names have been mutilated. It is a skeleton of a country. Despite the superb views there is something missing that no-one except a true Welshman can identify'.

So Jacques may lament a like lack (Libeskind, 1997: 110) in viewing the Void while Jay McInerney (1998) abandons the Gap for another brand and markedly misses the point. En route to the Hay-on-Wye literary festival, McInerney 'encountered a pack of young men on the sidewalk of a town with cobbled streets and lots of double consonants. All were dressed in baggy hip-hop gear and most were sporting sweatshirts with the name of designer Tommy Hilfiger emblazoned across the chest. So much for local colour. (Actually, after three days of bilingual signs, I was surprised the Hilfiger logo didn't have a Welsh translation printed underneath.)'

For others, the voids, the holes, the gaps are particularly meaningful precisely because they occur in unexpected places. Returning us to Richard Klein's catalogue of callipygean calligraphy, like a fold in the fat he so admires[3], or a crease in Carter's coruscating outback, is Lucian Freud's (Feaver, 1998) response to his own work.

'Big Sue, who sat for you so much a few years ago, became more tremendous from picture to picture'.

'Yes, she did. She is in her way very feminine and, as she says, luckily she's got a sensible gene. Initially, being aware of all kinds of spectacular things to do with her size, like amazing craters and things one's never seen before, my eye was naturally drawn to the sores and chafes made by weight and heat'.

The repetition here, and the implied willingness to be a model, suggest Big Sue has accommodated her craters, her size and her sores within her established sense of self, not so much disguising her supposed flaws with make-up as flaunting them in the foundation of her make-up. These fleshings of the word are not, then, a primarily imposed reading or the visible sign of some voyeur's belittling perspective, though Freud's – unconscious? – expression of his own artifice as a natural occurrence is hardly an objection to either. Nor, following our fine art sensibilities and Lucian's frame by frame enlargements, can we entirely exclude the flabby fetishism of Klein's

(1997: 52–54) 'chubby chasers'. Otherwise, Jekyll-and-Hyding on the darker side of overdevelopment with the unimpeachable Bill – Shagspere to his wife, since the heavens have shaped my body so, let Hell (1996: 16) make crooked my mind to answer it: 'They say obese women are the most sex-thirsty, which I believe, but any word with an x in it is sexy. Take axe'.

Manifestly, we accept, a means of consuming mass, yet Dada or gross disorder? More disturbing still, Lizzie Borden, what if axes – the horizontal, the vertical and the planes of colour they enclose – are the instruments, the warp and the weft, of universal harmony? Mondrian (1995: 103–105) maintains as much, sooner and surer than Corbusier in 'Vers Une Architecture' that a version of the 'machine aesthetic' (Mondrian, 1995: 65, 71, 97) would inevitably lead to a better balanced society (Mondrian, 1995: 107), with 'nature and non-nature in equilibrium', nothing less than paradise regained – on earth. Astonishingly, (1995: 89) Piet has not only preempted Carter's paradox of Western sight – 'inner vision is different from merely optical vision' – but also appreciated the significance of our everyday ability to see, for example, 'the room all at once in its entirety'.

In addition, Mondrian (1995: 77–78) emphasises, as Corbusier (1978: 31) does the forms our eyes were made to see, how in those individuals with a mature, that is, abstract rather than literal or realist, image of beauty, *'the particularities of nature have been transformed to unity in memory'*. Piet proclaims a parallel concurrence in structuring our outer world (Mondrian, 1995: 83–84), with, for instance, the six facing planes of a cell or chamber, the rectangular frames of wall, floor and ceiling, serving equally an architectural function – the enclosure and definition of space – and the more expansive pictorial role of representation. To complicate his own prognosis, or build in an emergency exit, Mondrian (1995: 94) admits that the necessary techniques and materials for such a duplication, or collapsing, of frames do not yet exist in toto, and artists are doubly handicapped as a result, with neither the means to educate us simpler folk in the new, improved beauty, nor the opportunity to achieve the appropriate degree of precision that this aesthetic engineering depends upon to embody its full significance and deliver the determined meaning in a finished artefact. For an enclosure to become a painting, Piet (1995: 88) insists it's not enough simply to place colours next to each other; this is still mere decoration. 'They must be the *right* red, blue, yellow, gray. Each right in *itself* and *right in mutual relation with the others'*. Alternatively, in articulating the space of Argyle Street:

'It's a nice fit. It's just a wee bit gaudy.'

'It's no gaudy. It's red, that's all.'

Mondrian is openly aware of, and unsettled by, the day-to-day difficulties involved in creating a balance between public places and private aesthetics (Mondrian, 1995: 106), a parity of personal perceptions and the popular psyche (Mondrian, 1995: 76, 80), in any hierarchical society based on exchange and mass production (Mondrian, 1995: 109–110) where, for some, even the most basic needs remain unmet (Mondrian, 1995: 73, 80–81). As Piet

(1995: 96) puts it in an acute opposition of antiquity and inequity, the slaves who built the Egyptian pyramids were probably not much penetrated by the spirit of their age. However, the wider significance of this rare counterpoint is lost for in accepting the monuments as inherently revelatory architecture, Mondrian is abandoning any attempt to link, say, dominant structures and structures of dominance, or to drive a critical wedge between cultures of construction and the construction of culture (Fauchereau, 1994: 31).

The painter's proffered option is suitably singular while very much in the spirit of his times, an artful performance of form amounting, almost, to a fascism of the self, a retreat into order reflected, some reckon (Wintle, 1997: 13), in readings of R.S. Thomas. From 1919 onward, whether in Paris, London or New York, Mondrian (Fauchereau, 1994: 29–30) 'had an *a priori* conception of the studio as *a whole in which to live*', a Piet-a-terre so to speak. Each of the artist's ateliers was laid out in strict accord with his (Mondrian, 1995: 82–88) published principles of the new equilibrium, the colours changing with his paintings of the period and a similar severity of line, but notably only employing easels as screens – the planes between axes – and mounts for finished canvases (Fauchereau, 1994: 29). In Paris at least, where the bulk of what is now his most acclaimed output was completed, the actual work was done flat on a table, Mondrian looking down on it like a map or a sand painting (Fauchereau, 1994: 29).

From a contemporary viewpoint, we would probably regard these bunkers as artistic landmarks in themselves, ur-installations (Fauchereau, 1994: 36) undoubtedly, but to Piet, each was a redoubt in his campaign against urban disorder, a considered restructuring of his original Parisian location, the 'calculated space where nothing happened by chance' (Fauchereau, 1994: 37). Yet Mondrian only moved in – from – the first place because a demolition order forced him out of his building on rue du Départ (Fauchereau, 1994: 43), no mean joke given Piet's fixation with fixity. Semiotic – seismic – slippage aside, this was a man for whom twentieth century modern meant music where he could dance along straight lines (Fauchereau, 1994: 10,35), the Tango included. Mondrian also prefigured Warhol's step from 'Dance Diagram' to wall-hanging by decades – 'Foxtrot A' was completed in 1930 and 'Broadway Boogie-Woogie' by 1943 – though these are signs of mass movement, not the individual consumption of space.

Despite the temptations of time, square corners and immediate gratification, we are as well not seeing Piet's pictures as 'naturalistic transpositions' (Fauchereau, 1994: 35) for the flickering coloured rectangles of his later framings are no more readily reduced to the neon signs and monoliths of Midtown Manhattan than the earlier planes are polder meadows and Dutch tiles. In reading Mondrian as a Modernist, it is axiomatic that we attempt an axial reading – horizontal and vertical lines in equilibrium across the margins of the plastic arts – as the pieces were assembled. The grids of Piet's New World – Order – paintings then appear as traffic flows and tail-lights together, simultaneously street plan and skyscraper, with all of the structure and none of the imbalances built into present boroughs. Understand these are schemata, not symbols of anywhere in particular but everywhere in general, universally applicable models of urban life as it will one day be lived in industrial societies across the globe.

Equally, while the works are not explicitly Cubist in style (Mondrian, 1995: 56), they are clearly three-dimensional projections: on to the canvas itself, though from a cartographer's perspective (Mondrian, 1995: 54) as much as the familiar Florentine, on to our intellectual landscape, extending that upright, Euclidean topology of presence which gives us all a sense of 'final place' (Barthes 1984: 205), and most importantly from Mondrian's point of view, on to the future he anticipates for everyone, without exception (Busignani, 1975: 25–26). Reversing the glance, we see a touch here of Thomas the Poet, particularly if Piet's plaint is perceived as a form of 'hiraeth' for the hereafter, a project like Libeskind's (1997: 34) Jewish Museum – each painting a 'preparation for future architecture' (Mondrian, 1995: 15), and a colonizing gaze, imposing his structures upon the unruly body of the world (Carter, 1996: 228–229) and the world of the unruly body.

Yet how much can this matter to us nowadays if De Stijl's style supremo, Piet the pattern-maker, has little value (Busignani, 1975: 11) as a theorist? Apart from the academically fraught question of why anyone should consume their own mass in amassing a volume of – unconsumed? – text, even an illiterate accepts that the written is a sign of the unwritten and the denial of a voice. These boundaries, and the bases of their definition, become singularly significant, and significantly far from singular, after Mondrian's trip to Spain in 1901. The visit was a complete failure and gave him no inspiration whatsoever; the light was too different from that of Holland and the people not engaging, with no relevance, hostile even, to the painter's slow way of thinking and his careful evolution of a new order (Busignani, 1975: 4).

Beyond Mondrian in a bad light and the likelihood that his disappearance of the personal (Mondrian, 1995: 97) disguises suppression as social reform, there is an obvious gap between any hoped-for equilibrium and the Iberian unrest which typifies, and promotes, some degree of organisation in every industrial society. With R.S. Thomas, we know this void is a paradox, the presence of God and an absence of Welsh understanding; with Mondrian, the paradox is to be avoided. It's overlooked, still, in certain high places, where a contemporary focussing of Piet's contemptuous gaze has provoked 'In the Dutch Mountains' (Nooteboom, 1995), a transcendent fable for our times which begins with some nameless central administration, 'the national government', running one enormous country very like latter-day Europe, from The Hague.

Written by Cees Nooteboom, who was born there and lives in Amsterdam when he's not in Spain, the medium for this incidental satire is one Alfonso Tiburón de Mendoza, nominally 'from the wilder regions the Dutch call the southern Netherlands' (Nooteboom, 1995: 2), meaning Aragon. Alfonso tells us: 'The northern landscape, like the desert, suggests absolutism. Except that in this case the desert is green and filled with water. There are no allurements, roundnesses, curves. The land is flat, exposing the people, and this total visibility is reflected in their behaviour'.

Consequently, Mendoza from Zaragosa tends to feel increasingly out of sorts the further he travels towards Den Haag – home, happily, to the International Court of Justice and a worldwide web of law – while the Dutch are similarly ill at ease in approaching the Mediterranean (Nooteboom, 1995: 3). Each is discomfited by their immersion in a culture of the excluded other, the disorder knowingly placed beyond some contingent interior margin of good taste and civilized conduct. Our modest Aragonese doesn't regard himself as inherently deficient, however, any more than R.S. Thomas' scorned compatriots do, though they're all encouraged to think that way by their awareness of life under a constant critical glare. And Nooteboom's Northerners are not notably less nervous at the slightest move away from an analagous position of accustomed advantage ....

Beyond their titular take-over, Cees' case study equates Hollanders' notions of organization and social cohesion with their everyday experience of mountains – Dutch uplands rise to sea-level – and an equivalent range of tolerable outlook and structure, remembering their own wars of independence against Spain (Schama, 1988: 83–93) and centuries of empire-building on a global scale. Nearer to home, Nooteboom's Netherlands are uniform enough, and sufficiently settled, to promote an appropriately proprietorial planar perspective; they are also a product of that levelling gaze, for even the ocean is subject to imperial order, leaving lacunae in Giorgione's Lagoon, and mudflats for seascapes.

No drain on meaning, though. We have already explored Thomas' High Welsh, his 'hiraeth', and Libeskind's Hollow-cast Walls from the outside, and been undone by them, with nothing left intact, because we cannot project ourselves into a script or a scene where all we are conscious of is the void in our own appreciation. So we experience these artefacts, these expressions of other cultures, not as a material gain but as a 'loss', a 'disappearance' (Barthes, 1984: 10), a giant step over some unsuspected march on our mental maps to beyond the twilight zone, where our sole Pole Star in a one-dimensional space is our complete lack of any further understanding. This, surely, is as close as we may come to a sufficient sense of absence, a knowledge of that greater nullity, when entire peoples ceased as our perceptions do, yet permanently.

In a like light, the Aborigines of Carter's Australia appear as a signally marginal exemplar. We cannot remain ourselves and infer their existence from our view of their homelands, nor on meeting them can we readily envisage how they might find fulfilment in what we take to be a void, empty to, and of, us. Compounding our perceived limitations, and the limitations of our perception, Libeskind and Thomas are also giving voices to civilizations and creativities, objects and assemblies, of which they themselves can never have been members. A further absence, then, in structures of meaning made to suggest a greater lack, a vacuum which contains another – the perfect counter to any industrialized society of accumulation and matter.

And pyramids of possessions do possess us with a pyramidic panorama, a widening one-way window upon the world which inclines us to turn a blind eye on ourselves as readily as we manipulate more distant geometries of mass. While we do see that an unblinkingly Modernist vista will not always end in Treblinka, we realize, too, the insufficiency of simple corrective lenses. Even Mondrian's flat acceptance of his own Lowlands outlook, whether painting in Paris or New Amsterdam, would not resolve a key, a Kitaj, question: are these fields of colour exile's art or foreign? And what of more subtle refractions such as Nooteboom's Iberian-inspired imaginings? His fabulous views of Europe, the entity not the entirety, are drawn up when physically in Amsterdam or Spain and commonly never quite as one with either culture, a tension Cees employs creatively to highlight the holes, and the multiplicities of interpretation, in our personal perspectives.

Mondrian, or something which passes for him, did die in New York; mine is the link with Lips and Skull, the Word and the Memory, making and selling music, an endless harmony of their own, from another hard cell elsewhere in the concrete city. Mine, too, the play of Piet's 'Victory Boogie-Woogie' (1993–1944: unfinished) as a fittingly offbeat finale for a jazz fan and a last gesture of defiance, an inspired – he's expired – riposte to the inevitable curtain-closer:

'O Death, where is thy sting-a-ling-a-ling,
O Grave, thy victoree?'

In preparing for all this, Mondrian wrote essays and articles about and between his accepted art; I've no idea if Nooteboom paints in between books.

On a less personal and more populous, if not more popular, scale, Cees' quasi-vertical axis, from Zaragoza to the Netherlands, can be overlaid on my horizontal yolking of Wales and Germany in the East – the East in Germany? – as easily as either or both may be added to Daniel's deconstructions of distance, time and space. These, it goes without saying, or with – that's the nature of things seen and things unseen – run from our immediate grasp to Manhattan and Central America on one extreme, Berlin and beyond the other. Libeskind is Polish in origin (Libeskind, 1997: 113) yet yearns for the use of his Yiddish as Derrida (Libeskind, 1997: 110) does his freedom of expression when sentenced without trial to solitary confinement in 'yr iaith fine' – the thin language. We, too, are walled up. Between Maastricht and matter out of place – the Antipodes as polar antipathies? – we are concerned about the folds and the contradictions of European cultural identity (Derrida, 1992: 44). If it is necessary to ensure that a centralising hegemony – the capital – should not be reconstituted, it is also necessary not to multiply the borders, meaning the movements – 'marches' – and the margins – 'marges'.

Marge is one small form of Margaret and one form of Margaret Small was jointly responsible for me and my rearing on the Marches, as well as my movements away. For a while there, we lived in a council house and my mummy is a Brummie with blue eyes, but ours is not the story of 'Border Blues'

(Thomas, 1987: 10–14) and the R.S. revealed by the writing is somebody else. The place where I grew up – became Small – is also gone though it's still on the map, a trace, a trait, I'd share were I less aware of erasing my raising. Not so Mondrian – any admission of omission will burst the bubble of our millennial doom and deny us our needful Modernity. Like Schönberg's Moses, Piet has a prospect of the promised land, neither the word nor its refutation, both, rather, and the denial of their contradictions.

His chiastic credo demands (Mondrian, 1995: 105) that artists should suffer the injustices and imbalances of an immediately imperfect world, along with the frustrations of outmoded art forms which remain well-thought-of (Mondrian, 1995: 114). Piet's personal expenses, meanwhile, are met through painting traditional watercolours of the style he publicly denounces (Faucher-eau, 1994: 31). Never explaining, Mondrian (1995: 132) makes plain planar meaning by discounting the Dadaist disorder described in his final –1920 – detailing of industrially identical objects as devices for demotic displays of individual difference. From a little restaurant somewhere in Paris, prototypical pan-European expansion emerges as soft, if not self, -centred, and hollow yet never utterly without import: 'The couple over there are sharing one *coeur à la crème*. This messenger boy has two *coeurs à la crème*. The foreigner over there is eating his *coeur à la crème* alone. A soldier. Has he a *coeur à la crème*? A *coeur à la crème* is not only soft but also white. 'Vous avez terminé, monsieur?' "

I think perhaps I have, for the moment, though it strikes me that while the centre may no longer hold, from Haussmann's perspective or those blue remembered hills, there are massy webs of meaning being made and unmade around Libeskind's Berlin, and Kitaj's diastrophic 'cult of the fragment'. Like 'Lexo saying to the barman, – Eight Becks, mate. Then he noticed a squad of scarfers come in from a bus. – Naw, make it Grolsch, eh, he said. He turned to me and winked, – Heavier boatils, eh.

They certainly were'.

(Irvine Welsh, 1995: 148)

1. Radioactive traces

In August 1945, Tatsuichiro Akizuki was the resident doctor at Urakami First Hospital, a small TB clinic which had been established in a Franciscan monastery situated on the northern edge of Nagasaki. This peculiar combination of calling and coincidence has allowed him to write an irradiated account of Oppenheimer's infernal encore, the A-bomb known as 'Fat Man' because of its cheerful rotundity and consequent association with Churchill (Akizuki, 1981: 21). The device was 3.5 metres long, weighed 4.5 tons, and had an explosive potential of 22 kilotons of TNT.

Beyond an implicit rebuttal of Klein's (1997: 38–39,102–103) correspondence between roundness and all-round well being, the fallout contains further elements of immediate, if disturbing, relevance. Six days after his birthplace was razed, Akizuki (1981: 97) had the unnerving experience of waking among the dead and the dying, to hear a Catholic mass being celebrated by consumptives and other survivors of an atomic weapon designed around notions – neurons to neutrons – of critical mass, to consume en masse. The sectarian undertow, of Christians immolating one another, has its own considerable half-life.

The city centre was so damaged that, like the banks of the flooded Nile (Singh, 1998: 8), nothing recognisable remained (Akizuki, 1981: 100–101). An area of about five kilometres in width had been reduced to a granular desert, a wasteland of pebble-sized pieces, where the only order apparent on the beach was an obscene geometry, marked out by gradations in the concentric circles of carbonized matter, and variations in the angles of inclination visible in slanting concrete walls or the raked iron frameworks of exploded factories. At the heart of Nagasaki, not even this; just the emptiness of ground zero, the word made void.

In an additional echo from earlier times, and lest we should forget, the street plan of Libeskind's Berlin (1997: 113) – the limits to flânage – was reclaimed from its kerbstones, which even carpet-bombing could not disturb. Nor are there books of the dead in Nagasaki. The final figure, the number of fatalities, (Akizuki, 1981: 147,151) is itself still fissile, unstable, any chance of symbolic closure as yet denied by those additional losses that have been attributed to less contentious causes, albeit induced by overexposure to radioactivity, and a degree of official disquiet – disgust – at discussing any aspect of nuclear-powered urban degeneration.

There are, however, texts like 'The Bomb and The General', by Umberto Eco and Eugenio Carmi (1989), a pacifist tract for children and understandably belittling of both atomic bombs and rampant militarism. On a note of academic abstraction, which Eco would surely be the first to appreciate, how are we to take such a lightweight item from a heavyweight among semioticians? Do we draw a line between him and Umberto the concerned adult and parent? Was either father to the book, or Eugenio the originator? Ché?

Some footnote, by the way.

2. Tho Mas

R.S. chose to write 'Neb' (1998: 25–110, originally 1985) – 'No-one in particular' or 'Anybody at all' – in Welsh rather than 'the thin tongue', the English of his upbringing, yet refers to himself in the third person throughout this gloss on over seventy years of life, while his wife, their son and four decades of marriage slip by almost incidentally. However, 'A year in Llŷn' (1998: 111–171, originally 1990), Thomas' token tally of his bird-watching amid the physical and political landscapes of Wales, is two thirds as long though it covers just twelve months, and in singularly personal terms too. Then again, Odysseus once called himself Nobody (Borges, 1986: 67) ....

226

3. Critical mass

In 'Fold', an exhibition of meticulously executed nude paintings by Alison Watt, which I saw in October, 1997, at the Fruitmarket Gallery, Edinburgh, the innate idealization of female form integral to several centuries of male Western art is subtly undermined by the selective introduction of those little peculiarities of feature and pose that make up a convincing image of individual self-identity. Watt focuses on the sheen of naked flesh and the sensuous folds of discarded drapery, taking her start from clinically erotic bath scenes by Ingres ....

Very much, and very deliberately, at the other end of the scale, Jenny Saville's self-portraits, like 'Branded' (1992) and 'Plan' (1993) in the Saatchi Collection, are colossi of nudes, so closeup her own body becomes more Ordnance Survey than ordonnance, overwritten with strap marks and creases, overripe and overrunning every frame. As for Klein's (1997: 243–246) Adipose Complex, it's true – his mother has played an unhealthily large part in his life.

Bibliography

Akizuki, T., (1981), *Nagasaki 1945*, London: Quartet Books.
Ayre, M., *Times Higher Education Supplement*, 3rd July, 1998.
Barthes, R., (1984), *Image – Music – Text*, London: Flamingo/Fontana.
Bataille, G., (1991), *The Accursed Share*, (Vol.1), New York: Zone Books.
Benjamin, W., (1997), *One-Way Street*, London: Verso.
Benjamin, W., (1992), *Illuminations*, London: Fontana/HarperCollins.
Borges, J.L., (1986), *Seven Nights*, London: Faber and Faber.
Busignani, A., (1975), *Mondrian*, London: Thames and Hudson.
Carroll, L., (1980), *The Hunting of the Snark*, Leicester: Windward/W.H. Smith.
Carter, P., (1996), *The Lie of the Land*, London: Faber and Faber.
Corbusier, Le, (1978), *Towards A New Architecture*, London: The Architectural Press.
Derrida, J., (1992), *The Other Heading: Reflections on Today's Europe*, Bloomington & Indianapolis: Indiana University Press.
Eco, U. and Eugenio, C., (1989), *The Bomb and The General*, London: Secker & Warburg.
Fauchereau, S., (1994), *Mondrian and The Neo-Plasticist Utopia*, Barcelona: Ediciones Poligrafa.
Feaver, W., *Observer Life*, 17th May, 1998.
Foucault, M., (1983), *This Is Not a Pipe*, Berkeley & Los Angeles: University of California Press.
Hell, R., (1996), *The Voidoid*, Hove: CodeX.
Hennig, J.-L., (1995), *The Rear View*, London: Souvenir Press.
Hill, C., (1996), *Liberty Against The Law*, London: Allen Lane.
Hopkins, A., *The Observer Review*, 16th August, 1998.
Hughes, R., (1981), *The Shock of the New*, London: British Broadcasting Corporation.
Jencks, C., (1982), *Modern Movements in Architecture*, Harmondsworth, Middlesex: Penguin.
Jencks, C., (1975), *Le Corbusier and the Tragic View of Architecture*, London: Allen Lane.
Klein, R. (1997), *Eat Fat*, London: Picador.
Kitaj, R.B., (1989), *First Diasporist Manifesto*, London: Thames and Hudson.
Libeskind, D., (1997), radix-matrix, Munich & New York: Prestel.
McInerney, J., *The Guardian*, 25th July, 1998.
Merrick, J., *The Independent*, 18th May, 1998.
Mondrian, P., (1995), *Natural Reality and Abstract Reality*, New York: George Braziller.
Nooteboom, C., (1995), *In the Dutch Mountains*, London: The Harvill Press.

Parks, T., (1998), *Europa*, London: Vintage.

Paulin, T., (1998), *Writing to the Moment*, London: Faber and Faber.

Ryan, R. and N. Stungo, *Blueprint*, July/August, 152, pp. 22–24.

Schama, S., (1988), *The Embarrassment of Riches*, London: Collins.

Shanes, E., (1993), *Warhol*, London: Studio Editions.

Singh, S. (1998), *Fermat's Last Theorem*, London: Fourth Estate.

Thomas, R.S., (1998), *Autobiographies*, London: Phoenix/Orion Books.

Thomas, R.S., (1993), *Collected Poems 1945–1990*, London: J.M. Dent/Orion Books.

Thomas, R.S., (1992), *Mass for Hard Times*, Newcastle upon Tyne: Bloodaxe Books.

Thomas, R.S., (1987), *Welsh Airs*, Bridgend: Poetry Wales Press.

Tzara, T., (1992), *Seven Dada Manifestos and Lampisteries*, London/New York: Calder Publications/Riverrun Press.

Virilio, P., (1991), *The Aesthetics of Disappearance*, New York: Semiotext(e).

Warhol, A., (1975), *The Philosophy of Andy Warhol (From A to B and Back Again)*, New York & London: Harcourt Brace Jovanovich.

Welsh, I., (1995), *marabou stork nightmares*, London: Jonathan Cape.

Wintle, J., (1997), *Furious Interiors*, London: Flamingo/HarperCollins.

Notes on contributors

Zygmunt Bauman is Emeritus Professor of Sociology at Leeds and the University of Warsaw. Known for *Legislators and Interpreters*, (1987), *Modernity and the Holocaust*, (1989), *Modernity and Ambivalence*, (1991), and *Postmodern Ethics*, (1993), he is the author of some 21 books in English and of numerous articles and reviews. He was awarded the Amalfi European Prize in 1990 and the Adorno Prize in 1998.

Rob Beeston is a doctoral student in the Centre for Social Theory & Technology at Keele University.

Robert Cooper is Research Professor in the Centre for Social Theory & Technology at Keele University. His current research is in cultures of information, theorising the impact of modern communication technologies on the nature of 'social mass' in the modern world.

Robert Grafton Small holds a CNAA doctorate on social aspects of consumption. Prematurely retired after posts in Marketing at Strathclyde and Organisational Symbolism at St. Andrews, he has been damned with high praise and a meagre medical pension. Currently an honorary professor at Keele University's Department of Management, he maintains an active interest in original research and still publishes regularly in several disciplines.

Heather Höpfl is Professor of Organizational Psychology and Head of the School of Operations Analysis and HRM at Newcastle Business School, University of Northumbria at Newcastle. Her research interests are primarily in the field of organizational performance and she has worked with a number of large organizations including British Airways and British Telecom.

Joanna Latimer draws together ethnography, textual analysis and post-structural theory to focus medicine as a key domain of Euro-American culture. Her recent book – *The Conduct of Care* – examines the multi-disciplinary practices and technologies which help make up the medical domain and which help form sometimes unexpected alignments, including the jointing of efficiency and morality. She is currently working on a new monograph – *Enhancement: The Human-Technology Relation*. Joanna lectures in social theory and the social study of medicine at Cardiff University's School of Social Science and is associate editor of *Gender, Work and Organisation*.

© The Editorial Board of The Sociological Review 2001. Published by Blackwell Publishers, 108 Cowley Road, Oxford OX4 1JF, UK and 350 Main Street, Malden, MA 02148, USA.

Nick Lee is a sociologist at Keele University and a Director of the Centre for Social Theory & Technology. He studies childhood and is author of *Childhood and Society: Growing Up in an Age of Uncertainty* (OUP 2001). He also publishes widely on issues of stability, integrity and regulation.

Rolland Munro is Professor of Organisation Theory and Director of the Centre for Social Theory & Technology at Keele University. He is currently writing a book on the Euro-American's cultural and social entanglement with technology, provisionally called *The Demanding Relationship*, to clarify ideas like motility, disposal, discretion and punctualising. He previously edited, with Kevin Hetherington, *Ideas of Difference: Social Spaces and the Labour of Division*, Sociological Review Monograph, Oxford: Blackwell, 1997.

Cristina Pallí Monguilod is a doctoral student of social psychology at the Universitat Autonoma de Barcelona. She also teaches in Science, Technology and Society at the Universitat Oberta de Catalunya. After carrying out fieldwork in a biology laboratory, she is currently researching issue of identity, community, mobility and ethnography.

Jane Parish is an anthropologist working in the School of Social Relations, Keele University. She has conducted fieldwork in Ghana on witchcraft, evil and misfortune. She is currently interested in perceptions of African religion 'abroad' and how West Africans living in Europe conceptualize misfortune and morality.

Dan Rose taught at the University of Pennsylvania where he is Professor Emeritus and was visiting professor of anthropology and American studies at the College of William and Mary, 2000–2001. In addition to writing articles and books and editing the Series in Contemporary Ethnography at the University of Pennsylvania Press, he has made and shown artist books in galleries and libraries. Over the last decade he has worked to theorize the material world and for the last five years has made physical objects, many using earth collected from sites worldwide. These works have been exhibited as installations in a number of art galleries in the US.

Doug Stuart teaches Sociology at the University of Greenwich. His research interests include the history of colonialism in Southern Africa and the creation of modern nationalism. This chapter relates aspects of these interests to the impact of new information technologies, and their relationship with the theoretical perspectives associated with post-modernity.

Index